Stetson University
[redacted]

Y0-ERI-289

WITHDRAWN

DATE DUE

HIGHSMITH #45230

Printed in USA

KIERKEGAARD'S CHRISTOCENTRIC THEOLOGY

ASHGATE NEW CRITICAL THINKING IN THEOLOGY & BIBLICAL STUDIES

Ashgate New Critical Thinking in Theology & Biblical Studies presents an open-ended series of quality research drawn from an international field of scholarship. The series aims to bring monograph publishing back into focus for authors, the international library market, and student, academic and research readers. Headed by an international editorial advisory board of acclaimed scholars, this series presents cutting-edge research from established as well as exciting new authors in the field. With specialist focus, yet clear contextual presentation, books in the series aim to take theological and biblical research into new directions, opening the field to new critical debate within the traditions, into areas of related study, and into important topics for contemporary society.

Series Editorial Board

Paul Fiddes, Regent's Park College, University of Oxford, UK
Anthony Thiselton, University of Nottingham, UK
Jeffrey Astley, NEICE, University of Durham, , UK
Timothy Jervis Gorringe, University of Exeter, UK
Alan Torrance, St Andrews University, UK
Adrian Thatcher, College of St Mark & St John, Plymouth, UK
Mary Grey, Sarum College, Salisbury, UK
Richard Roberts, University of Lancaster, UK
Judith M. Lieu, King's College London, UK
Terrence Tilley, University of Dayton, Ohio, USA
Rebecca S. Chopp, Emory University, USA
Miroslav Volf, Yale Divinity School, USA
Edward Farley, Vanderbilt University, USA
Stanley J. Grenz, Carey Theological College, Vancouver, Canada
Vincent Brummer, University of Utrecht, The Netherlands
Gerhard Sauter, University of Bonn, Germany

Kierkegaard's Christocentric Theology

TIM ROSE

Ashgate

Aldershot • Burlington USA • Singapore • Sydney

© Tim Rose 2001

All rights reserved. No part of this publication may be reproduced, stored in a retrieval system, or transmitted in any form or by any means, electronic, mechanical, photocopying, recording or otherwise without the prior permission of the publisher.

Published by
Ashgate Publishing Ltd
Gower House
Croft Road
Aldershot
Hants GU11 3HR
England

Ashgate Publishing Company
131 Main Street
Burlington, VT 05401-5600 USA

Ashgate website: http://www.ashgate.com

British Library Cataloguing in Publication Data
Rose, Tim
Kierkegaard's Christocentric theology. - (Ashgate new critical thinking in theology & biblical studies)
1.Kierkegaard, Soren, 1813-1855 2.Jesus Christ - Person and offices - Philosophy 3.Theology 4.Christianity - Philosophy
I. Title
230'.01

Library of Congress Control Number: 00-111410

ISBN 0 7546 1573 1

Printed and bound by Athenaeum Press, Ltd.,
Gateshead, Tyne & Wear.

Contents

Preface

This is a study of the theology of the Danish philosopher-theologian Søren Kierkegaard (1813-55), one of the most controversial figures in the history of Christian thought. It was originally begun as an examination of Kierkegaard's treatment of the relationship between faith and reason in *Philosophical Fragments*. However, as research progressed, it became increasingly apparent that Kierkegaard had developed important themes from *Philosophical Fragments* in later works such as *The Sickness Unto Death* and *Practice in Christianity*. Such works are more overtly theological than *Philosophical Fragments* and they provide great insights into Kierkegaard's more mature thought, something that is frequently neglected by scholars. In particular, I became fascinated by the centrality of Christology in any discussion of faith and reason in Kierkegaard's writings, and, how this was the basis for his rejection of natural theology as it is traditionally understood. The topic, and then the title, of the book therefore became *Kierkegaard's Christocentric Theology*, as the scope of the project was appropriately broadened.

The chapters are arranged as follows: The first chapter introduces the 'problem' of reading Kierkegaard: why it is that his interpreters must often deal with Kierkegaard's rhetorical eccentricities alongside the theological content of his works. It explains why he frequently chose to communicate his ideas indirectly through pseudonyms and how he employed the tactics of Socratic irony. Kierkegaard's thought is then placed in its historical and ideological context, explaining: the impact of his failed engagement upon his early writing, his ambiguous relationship with Romanticism, his hostile reaction against Hegelian Idealism and, finally, his criticism of the established Danish Lutheran Church. Finally, I introduce the diverse variety of works attributed to him known as 'the authorship' and show that Kierkegaard's later 'religious' works offer the clearest insight into his theology.

Chapter two is a theological introduction to Kierkegaard's thoughts on faith and reason. Beginning with his first detailed treatment of this topic, presented in *Philosophical Fragments*, it is shown that Kierkegaard holds the existence of human sin to be the major preventative factor in the search for knowledge of God. It shows that the alleged rebuttal of Socratic recollection in *Fragments* is actually a penetrating criticism of the immanentist theological epistemologies found in the rationalism and Idealism of Kierkegaard's contemporaries. In their place he proclaims a Christological epistemology, stating that humanity in need of God's activity both as teacher and as saviour.

In the light of this, I move on to discuss the complexities of Kierkegaard's Christology in chapters three and four. Chapter three examines Kierkegaard's Christological meta-concept 'the Absolute Paradox'. Traditionally this has been interpreted as a formal contradiction, either between the concepts of humanity and deity, or time and eternity. Rejecting these interpretations, I argue that 'the Absolute Paradox' of the Incarnation is not an irrationality, but a mystery. Drawing on evidence from some Patristic Christologies and the Chalcedonian Definition, I show that there has always been an indispensable element of mystery in this aspect of classical two natures Christology. On this point, despite his provocative use of 'paradox', Kierkegaard can therefore be seen to be operating within the mainstream of Christian theology.

Chapter four is entitled 'The Sign of Contradiction'. Beginning with Kierkegaard's 'Parable of the King and the Maiden' in *Fragments*, it shows that Christ comes to us 'like unto the lowliest'.[1] The nature of Christ's lowliness is explored in *Practice in Christianity*, where Kierkegaard discusses why humanity is so often offended at its saviour. I then explain why Kierkegaard was careful to stress that Christ is both Redeemer and Prototype. The final two sections consider the relationship between Kierkegaard's Christology, Kenotic Christology and then Luther's Theology of the Cross. Linking Kierkegaard to the latter, it is seen that Christ is 'the Sign of Contradiction' who reveals God *sub contrariis*.

This leads on to the twofold subject of Chapter five: Kierkegaard's doctrine of God, and, his critique of attempts to gain knowledge of God independently from faith in God through Christ. I begin by defending Kierkegaard against the charge that his theism is a product of pagan Greek philosophy. I claim instead that this is a trait of one of his non-Christian pseudonyms and that Kierkegaard himself adhered to traditional Christian theism. This then leads on to a rejection of the anti-realist interpretations of his theology put forward by Don Cupitt and D.Z. Phillips. Following this, I examine Kierkegaard's criticism of the pantheist conceptions of God found in nineteenth century Idealism

[1] Søren Kierkegaard, *Philosophical Fragments*, ed. and trans. Howard and Edna Hong (Princeton: Princeton University Press, 1985), p. 32 (abbreviated to *Fragments* in future footnotes).

and his resultant affirmation of God's transcendence and omnipotence. The discussion of Kierkegaard's theism ends with the subject of God's love. It shows that, working from 'the thesis of Christianity' that 'God loves - and wants to be loved',[2] he argues that our knowledge of God derives from, and is motivated by, our love for him. This leads to the subject of natural theology and the knowledge of God. I examine Kierkegaard's verdict upon the validity of proofs and demonstrations for Christian faith before focusing on his treatment of the ontological argument and the argument from design. His rejection of natural theology has led some to claim that Kierkegaard may be classed as a negative ('apophatic') theologian. Against this I argue that Kierkegaard's criticism of natural theology stems instead from his Lutheran heritage, which, as clarified in Chapter four, focuses on God's self-revelation in Christ.

The final chapter examines the nature of faith in Kierkegaard's theology and whether this really does lead him into irrationalism or fideism as is commonly supposed. I begin by discussing the nature of his 'anti-rationalism' and discuss his relationship with three other figures in the history of ideas who have developed similar theologies: Luther, Pascal and Hamann. Following this, the chapter considers the importance of whether Kierkegaard saw faith as being above, or against, 'reason' or 'understanding'. In order to do this I place his thought in the context of Kantian, Hegelian and Coleridgean philosophies. I then discuss the significance given by Kierkegaard to knowledge, volition and subjectivity in his doctrine of faith.

---

[2] *Søren Kierkegaard's Journals and Papers*, ed. and trans. Howard and Edna Hong (Princeton: Princeton University Press, 1967-78), 1446, XI 2 A 99 *n.d.*, 1854.

Acknowledgements

Work on this text was carried out over four years in the universities of both Wales and London. The project began in 1994 as a part-time MPhil study based in the Philosophy Section at the University of Wales, Cardiff. I am grateful to Professor Christopher Norris and Dr Stephen Moller, and especially to Mr Michael Durrant for their supervision, advice and encouragement at this time. In 1996 registration was upgraded to that of part-time PhD study and supervision was transferred to the Reverend Paul Ballard from the Department of Religious and Theological Studies at Cardiff. I am grateful to Paul for his significant help, but also to introducing me to Kierkegaard's thought during my first year as an undergraduate in Cardiff. In the summer of 1997 I transferred to full-time study in the Department of Theology and Religious Studies, King's College, London, where I enjoyed the supervision and guidance of the Reverend Dr Alan Torrance. Material from chapters two and five were presented as a seminar and conference paper respectively at King's, and I benefited from the constructive criticism offered by the staff and research students on these occasions. The thesis was prepared for publication during my training for ordination at Wycliffe Hall, during which time I received support and encouragement from several members of staff and students at Oxford University, most notably Professor John Webster in Christ Church. I am grateful to my parents and latterly to my wife for their support during these years of study; to my father Dr Edward Rose and my father-in-law the Reverend Dr John Colwell for commenting on early drafts of the thesis; and to my wife Sarah, who not only proof read the final draft, but has provided much practical support and encouragement in the last five years.

Chapter One

Introduction:
On Reading Kierkegaard

Kierkegaard's works are not easy to read, but maybe that was his intention. He wrote in an obscure, highly rhetorical style, whilst he frequently adopted pseudonyms in order to distance himself from publications that are often full of irony and satire. The purpose of this introductory chapter is to provide a framework for a correct interpretation of Kierkegaard's writings. It will be shown that, to a certain extent, *how* he presented his arguments in a text can be more important than the outward content of what it says literally.

Kierkegaard's writings can be divided into three distinct groups.[1] Most speculation, not to mention controversy, centres around the first group, his pseudonymous works, sometimes also referred to as the 'indirect communication'. From *Either/Or* in 1843 to *Practice in Christianity* in 1850, these books present us with a variety of different authors, editors, life-views and puzzles.[2] In these pseudonymous works we are always left wondering just where Kierkegaard stands in relation to what is written on their pages. Kierkegaard also published numerous works under his own name, and so we may refer to this second group as the signed works, or 'direct communication'. Within this particular category we may include Kierkegaard's MA thesis *The Concept of Irony*,

---

[1] I am here largely following the classification suggested by Julia Watkin (cf. Julia Watkin, *Kierkegaard* (London: Geoffrey Chapman, 1997), pp. 46-49). However, there have been several different methods used to clarify the types of literature within Kierkegaard's literary corpus. Cf. for instance Mark C. Taylor, *Kierkegaard's Pseudonymous Authorship, A Study of Time and the Self* (Princeton: Princeton University Press, 1975), pp. 11-13 and Alastair Hannay, *Kierkegaard* (London: Routledge, 1991) pp. 16-17.

[2] Watkin does list earlier works within this category: the articles by A and B written from 1834-36, and *From the Papers of One Still Living* which Kierkegaard wrote in 1838. However, Kierkegaard himself did not regard these as being important for his later authorship (cf. Søren Kierkegaard, *The Point of View*, trans. Walter Lowrie (London: OUP, 1950), p. 10), and it is therefore customary to cite his first major work *Either/Or* as being the first pseudonymous work of the authorship proper (cf. Watkin, *Kierkegaard*, pp. 47f).

the numerous *Upbuilding Discourses*, plus the polemical articles and discourses written in the early 1850s till his death in 1855. The *Upbuilding Discourses* are a collection of Christian essays, almost homilies, which he published parallel to the early pseudonymous works. Unlike the pseudonymous works they more obviously bear clear witness to his own Christian faith. Finally, forming the third group of Kierkegaard's works, there are his multi-volume *Journals* and other unpublished material. These cover a diverse range of topics and help to give us an insight into his most personal thoughts and beliefs from adolescence till the last days of his life.

In order to tackle the problem of how we may approach this vast and varied authorship, the first task is to evaluate some of the methods of interpretation offered by scholars. It will then be appropriate to explain my reasons for adopting what may be termed the literary-theological approach as a solution. I then discuss the most significant motives behind Kierkegaard's authorship as a whole: his relationship with his former fiancée Regine Olsen, his dissatisfaction with aspects of Romanticism, his rejection of Hegelian Idealism, and lastly, his 'direct or indirect polemic against the monstrous illusion we call Christendom, or against the illusion that in such a land as ours all are Christians of a sort'.[3] Following this background information, I will offer some explanation of Kierkegaard's use of irony and pseudonymity, literary tactics employed throughout the 'indirect communication' as a means of creating a certain distance between himself and the views expressed within the works themselves. This will be illustrated with reference to his famous 'stages of existence', or life-views, as portrayed by some of his pseudonymous authors within the early works of the 'indirect communication'. There then follows a section in which I briefly introduce what I believe to be the most theologically insightful of his writings. I have therefore entitled these 'the religious works'. Some of these texts are pseudonymous, whilst others were published quite openly as Kierkegaard's own works. Within this section I will also include some discussion of his *Journals* and papers, showing their theological importance within the authorship.

1. The Authorship and a Matter of Interpretation

There are several different approaches to Kierkegaard's works (normally referred to as 'the authorship' in most studies) currently circulating in English-language scholarship. Rather than referring to each theory specifically, I have chosen to summarize the most

[3] *The Point of View*, p. 6.

influential methods under three general headings. I am of course aware that some people will wish to disagree with such a generalization (one article claims that there could be nine ways of reading *Philosophical Fragments* alone![4]), especially with the current trend of offering a variety of post-modernist or post-structuralist readings of any one text. However, my intention is to clarify the position to be employed here without digressing too far into the detailed field of literary theory at this stage. The finer details of this position will be illustrated as they are applied within the context of each chapter. So, in the rest of this section I have chosen to adopt the quite broad definitions offered by the American philosopher C. Stephen Evans in order to clarify the most significant methods of interpretation.

The 'Philosophical' Method

The first method, Evans suggests, may be referred to as the 'philosophical method'. This particular method seeks to appreciate Kierkegaard's texts as being primarily philosophical. Little significance is given to the pseudonyms under which he wrote various works and so each one is interpreted as representing the content of Kierkegaard's own personal viewpoint, despite the extreme contrasts between the views of the different pseudonyms and regardless of the obvious discrepancies between them and the signed works. It is deemed possible to construct a picture of what Kierkegaard thought from a literal interpretation of his entire authorship, something which proponents of this method would consider to be a continuous, long term project.[5]

In a similar vein, there are those who seek to adopt the same method, albeit from a more theological viewpoint, such as David Law.[6] According to Law, 'although Kierkegaard may not personally occupy

---

[4] Jens Glebe-Møller, 'Wittgenstein and Kierkegaard', *Kierkegaardiana* 15 (1991), p. 55.

[5] C. Stephen Evans, *Passionate Reason, Making Sense of Kierkegaard's* Philosophical Fragments (Bloomington and Indianapolis: Indiana University Press, 1992), p. 2. Good examples of this view are Walter Lowrie, *A Short Life of Kierkegaard* (Princeton: Princeton University Press, 1970) and David Swenson, *Something About Kierkegaard* (Macon: Mercer University Press, 1983). Regarding the more recent scholars in this category, Evans lists the following texts as examples: John Elrod, *Being and Existence in Kierkegaard's Pseudonymous Works* (Princeton: Princeton University Press, 1975); Stephen Dunning, *Kierkegaard's Dialectic of Existence: A Structural Analysis of the Theory of Stages* (Princeton: Princeton University Press, 1985); Louis Pojman, *The Logic of Subjectivity: Kierkegaard's Philosophy of Religion* (Alabama: University of Alabama Press, 1984); Mark C. Taylor, *Kierkegaard's Pseudonymous Authorship: A Study of Time and the Self* (Princeton: Princeton University Press, 1975).

[6] David Law, *Kierkegaard as Negative Theologian* (Oxford: Oxford University Press, 1993). On this point he is largely following Mark C. Taylor. (Cf. Law, *Kierkegaard as Negative Theologian*, p. 5.)

the positions advocated in his works, they nevertheless form an integral part of his thought. In this sense we can ascribe them to him even if he himself has rejected them as possibilities for his own existence.'[7] However, it is a mistake to form too close a link between ideas delivered through the mouths of the pseudonyms and those of Kierkegaard himself as the pseudonyms are caricatures of views he criticized. The weaknesses of each pseudonym represent a corresponding weakness in the view under attack, indirectly giving support to Kierkegaard's own, frequently quite different views.

The 'Literary' Method

On the other hand, it is possible to take the literary forms of Kierkegaard's texts very seriously indeed, even up to the point where they dominate all else. This 'literary method' represents a diverse body of scholars who see Kierkegaard as primarily a literary artist, or poet. One of the first to do this was Louis Mackey in his book *Kierkegaard: A Kind of Poet.*[8] However more recent authors have moved beyond Mackey's original thesis and attempt to relate Kierkegaard to contemporary developments in deconstructionism, post-structuralism and other literary movements.[9] Taken to its logical conclusion this method ultimately serves to deny any definitive reading of Kierkegaard's texts and Evans therefore entitles it the 'ironic method'. For instance, Roger Poole, referring to the various rhetorical devices employed in the aesthetic authorship, claims 'Kierkegaard's writing has made all solutions impossible', because, 'trained in the school of Romantic irony, Kierkegaard was an adept at displacing and "deferring" meaning. Indeed, it is Kierkegaard, a century before Derrida, who demonstrates that a meaning can be so long deferred that it would finally be merely naive to ask for it.'[10] Poole therefore states: 'a new reading of Kierkegaard should discover that the aesthetic texts do not mean but are.'[11]

---

[7] Ibid.

[8] According to Mackey, 'In a word Kierkegaard is not a philosopher and theologian who puts up poetic advertisements to recommend his product. More Dante than Thomas Aquinas, he is a poet whose orientation is primarily philosophical and theological.' (Louis Mackey, *Kierkegaard: A Kind of Poet* (Philadelphia: University of Pennsylvania Press, 1971), p. 259).

[9] Cf. Evans, *Passionate Reason*, p. 2. Some good examples of work in this category are Christopher Norris, 'De Man Unfair to Kierkegaard? An Allegory of (non)-reading', in *Kierkegaard Conferences I*, (ed.) Brigit Bertung (Copenhagen: C.A. Reitzel, 1989), and Roger Poole, *Kierkegaard: The Indirect Communication* (Charlottesville and London: University Press of Virginia, 1993).

[10] Poole, *Kierkegaard: The Indirect Communication*, p. 2.

[11] Ibid., p. 5.

There is evidence from the authorship to support some aspects of this position. For instance, on some occasions Kierkegaard did describe himself as 'merely a poet'.[12] Also, when, if at all, is it safe to take him literally? In the posthumously published *The Point of View For My Work as an Author* he allegedly explains the nature and purpose of his authorship, doing so without a pseudonym and (apparently) without irony. Kierkegaard also admits his responsibility for the pseudonymous authorship and appears to explain his writings in a note entitled 'A First and Last Explanation', which he appended to the pseudonymous *Concluding Unscientific Postscript*. Yet, as Christopher Norris argues, 'irony is not so easily laid to rest, especially when Kierkegaard has himself provided such a range of sophisticated ruses, alibis and narrative pretexts for *not* taking him at his word.'[13] Therefore, 'One could treat *all* of Kierkegaard's texts (including the ethical, religious and 'edifying' discourses) as belonging to the order of aesthetic production, as written - and who is to prove otherwise? - from some pseudonymous, ironic, or noncommital standpoint, and therefore as open to post-modern reading, indifferent to questions of ultimate truth.'[14]

The 'Literary-Philosophical' Method

To a certain extent I would agree with the literary method, namely, in that it is very important to do proper justice to the literary forms of the texts. However, the tendency of some scholars within that category to reject the possibility of one definitive reading of Kierkegaard's texts does seem to miss the whole point of the exercise. Additionally, the literary method frequently attempts to avoid treating the theological material with any seriousness.[15] Yet I indicated earlier that the philosophical method has its weaknesses too. Therefore I agree with Evans that a 'literary-philosophical' method, combining the best aspects of both approaches, offers a better solution to the problem. Allowance is made for the literary forms of the texts, being especially mindful of the role and extent of irony where appropriate, and the significance of any pseudonyms used. At the same time it is also recognized that Kierkegaard had a philosophical purpose in writing what he did and when he did. However, as my concern is to consider Kierkegaard's theology, I have chosen to adopt a 'literary-theological'

---

[12] *Journals and Papers*, 2301, X4 A 247 *n.d.*, 1851.

[13] Norris, 'De Man Unfair to Kierkegaard? An Allegory of (non)-reading', p. 92.

[14] Ibid., p. 91.

[15] Cf. for instance Poole's cautionary statement 'we, as modern skeptics', which he voices when discussing the Incarnation in Kierkegaard's writings (Poole, *Kierkegaard: The Indirect Communication*, p. 252).

method as I would argue that Kierkegaard's philosophical concerns arise largely within the context of his theological enquiries.

This point may best be illustrated by considering the composite nature of Kierkegaard's literary output as a whole. Alongside the aesthetic works stand his *Upbuilding Discourses*, his unpublished *Journals* and various published works on specific Christian themes such as *Christian Discourses*, *For Self-Examination* and *Judge For Yourself!*[16] The style, content and nature of these works differ very much from that of the pseudonymous works. For instance, each group of the sermon-like *Upbuilding Discourses* was published under Kierkegaard's own name, and, more importantly, the time of each publication was practically parallel with a pseudonymous aesthetic text. He therefore seems to have presented his readership with a clear indication of his beliefs from the outset, regardless of the statements of any pseudonym to the contrary. Added to this is the fact that his two later pseudonymous works, both attributed to Anti-Climacus, are overtly Christian in theme, clarifying and developing topics introduced by some of the earlier pseudonyms. When taken together these two facts give weight to his claim, expressed in *The Point of View For My Work as an Author*, that he had always written from a primarily theological concern.[17] We can read his works with a view to finding out what his ideas really were. Yet, this can only be done if care is taken to understand what Kierkegaard's motivations were for adopting this means of communication, and in this way discern what each one of the various pseudonyms represent.

2. The Critical Purpose of the Authorship

The situation that led to Kierkegaard embarking upon his writings was complex indeed. There were several significant causes behind his decision to write in such an extravagant and sometimes heavily polemical manner. The first was a personal motive, namely his failed relationship with Regine Olsen. It was this that had largely propelled him into composing some of the earliest pseudonymous works, such as: *Either/Or*, *Fear and Trembling* and *Repetition* (all of which were

---

[16] We could also add to this category some of the less known items from the last phase of Kierkegaard's literary output such as *What Christ's Judgement is About Official Christianity*, Kierkegaard's various articles in *The Fatherland*, etc. These are normally referred to as the 'Attack Literature' and they form the final and most vitriolic component of Kierkegaard's direct polemic against the state of Christianity in Denmark at the time. Cf. Søren Kierkegaard, *Attack Upon 'Christendom'*, trans. Walter Lowrie (Princeton: Princeton University Press, 1968).

[17] *The Point of View*, pp. 10ff.

published in 1843). The second motive, which was both personal and ideological, was Kierkegaard's wish to deliver a theological critique of contemporary thought and values. As is explained retrospectively in *The Point of View*, he sought to address 'the problem "of becoming a Christian", with a direct or indirect polemic against the monstrous illusion we call Christendom, or against the illusion that in such a land as ours we are all Christians of a sort.'[18] This led him into conflict with two distinguished opponents: speculative Idealist philosophy, primarily as represented by Hegelianism, but also by various forms of Romanticism, and, later in life, the established Evangelical Lutheran Church of Denmark. Pseudonymous works that are of particular relevance to this category are *Philosophical Fragments* (1844), *Concluding Unscientific Postscript to Philosophical Fragments* (1846) and *Practice in Christianity* (1850).

Regine Olsen

The first meeting between Kierkegaard and Regine occurred in 1837. She was only fourteen years old and he was ten years her senior, yet despite this age gap he was captivated by her from the start. A few years later he courted her and their engagement was announced on September 10, 1840, but any hope of marriage was soon ruled out. Kierkegaard had always been of a melancholy temperament, something he inherited from his father, and very swiftly he realized that he could not go on with the engagement.[19] Instead he believed that his life should be spent as a solitary writer, in detachment from the world. Nevertheless, it was not until October 11 the following year that he was able to break the engagement. In so doing he devastated his young fiancée and caused a scandal so great that he alienated himself from most of society. However, as it was considered to be a gross insult to the honour of any woman to be treated in this way, Kierkegaard did his best to ensure that the blame lay squarely on his shoulders. In order to do this he acted the part of a heartless scoundrel in public, and so turned opinion against him, though of course this hurt her even more.[20]

The guilt of this episode haunted him till the end of his life. He never really stopped loving her and for many years he held some hope

[18] Ibid., p. 6.

[19] *Journal and Papers*, 6472, X 5 A 149 *n.d.*, 1849.

[20] Ibid. Interestingly 'The Seducer's Diary', in *Either/Or* vol. 1, pp. 301-445, was written for this purpose. Through it Kierkegaard indirectly attempted to portray himself as a callous seducer (Johannes) and Regine as his innocent victim (Cordelia). Although he may well have upset Regine by it, Kierkegaard despairingly relates in the journal how he then went up in the public's estimation because of this particular publication! (*Journals and Papers*, 6472 §19, X 5 A 159 *n.d.*, 1849.)

of reconciliation, until she finally married a childhood sweetheart 'Fritz' Schlegel. Prevented from speaking to her directly by social custom and, no doubt severe embarrassment, he sought an alternative way to explain his conduct. Kierkegaard was in many respects an eccentric character and his solution to the problem was in keeping with this description. Possessing an exceptional literary ability and a vivid imagination, he embarked on the aesthetic works. He therefore wrote some of his earliest works for Regine, cryptically conveying personal information through the illusions of Romantic fiction.

Hegelianism

In order to placate his devoutly religious father Kierkegaard had originally begun his years at Copenhagen University as a theology student. It soon became apparent that his interests were in fact much broader than this and his attention shifted to a range of other subjects, notably philosophy and literature, with him remaining a student for ten years. Denmark was culturally very much influenced by Germany. In both countries Enlightenment Rationalism had largely been superseded by the philosophies of Kant and Hegel, and Hegel's thought was being warmly received by several academics in Copenhagen whilst the young Kierkegaard studied there. The most central figure to make Hegelianism the prominent school of thought in Denmark at this time was Kierkegaard's tutor, Hans Martensen.[21] As a young student Kierkegaard had lost faith in Christianity, and for a brief time he too embraced Hegelianism as he turned to philosophy for solace instead.

This enthusiasm was short-lived. Criticism of Hegelian philosophy (often referred to by him as 'the system') occurs throughout Kierkegaard's *Journals* and the *Concluding Unscientific Postscript* in particular, although to a lesser extent it permeates the entire authorship. His main criticism of Hegel was that he had presented a distorted idea of reality in order to attempt to describe everything neatly within one philosophical system. In a journal entry of 1844 he wrote, 'If Hegel had written his whole *Logic* and written in the preface that it was only a thought-experiment, in which at many points he still avoided some things, he undoubtedly would have been the greatest thinker who has ever lived. As it is he is comic.'[22] As Kierkegaard saw it, Hegel and his followers were lost in vacuous speculation on the objective universe, instead of addressing the problems of human existence in the real world.[23] Within this philosophy he claimed Christianity was reduced to but an intellectual exercise, a minor component of an elitist

---

[21] Watkin, *Kierkegaard*, pp. 15-16.

[22] *Journals and Papers*, 1605, V A 73 *n.d.*, 1844.

[23] Watkin, *Kierkegaard*, p. 16.

metaphysical system. Yet the Christianity embraced by Kierkegaard may be defined as a relationship with God, one that demands total commitment in opposition to secular standards of rationality and ethics, and because of this it cannot be defined purely intellectually. Kierkegaard proclaimed a Christian faith that could never be rid of mystery and so he constantly found himself at odds with Hegel's paradox-free rendition of religion. However, although there are numerous references to Hegel and Hegelianism throughout the authorship, Kierkegaard's attack upon 'the system' was primarily directed against Hegel's Danish followers with whom Kierkegaard frequently came into contact both during, and after, his university days.[24] He had little interest in critiquing German thought in Germany, rather his interests were far closer to home as he sought to stem the influence of Absolute Idealism in his own country.

Romanticism

Contemporary with Hegel was the development of German Romanticism. Just as Hegel set himself against the aridity of Enlightenment philosophy, so too did the Romantics attempt to breathe new life and vitality into the arts and humanities during the early nineteenth century. Theologically the movement was best represented by Friedrich Schleiermacher in his two most significant works *On Religion: Speeches to its Cultured Despisers* and *The Christian Faith.* However, Idealism soon became its dominant philosophical framework, developed largely by Fichte and Schelling.[25] It is debatable whether Hegel can really be classed as a Romantic himself, but aspects of his philosophy swiftly passed into the mainstream of German Romanticism. This served to influence the development of Danish thought in the early nineteenth century, which, as mentioned above, is often the main butt of Kierkegaard's critique rather than Hegel himself.

However, there were times when German Romanticism did become the direct object of Kierkegaard's attack. When this occurred his thoughts were focused upon what was called the Romantic Ironists, a group of scholars, writers and poets that included Novalis, Tieck, Solger and the brothers A.W. and Friedrich Schlegel. This group had come together in the University of Jena during the 1790s, drawing much of their literary inspiration from Shakespeare.[26] Schlegel and his associates

---

[24] Poole *Kierkegaard: The Indirect Communication*, p. 2.

[25] Cf. Niels Thulstrup, *Commentary on Kierkegaard's* Concluding Unscientific Postscript (Princeton: Princeton University Press, 1984), p. 43.

[26] E. Behler, *German Romantic Literary Theory* (Cambridge: CUP, 1986), pp. 14ff; Kathleen Wheeler, *Romanticism, Pragmatism and Deconstruction* (Oxford: Basil Blackwell, 1993), p. 27.

challenged Enlightenment values and traditions through works such as his revolutionary novel *Lucinde*. In this work Schlegel used the characters to break with traditional role models, developing in their place life-views that owe their inspiration to desires and feelings, giving free reign to the imagination. However, even for a Romantic author, Schlegel was extreme. According to Kierkegaard, who found much to inspire him in the movement at its more general level, the Romantic Ironists had gone so far in their ironic subversion of traditional values and truth claims that they verged upon moral nihilism. Their rejection of rationalist claims to objectivity and systematic knowledge led them to posit notions of incomprehensibility and paradox far too freely.[27] In so doing, he believed that their attempts to reach freedom beyond restraint had ultimately loosened their grasp of reality.

'Christendom'

Kierkegaard's final object of polemic was something he referred to as 'Christendom'. The official state religion of Denmark since 1536 has been Lutheranism. In Kierkegaard's time it was a requirement that all Danish citizens be baptized and confirmed into the Evangelical Lutheran Church.[28] To Kierkegaard the church had become just a facet of the royal administration, instead of the community of believers, with entry to it being a requirement under civil law (although certain limited freedoms were given to other religious groups). As Kierkegaard developed his theology he had serious difficulties in accepting this as being a valid manifestation of the church. Christianity is chosen by an individual through faith, not something to be born into,[29] nor could it be imposed on others by force of state or society in general. This idea of the state church, or Christian nation, was Kierkegaard's 'Christendom' and although he levels some indirect attacks against it in the 1840s, it was to become the recipient of his harshest, most scathing attacks towards the end of his life.

3. The Aesthetic Works and Indirect Communication

So, it can be seen that on one level the authorship arose out of Kierkegaard's eccentric, yet covert attempts to enable Regine to understand his position. Besides this, he also wanted to criticize the main religious and intellectual establishments of his society. On one hand Hegel was attacked for his claim to have presented an all-

---

[27] Cf. Wheeler, *Romanticism, Pragmatism and Deconstruction*, p. 29.
[28] Watkin, *Kierkegaard*, p. 13.
[29] Cf. *Journals and Papers*, 3966, XI 1 A 219 *n.d.*, 1854.

embracing philosophical system, free from contradictions, where everything formed a coherent whole. On the other hand, the Romantic Ironists seemed to have fled to the opposite end of the spectrum. Their ironic subversion of accepted values approached nihilism, whilst their rejection of systematic philosophies left them submerged beneath a philosophy of paradox and uncertainty. As for the state church, to Kierkegaard it seemed to give the impression that Christianity was something to be born into or to be embraced in order to fit in with society.

This was Kierkegaard's background and reasons for writing, yet what can be said about the singular manner in which he delivered the pseudonymous works? Did he intend for his works to be taken seriously? Or, did he really wish to prevent his readers from making actual conclusions from what is said? In his *Philosophical Rhetoric* Jeff Mason warns against taking Kierkegaard too literally:

> Kierkegaard is extremely devious in his use of rhetorical strategies and tropes. He makes great use of circumlocution. We are never given formulas or recipes we can just accept and use. Everything must be questioned, nothing taken for granted ... He is not above using invective, satire, irony, jokes, parables, and all the rest to lead us back to ourselves by a circuitous route that only we can follow.[30]

For those who are used to a far more straight-forward approach this may certainly give rise to concern. Before attempting to grasp what might be said in or through a text, we are required to examine the matter of how it is said. Is there a pseudonym, if so, who is this pseudonym and what is he alleged to represent? From what position is he coming? To what extent, if any, does irony subvert the apparent content of the argument? Such questions continue, without them any correct appraisal of one of Kierkegaard's works (especially the pseudonymous texts) would not be possible.

Pseudonymity

A pseudonym permits the author a certain amount of freedom. For example, if I were to present this text to a friend for her to read it, she would proceed to take into account any knowledge of me as an important factor. There would exist a definite bias in her interpretation, either for or against me. She would have some knowledge of my views and beliefs. She would perhaps recognize my preconceptions and style, possibly even go some way to predict my

[30] Jeff Mason, *Philosophical Rhetoric, The Function of Indirection in Philosophical Writing* (London and New York: Routledge, 1989), p. 29.

conclusions. Yet if I offered this same text to the same friend under the pretence that the author was anonymous, my friend would not have the same privileged position. This approach would allow her to take the text entirely on its own merits and so interpret what is said (hopefully) without bias.

Kierkegaard's employment of pseudonymity was rather on the subtle side. In a sense he was already known to be the author of his works, having been required to notify the Stationer's Register in Copenhagen of his true identity as a legal formality.[31] Certain secrets of his authorship were also made known to his secretaries and a few close friends. Although *The Point of View for My Work as an Author* explained his intentions, he felt unable to publish it during his lifetime (although this was published by his brother after his death); but he did provide 'A First and Last Explanation' in the *Postscript* in 1846 when he felt his aesthetic authorship had come to an end. However, to the resident of Copenhagen glancing along the shelves of the book shops, no immediate indication of his responsibility for the works would be visible. Instead the title pages would exhibit various bizarre names in his place - Victor Eremita, Johannes de Silentio, Vigilius Haufniensis, Johannes Climacus, or even Anti-Climacus. These were never intended to masquerade as real names, but instead to hold a symbolic function. The precise details of some of these pseudonyms will be discussed with reference to the works to which they were attached in the remaining sections of this chapter. For the present it is sufficient to say that each one of them personifies a life-view wholly different from that held by Kierkegaard at the time of writing. He did not want to be associated directly with the contents of the views themselves. As he explained, 'one will perceive the significance of the pseudonyms and why I must be pseudonymous in relation to all aesthetic productions, because I led my life in entirely different categories and understood from the beginning that this productivity was of an interim nature, a deceit, a necessary process of elimination.'[32]

Each text is used to set forth a critical argument. To read the entire pseudonymous output in chronological order, and then claim that it faithfully represents Kierkegaard's own philosophy or theology would be a serious mistake. Anyone who claims that he adhered to all that is expressed in these works would have to view him as, at best inconsistent, or at worst as one who suffered from some form of multiple personality disorder. What Kierkegaard really did was to offer his readership caricatures of the life-views he wished to review. For this purpose, each pseudonym is in fact a rhetorical exaggeration through which he allowed

[31] Mackey, *Kierkegaard: A Kind of Poet*, p. 249.
[32] *The Point of View*, pp. 5-6.

the effects of metaphor and hyperbole to play upon the reader.[33] This tactic was intended to give Kierkegaard greater authorial freedom. As he explains, each pseudonym 'has his definitive life-view, and the lines, which understood in this way could possibly be meaningful, witty, stimulating, would perhaps sound strange, ludicrous, disgusting in the mouth of a particular factual person.'[34]

In absolving himself from personal responsibility for their views, he allowed the pseudonyms to illustrate points that were designed to shock, even offend a readership that may have existed within the life-views he derided. In case of complaint, Kierkegaard could argue in his defence that he was merely engaging in a rhetorical experiment and so meant no harm. He declared,

> What has been written then, is mine, but only insofar as I, by means of audible lines, have placed in the life-view of the creating, poetically actual individuality in his mouth, for my relation is even more remote than that of a poet, who poeticizes characters and yet in the preface is himself the author. That is, I am impersonally or personally in the third person a *souffleur* [prompter] who has poetically produced the authors, whose prefaces in turn are their productions, as their names are also. Thus in the pseudonymous books there is not a single word by me.[35]

In the same passage from which this is taken (in which he openly acknowledges his responsibility for the pseudonymous works to that date), he asks that,

> If it should occur to anyone to want to quote a particular passage from the books, it is my wish, my prayer, that he will do me the kindness of citing the respective pseudonymous author's name, not mine - that is, of separating us in such a way that the passage femininely belongs to the pseudonymous author, the responsibility civilly to me.[36]

The failure to appreciate this is widespread and illustrated by the secondary sources listed within the 'philosophical' tradition of reading Kierkegaard.[37] Those in this category have quoted from the pseudonymous works supposedly offering 'Kierkegaard's philosophy of *x*' when in fact they are only relating what is said by, for instance, Johannes the Seducer. To find the real content of Kierkegaard's

---

[33] John Mullen, *Kierkegaard's Philosophy, Self-Deception and Cowardice in the Present Age* (London: University Press of America, 1995), p. 39.

[34] Søren Kierkegaard, *Concluding Unscientific Postscript to* Philosophical Fragments, vol. 1, ed. and trans. Howard and Edna Hong (Princeton: Princeton University Press, 1292), pp. 627f.

[35] Ibid., p. 626.

[36] Ibid., p. 627.

[37] See p. 6 above.

thought we have to look beyond the text. We also have to compare what is said by him in his nonpseudonymous writings - like his *Journals*, or the *Upbuilding Discourses*. However, pseudonymity is only one factor of Kierkegaard's indirect communication. The greater importance is reserved for his use of irony.

Irony

Josiah Thompson entitles Kierkegaard 'the Master of Irony'.[38] In fact Kierkegaard had displayed a biting, ironic wit from an early age, allowing him to engage in dialogue with others at their frequent expense.[39] The youngest member of a large family, Kierkegaard frequently resorted to teasing in this manner both at home and at school, and had earned himself the nickname of 'the fork' as a result. Even at university he carried on employing a devastating irony against his teachers and other public figures.[40] In Kierkegaard's writings 'irony' swiftly begins to take on a far more profound meaning than is normally encountered in everyday English. I will show how and why this arises and, in the process, illustrate the nature of Kierkegaard's ambiguous relationship with some of the streams within German Romanticism that he had come across during his studies.

(a) Classical Irony Kierkegaard was able to develop his concept of irony through acquainting himself with authors both classical and Romantic. For instance, in *The Art of Rhetoric* Aristotle talks of irony as being a rhetorical device, a form of jest possessing an almost aristocratic air.

> As for jests, since they may sometimes be useful in debates, the advice of Georgias was good - to confound the opponents' earnestness with jest and their jest with earnestness. We have stated in the *Poetics* how many kinds of jest there are, some of them becoming a gentleman, others not. You should therefore choose the kind that suits you. Irony is more gentlemanly than buffoonery; for the first is employed on one's account, the second on that of another.[41]

Amongst Latin authors, it can be observed that Cicero limited irony to dissimulation, but Quintillian kept closer to the Greek understanding and

---

[38] Josiah Thompson, *Kierkegaard* (London: Victor Gollancz, 1974), pp. 138ff.

[39] Cf. M. Holmes Hartshorne, *Kierkegaard Godly Deceiver, The Nature and Meaning of His Pseudonymous Works* (New York: Columbia University Press, 1990), p. 6.

[40] Bruce Kirmmse, ' "Out with It!": The modern breakthrough, Kierkegaard and Denmark', in Alastair Hanny and Gordon Marino (eds.), *The Cambridge Companion to Kierkegaard* (Cambridge: CUP, 1998), p. 24.

[41] Aristotle, *The Art of Rhetoric*, trans. J.H. Freese (London: Heinemann, 1926), p. 447.

thereby allowed for a broader concept.[42] He put irony into the category of a figure of speech, whilst Cicero saw it as a trope. However, Quintillian's definition does not require irony to remain within the bounds of rhetoric, but, it may be seen instead to refer to the nature of a person's character. In this sense that person can be said to embody irony through his attitude to life. Quintillian discusses this in his *Oratorical Education*, presenting Socrates as an example of irony in this sense.

> In the trope the conflict is purely verbal, while in the figure the meaning, and sometimes the whole aspect of our case, conflicts with the language and the tone of the voice adopted; nay, a man's whole life may be coloured with irony, as was the case with Socrates, who was called an ironist because he assumed the role of an ignorant man lost in wonder at the wisdom of others.[43]

(b) Socratic Irony It was to Socrates that both the Romantics and Kierkegaard had turned to as being the greatest of all ironists. Plato and Xenophenon have handed down to us the picture of Socrates as confounding his opponents in an unusual manner of debate. This may be referred to as Socrates' maieutic method, though some also call it dialectic, or eristic. Socrates would not begin a debate in the straightforward manner by first marking his position, and then defending it. Instead, he would begin by allowing his opponent to outline his position on a topic or issue. Socrates would then focus on his opponent's claims, and then proceed to demolish them by questioning his opponent in such a way that, through their answers he would force them to reveal the inconsistencies of their position. In this manner the opponent is compelled to retract his former argument, and then to begin the search for a new answer. Socrates' irony lay in the fact that he always began a debate as if he were the one ignorant of the matter in question, yet the end result always served to illustrate that he had a better grasp of the subject than any others who were present.

Kierkegaard greatly admired this method in that it forced the reader to follow the process of questioning the matter himself, as opposed to the mindless repetition of a ready-made formula or solution:

> The fact that many of Plato's dialogues end without a result has a far deeper reason than I had thought earlier. They are a reproduction of Socrates' maieutic skill which makes the reader or hearer himself active, and therefore they do not end in a result but in a sting. This is an excellent parody of the

---

[42] S. Alford, *Irony and the Logic of Romantic Imagination* (New York: Peter Lang, 1984), p. 20.

[43] Quintillian, *Oratorical Education*, trans. H.E. Butler (London: Heinemann, 1920), p. 401.

> modern rote-method which says everything the sooner the better and all at one time, which awakens no self-action but only leads the reader to rattle it off like a parrot.[44]

So, instead of proclaiming himself to be an expert in complex matters, Socrates ironically questioned even the most basic of truths. Hence, whilst many of his interlocutors believed themselves to be knowledgeable in everyday facts, Socrates' seemingly innocent questioning was able to show up numerous gaps in their knowledge. Apparently 'lost in wonder at the wisdom of others', he subverted the very 'wisdom' they held so dear. Turning again to Kierkegaard's *Journals* we find the following paragraph on the subject:

> In what did Socrates' irony really lie? In expressions and turns of speech, etc.? No, such trivialities, even his virtuosity in talking ironically, such things do not make a Socrates. No, his whole existence is and was irony; whereas the entire contemporary population of farmhands and business men and so on, all those thousands, were perfectly sure of being human and of knowing what it meant to be a human being, Socrates was beneath them (ironically) and occupied himself with the problem - what does it mean to be a human being? He thereby expressed that actually all the *Treiben* [bustle] of those thousands was an hallucination, tomfoolery, a ruckus, a hubbub, busyness, etc., worth a zero in the eyes of the ideal, or less than zero, inasmuch as these man could have used their lives to concentrate upon the ideality.[45]

Kierkegaard's fascination with Socratic irony was so great that he decided to choose it as the subject for his MA thesis (the equivalent to a modern Ph.D.), choosing as his title *The Concept of Irony, with Continual Reference to Socrates*. This was submitted in 1841, but was probably written in 1838-9. He did not consider it to be very significant alongside his later literary output and rarely referred back to it in his *Journals*. However, an examination of its manner and contents serves to shed much light on his future tactics and anticipates several later projects. For instance, comments regarding Romanticism are echoed in the aesthetic life-view in *Either/Or*, and the comparison he makes between Socrates and Christ hints at the topic of *Philosophical Fragments*. The dissertation is composed of two main sections. The first discusses the position of Socrates as irony, whilst the second tackles the subject of Romantic irony.

In his discussion of Socratic irony Kierkegaard draws upon the writings of Plato, Xenophenon, Aristophanes and Aristotle. Irony is described by Kierkegaard as the 'infinite absolute negativity' which

---

[44] *Journals and Papers*, 4266, VII 1 A 74 *n.d.*, 1846.
[45] Ibid. 1767, XI 2 A 189 December 3, 1854.

provides a certain freedom from reality.[46] 'The concept of irony makes its entry into the world through Socrates', who embodied the concept in that 'he walked through life continually between a caricature and the ideal'.[47] Just as he was to use the pseudonyms to embody various life-views in later works, so in his thesis Kierkegaard uses Socrates as the personification of irony.

(c) Romantic Irony As Kierkegaard explains the role of irony and the 'negative freedom' which it brings to its user, he provides a clarification of his own literary tactics:

> When I am aware as I speak that what I am saying is what I mean and that what I have said adequately expresses my meaning, and I assume that the person to whom I am talking grasps my meaning completely, then I am bound in what has been said - that is, I am positively free therein. Here the old verse is appropriate: *semel emissum volat irrevocabile verbum* [the word once set free flies beyond recall]. I am also bound with respect to myself any time I wish. If, however, what is said is not my meaning or the opposite of my meaning, then I am free in relation to others and to myself.[48]

We must be mindful that the thesis is not only about irony but is also itself ironic. At one point he eulogises irony for giving him the ability to distance himself from what has been written. At another point he is seen to be ironically deriding ironists. Consider the following example: 'Just as kings and princes speak French, the higher circles (this, of course, must be understood according to an intellectual ordering of rank) speak ironically so that lay people will not be able to understand them, and to that extent irony is in the process of isolating itself; it does not wish to be understood.'[49] In the past regal circles had spoken French as an indication of rank and in order to preserve a certain aloofness from their subjects. The 'higher circles' who speak ironically refers to intellectuals, principally those holding posts at Copenhagen University, whom Kierkegaard felt to have been so caught up in the details and terminology of (primarily Hegelian) academic philosophy that they had created a gulf between themselves and most of reality. This was perhaps a little bold, if not indeed rash, when one realises that Kierkegaard was only too aware that these were the academics who would be marking the thesis on its completion. Ironically enough, it was his favourite target,

---

[46] *The Concept of Irony, with Continual Reference to Socrates*, ed. and trans. Howard and Edna Hong (Princeton: Princeton University Press, 1989), p. 259.
[47] Ibid., p. 13.
[48] Ibid., pp. 247-8.
[49] Ibid., pp. 248-9.

Hans Martensen, who was to be given the final say over whether the thesis would pass.[50]

Returning to the text, Kierkegaard's criticism of contemporary trends broadens, when, in a footnote, he admits 'throughout this whole discussion I use the terms "irony" and "ironist"; but I would just as well say "Romanticism" and "Romanticist".'[51] He then clarifies the specific objects of his critique by presenting sections on the Romantic Ironists Friedrich Schlegel, Tieck, Fichte and Solger. Most of his attention is directed towards Schlegel and his novel *Lucinde*. To Kierkegaard this work served to capture the very essence of Romantic irony, turning it into a life-view that moved far beyond the Socratic manifestation of the concept. Through *Lucinde*, the allegorical novel representing his love affair with Dorotheia Veit, Schlegel sought to deliver a near utopian vision of Romanticism that would supersede all previous life-views.[52] For Kierkegaard the novel is a failure. Rather than achieving its aim, he found it to be 'immoral', 'unpoetic' and even 'irreligious'.[53] Schlegel's attempts to portray a higher, more liberated morality had resulted in his being ensnared by the carnal forces he wished to transcend. For Kierkegaard this typified Schlegel's extremist strain within Romanticism: 'the oddity about *Lucinde* and the whole trend associated with it is that, by starting from the freedom and the constitutive authority of the I, one does not arrive at a still higher spirituality but comes only to sensuousness and consequently to its opposite.'[54]

(d) 'Mastered' Irony and Fragments of Truth By the time of his writing the thesis Kierkegaard was gradually returning to Christianity. Due to this he increasingly sought to ground any intellectual or moral reasoning in the reality of God. Yet Schlegel, and with him the rest of the Romantic Ironists, had no such sense of grounding (although Schlegel was, like many Romantics, to embrace Roman Catholicism later in life). The Romantic Ironists advocated a relativism that denied absolute, objective standards of truth or knowledge.[55] In place of systematic philosophy they offered what they called 'Symphilosophy'. Rejecting formal doctrines and abstract ideas they argued that philosophy was a matter more of living and experiences, an art form rather than a science.[56] Within this they extolled the importance of what was termed the 'fragment' form, something similar to the aphorism or the pensée.

[50] Cf. Poole, *Kierkegaard: The Indirect Communication*, p. 38.
[51] *The Concept of Irony*, p. 275.
[52] Behler, *German Romantic Literary Theory*, pp. 290, 297.
[53] *The Concept of Irony*, p. 301.
[54] Ibid.
[55] Wheeler, *Romanticism, Pragmatism and Deconstruction*, p. 27.
[56] Ibid., p. 33.

They used this short, staccato formulation of thought as an ironic subversion of the truth-claims of more traditional philosophy.

> The fragment form expressed the nature of language and communication as indirect, imperfect and rhetorical. Indeed, incomprehensibility became a way of parodying the literal language and immediate comprehension (demanded by some readers) as a delusion and as utterly unproductive of thought. Like Socrates, ironists sought to stimulate readers to think for themselves, not to seek solutions from the author.[57]

The ambiguity of Kierkegaard's relationship with Romanticism now begins to become apparent. He might have rejected the general Romantic views on reality, but he did employ some of the tactics of the Romantic Ironists (this will become clearer when I discuss the aesthetic life-view in the next section). Of notable interest is the fact that Schlegel used the concept of paradox in order to express 'the non-absolute, incomplete nature of truth, the absurdity and in-comprehensibility of notions of transcendent reality or being, and especially for expressing the extent to which human beings have not yet comprehended or cultivated themselves'.[58] He declared in his *Critical Fragments* in 1797 that, 'irony is the form of paradox. Paradox is everything simultaneously good and great.'[59] The important thing was not to comprehend a set of truths, but to exercise the imagination and put some effort into the process. Objective certainty could not be attained, so self-knowledge and self-development became the focus of attention.

This was where Kierkegaard was to part company with the Romantic Ironists. It seemed that they were striving for striving's sake without any genuine direction. Their development from Socratic irony took them nowhere, as, 'to know that one is ignorant is the beginning of coming to know, but if one does not know more, it is merely a beginning.'[60] According to Terry Eagleton, 'Socratic irony raises the subject out of its mindless communion with the world, critically unhinging it from the real; but since it yields no positive alternative truth it leaves the subject giddily suspended between actual and ideal, in and out of the world simultaneously.'[61] In the conclusion of his thesis Kierkegaard stresses the importance of the fact that irony must have its limits; it must be controlled, 'a mastered moment'. Only if this

---

[57] Ibid., p. 31.
[58] Ibid., p. 32.
[59] Schlegel, in D. Simpson (ed.), *The Origins of Modern German Critical Thought - German Aesthetic and Literary Criticism from Lessing to Hegel* (Cambridge: CUP, 1988), p. 189.
[60] *The Concept of Irony*, p. 269.
[61] Terry Eagleton, *The Ideology of the Aesthetic* (Oxford: Basil Blackwell, 1991), p. 174.

criterion is to be respected may irony be employed and nihilism avoided. The failure to appreciate irony as 'a mastered moment' has led to the extremes within the 'literary approach' to Kierkegaard that I mentioned earlier, with its adherents missing the theological significance of his writings.

The pseudonymous and 'signed' literary output up to 1848 received an evaluation in Kierkegaard's apologetic *The Point of View for My Work as an Author* (written in 1848, but published by his brother posthumously in 1859), and in 1851 he wrote *About My Activity as a Writer* for similar purposes. Both form part of his 'direct communication' and represent his attempts to educate his readers on the true nature of his authorship. He was sure that he had been misunderstood and that people were divided as to how to interpret what he had written.[62] Although it is debated whether Kierkegaard may be taken seriously, even in these works, I believe that they represent a clear defence of his position and are therefore vital for forming a correct interpretation of his works. Whereas the *Concept of Irony* illustrates that he wished to criticize the Romantic Ironists and the intellectual elite of Copenhagen, these other two show his theological premises for writing, and are closely supported by journal entries from the late 1840s onwards. It is declared in his journal that his task was that of 'trying to introduce Christianity into Christendom, albeit poetically and without authority (that is, not making myself into a missionary)'.[63] I have already explained the details of why he felt this to be necessary, yet instead of confronting his readers directly he used his irony and pseudonyms to shatter the illusion of Christendom through an ironic deception.

> The aesthetic work is a deception ... One can deceive a person for the truth's sake, and (to recall old Socrates) one can deceive a person into the truth. Indeed, it is only by this means, i.e., by deceiving him, that it is possible to bring into the truth one who is under an illusion ... What does it mean, 'to deceive?' It means that one does not begin directly with the matter one wants to communicate, but begins by accepting the other man's illusion as good money. So ... one does not begin thus: I am a Christian; you are not a Christian. Nor does one begin thus: It is Christianity I am proclaiming; and you are living in purely aesthetic categories. No, one begins thus: Let us talk about aesthetics.[64]

The irony lies in the fact that, whilst a pseudonym might be a vociferous champion of the aesthetic life-view, Kierkegaard is destroying the credibility of that very view through the same

---

[62] Watkin, *Kierkegaard*, p. 51.

[63] *Journals and Papers*, 6356, X 1 A 138 *n.d.*, 1849.

[64] *The Point of View*, pp. 40-1.

pseudonym. A reader would follow the text, possibly agreeing with its contents as he recognizes his views portrayed on the page. Then suspicion would begin to gradually build up as deliberate flaws were perceived in the view of the pseudonym, showing that what had at first appeared certain, was now lacking in credibility. Kierkegaard hoped that this would lead to the reader abandoning such views and instead turn his attention towards the Christian faith, something implicit within the body of the text. To this end he added a less subtle signpost, his later pseudonymous works were penned by Anti-Climacus who presented Christianity in its most Idealistic and challenging form;[65] thereby confronting the reader with what Kierkegaard felt to be the best option, but in such a way that he was able to make the choice himself. Kierkegaard is not the preacher in this process, but, like Socrates' maieutic method, he attempts to allow the reader to find out the truth himself, even if he indirectly guides him to the place where the choice is to be made.

> The maieutic attitude lies in the relationship between aesthetic works as a beginning and religion as τελος [goal]. The point of departure was the aesthetic, wherein possibly the majority have their being; and then the religious is introduced so unexpectedly that they who were moved to follow along the attraction of aesthetics suddenly find themselves in the midst of the most decisive definitions of Christianity and are obliged at least to take notice.[66]

That this was his intention from the start, and not a later religious gloss over the whole pseudonymous enterprise, can be seen from a similar passage written five years earlier in the *Journals*, the year he published *Either/Or*:

> My destiny seems to be to discourse on truth as far as I can discover it but in such a way as at the same time to demolish all possible authority on my part. Since I then become incompetent and to the highest degree unreliable in men's eyes, I speak the truth and thus place them in the contradiction from which they can be rescued only by appropriating the truth themselves.[67]

---

[65] Cf. *Journals and Papers* 6432, X 1 A 513 *n.d.*, 1849.
[66] *The Point of View*, pp. 148-9.
[67] *Journals and Papers*, 5646, IV A 87 *n.d.*, 1843.

4. The Stages of Existence

Within Kierkegaard's pseudonymous works published between 1843-6 we encounter the three stages of existence: the aesthetic, the ethical, and the religious. Quite understandably the latter stage is of the most concern for his theology, but a brief synopsis of the theory of the stages will serve to support my interpretation of Kierkegaard's works considered, in addition to placing the religious stage in its context. Care must be taken not to read too much into the theory of the stages as they only appear in the pseudonymous works up to the *Concluding Unscientific Postscript* and important theological texts such as *Practice in Christianity* do not mention them at all. Some have argued that Kierkegaard saw these as progressive levels in a person's development. Others see them as portraying stages in the development of his own life. Yet in both cases this would be to confuse the views of the pseudonyms with those of Kierkegaard himself. As far as he was concerned, there were only really two alternatives in life: either Christianity, or not. He shows this in *The Point of View* when he states that most people exist in aesthetic categories as opposed to the 'ethical-religious', or Christianity.[68]

The Aesthetic Stage

The best exposition of the aesthetic stage of existence can be found in the first volume of *Either/Or*, Kierkegaard's first 'official' pseudonymous publication, which came off the press in 1843. This volume contains several sections, as I explained earlier one of these, 'The Seducer's Diary', supposedly composed by Johannes the Seducer, was designed to repel Regine. It relates the details of a tragic love-affair in which Johannes treats his young lover very badly, and bears some similarities with the Kierkegaard-Regine episode. Another section, the 'Diapsalmata' is reminiscent of Friedrich Schlegel's various collections of fragments, with the ironic stance taken to nihilism in the character of the pseudonymous author, a certain Mr A. For example, he declares, 'My life is utterly meaningless. When I consider its various epochs, my life is like the word *Schnur* in the dictionary, which first of all means a string, and second a daughter-in-law. All that is lacking is that in the third place the word *Schnur* means a camel, in the fourth a whisk broom.'[69] Cynicism and scepticism fill his words, he is unable to recognize the objective status of values and denies their reality.[70] Mr A

---

[68] Watkin, *Kierkegaard*, p. 53.

[69] Søren Kierkegaard, *Either/Or* vol. 1, ed. and trans. Howard and Edna Hong (Princeton: Princeton University Press, 1987), p. 36.

[70] Cf. Holmes Hartshorne, *Kierkegaard Godly Deceiver*, p. 17.

cannot offer any hope of clarity or purpose, his only aim in life is to achieve pleasure without getting bored.[71] The aesthetic stage, or life-view, is a passive phenomenon. Those within it feel themselves caught up in life's processes, incapable of taking the initiative. At best they escape into the theoretical, the realm of possibility, guided by fancies and desires. In this way they hope to avoid life's duties and responsibilities.[72] The only real values for the aesthete are those temporally adhered to in order to keep the boredom away. Yet there is no substance to this stage, life becomes merely a chain of unconnected possibilities, fragments that are neither linked nor form a coherent whole.

The Ethical Stage

The ethical stage forms a stark contrast to the aesthetic, as can be seen in the second volume of *Either/Or* and its pseudonymous author Judge William. Life in this stage can only be a well ordered, carefully planned-out whole. There must be no irregularities, no contradictions. This philosophy of life is explained in the tortuous 'The Balance between the Aesthetic and the Ethical in the Development of the Personality', a letter of quite considerable length addressed to Mr A, which constitutes a substantial part of the volume. Its long, deliberately ponderous style contrasts with the short, sharp, witty comments of the 'Diapsalmata', and part of the irony lies in the fact that Mr A would probably get bored before reaching the end of even the first of its pages and give up.

The Judge seeks to affirm all that the aesthete would deny and Kierkegaard uses the Judge to mimic the over-confident stance of Enlightenment (German *Aufklärung*) rationalism and Hegelian philosophy. Judge William talks of responsibility, marriage, duty, loyalty to the establishment, all in an effort to become what he calls 'the universal'.[73] One simply *is* aesthetic, but one must *become* ethical, become 'the universal' by force of human character.[74] Yet the Danish word used by the Judge for 'the universal' is *det Almene*, which, somewhat ironically, implies something that is ordinary, common, banal.[75] Kierkegaard was critical of the over-confidence in human reason that had been exhibited by Enlightenment thinkers and Hegelian philosophy, and he rejected any claims to complete autonomy that they made. Also, his attack is directed against the small-mindedness that refuses to look beyond the surface of local convention. In the end,

---

[71] Cf. the section entitled 'Rotation of Crops', *Either/Or*, vol. 1, pp. 281-301.
[72] Ibid., pp. 295ff; cf. Taylor, *Kierkegaard's Pseudonymous Authorship*, p. 128.
[73] *Either/Or*, vol. 2, p. 255.
[74] Ibid., p. 258.
[75] Hannay, *Kierkegaard*, p. 62.

Judge William is found largely to be following the dictates of his environment and we are left wondering how 'universal' his standards really are. So, despite its apparent confidence in itself, the ethical stage is seen to be little better than the aesthetic, and Kierkegaard used the religious stage to bring its preconceptions crashing down.

Religiousness A - Immanent Religion

We first encounter the religious stage in *Fear and Trembling*, which was published in 1843. Its pseudonymous author Johannes de Silentio (John of Silence) examines the story of Abraham and Isaac in Genesis 22:1-19. Johannes' concern is with the paradox that, once God finally blesses Abraham and Sarah with their only son, Isaac, he then demands him as a sacrifice. This seems to run counter to all God's promises of Abraham becoming the father of many nations through countless descendants. However, Abraham retains his faith in God despite the risk involved, and this Johannes cannot fathom - but that is where the irony lies. Consider this from the preface:

> The present author is no philosopher, he has not understood the System, nor does he know if there really is one, or if it really has been completed. As far as his own weak head is concerned the thought of what huge heads everyone must have in order to have such huge thoughts is already enough. Even if one were able to render the whole content of faith into conceptual form, it would not follow that one had grasped faith, grasped how one came to it, or how it came to one. The present author is ... a freelancer ... He writes because for doing so is a luxury.[76]

Johannes does not claim to have faith, therefore he describes something outside of his own experience and personal knowledge. From the start he points out that he is largely ignorant of this particular topic and that he writes merely out of entertainment value, treating the subject as a logical puzzle, not something of any great importance. It is therefore quite ironic that he chooses to write about faith at all, and hardly surprising that he reaches a negative verdict:

> What I intend now is to extract from the story of Abraham its dialectical element, in the form of problemata, in order to see how monstrous a paradox faith is, a paradox capable of making a murder into a holy act well pleasing to God, a paradox which gives Isaac back to Abraham, which no thought can grasp because faith begins exactly where thinking leaves off.[77]

---

[76] Søren Kierkegaard, *Fear and Trembling*, pp. 42f.
[77] Ibid., p. 82.

Johannes is unable to conceive of anything higher than the ethical stage, so the faith of Abraham, as part of the religious stage, is totally beyond his comprehension and therefore a 'paradox' which reduces him to silence (hence the pseudonym). Kierkegaard uses him to illustrate that religious faith could well make demands upon its adherents that are beyond those recognized by their society. Active discipleship will not only lead the believer beyond recognized conventions, but sometimes even against them, if that is understood to be the will of God. This Johannes terms the 'teleological suspension of the ethical',[78] by which Kierkegaard implies that it is the ethical *stage* as exemplified by Johannes, with its purely secular loyalties, that is to be superseded by the religious stage with its absolute loyalty to God. There was a significant message for Regine too, namely that he had broken their engagement because of his divine vocation, not because of her. What he was not advocating was the rejection of ethics itself - such would have placed him on a par with the worst moral nihilism in the aesthetic stage.

The religious stage, as exemplified by Abraham, is not intended to represent Christianity and was later to be entitled religiousness A in the *Concluding Unscientific Postscript* in 1846. Religiousness A represented religion without the Incarnation, and may be referred to as 'immanent religion' on the grounds that it finds its relation to God within itself instead of relating to God in Christ.[79]

Religiousness B - Transcendent Religion and Christianity

Next is religiousness B, the 'transcendent' or 'paradox religiousness'.[80] This actually turns out to be Christianity, and it is first introduced, albeit indirectly, in *Philosophical Fragments* (published in 1844) by the pseudonym Johannes Climacus (John the Climber), a representative of stage A, who also 'wrote' the *Concluding Unscientific Postscript*.[81] Climacus' seemingly carefree attitude is similar to Johannes de Silentio, and he regards religiousness B as only a hypothesis, invented as an improvement upon a form of immanent religion (hypothesis A, or the 'Socratic'). He pretends to have invented it, which is Kierkegaard's satirical comment on the claims of philosophers who would degrade Christianity as being inferior to their schools of thought.[82] John the

[78] Ibid., p. 54.
[79] Merold Westphal, *Becoming a Self: A Reading of Kierkegaard's* Concluding Unscientific Postscript (West Lafayette: Perdue University Press, 1996), p. 176. Cf. also C. Stephen Evans, *Kierkegaard's Fragments and Postscript: The Religious Philosophy of Johannes Climacus* (New Jersey: Humanities Press, 1983), p. 45; David Gouwens, *Kierkegaard as Religious Thinker* (Cambridge: CUP, 1996), p. 110.
[80] Evans, *Kierkegaard's Fragments and Postscript*, p. 13.
[81] Cf. *Concluding Unscientific Postscript*, vol. 1, p. 557.
[82] *Journals and Papers*, 5827, VI A 84 *n.d.*, 1845.

Climber is ironic in that he attempts to climb to heaven by his own intellectual efforts alone, even though he knows it cannot be done.

The titles, and sizes, of the works further serve to exhibit Kierkegaard's irony. *Philosophical Fragments*, as a title, is reminiscent of the fragment form of the Romantics' 'Symphilosophy', although the Danish word used here for fragments (*smuler*) is better translated 'crumbs', or even 'titbits'.[83] In this sense it stands in contrast to the claims of any who claim to offer a truly comprehensive systematic treatment of existence (for which Hegel's *Encyclopedia of the Philosophical Sciences*, or *Phenomenology of Mind* could count as relevant examples). The *Concluding Unscientific Postscript* is five times larger than *Fragments*, so can hardly be its postscript. Also, the Danish word used, *uvidenskabelig*, would be better understood to mean 'unscholarly' instead of 'unscientific', thereby denoting something of an amateurish composition.[84]

Climacus, although he seems to know many of the fine details, cannot comprehend the real significance of Christian doctrines such as the Incarnation or the Atonement, so, just like Silentio when confronted with the facts of faith, he stands back and declares them to be paradoxes.[85] Hence Christianity is therefore perceived as the 'paradox religious'. These works differ from the earlier pseudonymous texts in that Kierkegaard's name appears on the title pages as their 'editor'. Kierkegaard wished to indicate a closer relation to the views expressed in the two Climacus texts, yet he still maintains a distance from what is said within them. Climacus remains a 'fantastic figure' who does not actually exist, claiming to know all about Christianity yet is without any faith.[86]

5. The Religious Works and Direct Communication

The stages of existence, irony and pseudonymity are all primarily related to Kierkegaard's pseudonymous, or aesthetic texts. It is these works which all too frequently form the main subject matter of the philosophical, theological and (especially) the literary discussions of Kierkegaard. However, I have also referred to other, pseudonymous and non-pseudonymous texts within Kierkegaard's authorship which do not fall into the aesthetic category. It is within the non-aesthetic works in particular that it is possible to find a tremenous wealth of material that

---

[83] Hannay, *Kierkegaard*, p. 95.
[84] Holmes Hartshorne, *Kierkegaard Godly Deceiver*, p. 35.
[85] E.g. *Fragments*, p. 58.
[86] Murray Rae, *Kierkegaard's Vision of the Incarnation, by Faith Transformed* (Oxford: OUP, 1998), p. 4.

can serve to illuminate and explain Kierkegaard's own theological position. It is therefore appropriate to offer a brief explanation of the significance of this component of the authorship. I will begin by discussing the works by Anti-Climacus, then I will discuss the nature and purpose of the various *Discourses* and other signed works, before concluding with some treatment of the *Journals and Papers*.

Anti-Climacus

The two writings attributed to Anti-Climacus are *The Sickness Unto Death* (1848) and *Practice in Christianity* (1850). Within these two works Kierkegaard allows his pseudonym to develop and elaborate upon the main theological ideas introduced in the Climacus texts. The 'Anti', does not mean that Anti-Climacus is against Climacus, rather it denotes 'prior to' (like the English 'ante-') or 'before' in the context of rank, thereby denoting that Anti-Climacus is higher than Climacus. Unlike Climacus, Kierkegaard describes Anti-Climacus as being 'a Christian to an extraordinary degree'.[87] He chose to use Anti-Climacus to present Christianity in its ideal form,[88] something Kierkegaard's humility and lack of self-confidence prevented him from doing at this point in his life. Whether it is safe to interpret Anti-Climacus' theology as being a faithful representation of Kierkegaard's theology is a topic of debate. However, like the Climacus texts, the title pages of both the works by Anti-Climacus also carried Kierkegaard's name as their editor, so they too are closer to his views than the earlier pseudonymous works. In his *Journals* Kierkegaard claimed that he felt himself to be 'higher than Johannes Climacus, lower than Anti-Climacus'.[89] He did at first consider publishing the Anti-Climacus texts directly under his own name, yet he rejected this on the grounds that his readership would take him less seriously if he attempted to claim that he was worthy of being such a Christian. By keeping the texts pseudonymous, however thinly veiled that pseudonymity might be, he was able to maintain a certain distance in the hope that the texts would still be considered on their own merits.[90] It is therefore safe to interpret Anti-Climacus as saying what Kierkegaard would like to say himself if he had had the confidence, yet

[87] *Journals and Papers*, 6431, X 1 A 510 *n.d.*, 1849; cf. the comments regarding 'Anti-' in Howard and Edna Hongs' introduction to Søren Kierkegaard, *The Sickness Unto Death*, ed. and trans. Howard and Edna Hong (Princeton: Princeton University Press, 1980), p. xxii.
[88] Søren Kierkegaard, *Practice in Christianity*, ed. and trans. Howard and Edna Hong (Princeton: Princeton University, 1991), p. 7. Cf. also *Journals and Papers*, 6439, X 1 A 530 *n.d.*, 1849.
[89] *Journals and Papers*, 6433, X 1 A 517 *n.d.*, 1849.
[90] Ibid. 6527, X 2 A 183 *n.d.*, 1849; 6464, X 1 A 615 *n.d.*, 1849.

he felt it inappropriate to do so directly due to the seriousness of the subject and the nature of his own life.

Discourses and Signed Works

Alongside all of the various different pseudonymous texts discussed above stand the groups of discourses and other signed works. These differ from the pseudonymous works in that they were written for those of his readers, however few they might be, who had begun to take notice of the issues he sought to address.[91] This is a large and diverse body of writings and I will now briefly describe some of those which I have chosen to use in the following chapters. From 1843-44 Kierkegaard published a total of eighteen *Upbuilding Discourses*. These are fascinating in that they present us with his Christian beliefs from the start of his authorship. They were published in groups at the same time as certain aesthetic texts were also published and each discourse tackles a subject to be treated by one of the various pseudonyms, yet the discourses do this from Kierkegaard's own theological position. In this way he was able to illustrate the differences in life view between him and the pseudonyms in question. In 1848 he published his *Christian Discourses*, an important collection of homilies that he intended to accompany the Anti-Climacus writings. Also in this category are the two theological works *For Self-Examination* and *Judge For Yourself!* In these two, too often neglected books, Kierkegaard presents some of his most penetrating and insightful Christology and teaching on the nature of faith, both of which clearly illustrate his theological debt to Luther.

The Journals and Papers

The final group of writings to be discussed are the *Journals* and papers. These offer an enormous wealth of information. Kierkegaard kept his *Journals* throughout his late teens and adult life, recording numerous personal details and theological reflections. Whilst some entries present Kierkegaard's thoughts, there are times when he used the *Journals* to make drafts for his various publications. Because of this it is possible to discover similar, or even identical, passages in the *Journals* and other works. Interpreters of Kierkegaard's thought therefore need to be careful of this and so distinguish between these passages and Kierkegaard's own thoughts and beliefs.[92]

---

[91] Mullen, *Kierkegaard's Philosophy*, p. 39.
[92] Cf. Peter Vardy, *Kierkegaard* (London: Fount, 1996), p. 39.

6. Conclusion

In conclusion, we can see that the task of interpreting Kierkegaard's writings leads us into theology, philosophy and literary theory. Most importantly for this thesis is the fact that he was motivated by theological and philosophical concerns, wishing to deliver his critique upon the philosophical and intellectual trends of his time, and on the nature of the established Evangelical Lutheran Church in Denmark. He sought to defend a personal, Christian faith in the face of, as he saw them, these competing errors within society. To a lesser extent Kierkegaard also wanted to communicate with his ex fiancée, Regine Olsen (although this primarily concerns *Either/Or* and *Fear and Trembling* rather than other works mentioned in this chapter). For all these purposes he published a variety of ironical works under pseudonyms, in doing so he ironically employed the literary tactics of the Romantic Ironists. Some details within his earlier texts would be perceived by Regine as pertaining to their relationship. On another level, yet often within the same text, the general reader would be able to discern the critical, polemical nature of the texts. Unsure whether all his readers would understand what he published, he wrote some explanatory works such as 'A First and Last Declaration', and *The Point of View* as a means of rectifying the situation.

In order to examine Kierkegaard's Christocentric theology, I have chosen to use the following works. First, the pseudonymous *Philosophical Fragments* and *Concluding Unscientific Postscript*, through which Kierkegaard ironically introduces Christianity, under the guise of religiousness B. This is where he begins to deal with the problem of religious knowledge, and the nature and purpose of the Incarnation. Yet, although some attribute the views found therein to Kierkegaard, they are only those of his pseudonym, Johannes Climacus, through whom Kierkegaard introduces particular themes. Therefore, I will use material from the Climacus texts to form but a starting-point for discussing Kierkegaard's theology. I will then proceed to develop the argument with important material taken from Anti-Climacus' texts, the *Journals*, and some of the signed works and discourses which were also published under his own name. In this way I hope to be able to delve beneath the rhetorical devices of the authorship and illustrate how the Christocentricity of Kierkegaard's religious thought continues to make an important and constructive contribution to contemporary theology.

Chapter Two

Reason and Revelation: Can the Truth be Learned?

Kierkegaard stands out as a radical critic of his time. John Macquarrie describes him as 'a lone protester' swimming against the stream of nineteenth century theology.[1] During Kierkegaard's lifetime Denmark was largely in intellectual and cultural debt to its German neighbours, so it is hardly surprising that we frequently find his writings set against a background of German thought. Although he may have embraced a broadly Lutheran theology, he wholeheartedly rejected the philosophical approaches to religion then in circulation within that tradition. This was largely on the grounds that they were the product of Idealism, whether of the Romantic, Hegelian, or other variants of that strand of philosophical thought. We have to allow for this important factor if we are to appraise Kierkegaard's response to such approaches with any clarity.

The Rationalist philosophers of the German Enlightenment (*Aufklärung*) in the previous century had stressed either the authority of the unaided human reason or of sense experience. In theological matters this had set them against allowing for divine or supernatural revelation. Traditional sources of revealed theology therefore tended to be disregarded, as faith was subordinated to knowledge in order to promote the alleged validity of what was deemed to be truly 'objective' and 'rational'. Echoes of such theological rationalism were heard in the early nineteenth century with the development of Hegel's Absolute Idealism. Largely through the work of Kierkegaard's undergraduate tutor, the pastor and theologian Hans Martensen, Hegelian Idealism had become, by the time of Kierkegaard's undergraduate studies, the dominant philosophy in Denmark.[2] As explained in the first chapter, Danish Hegelianism was to find itself the principal target of Kierkegaard's polemic in his early pseudonymous writings. Yet at times his critical eye also turned to certain aspects of the Romanticist

[1] Macquarrie, *Jesus Christ in Modern Thought* (London: SCM, 1990), p. 236.
[2] Watkin, *Kierkegaard*, p. 16.

theology of Schleiermacher. Kierkegaard had been introduced to Schleiermacher's *The Christian Faith* by Martensen during his studies in 1834.[3] By seeming to reduce religion to an affective, subjective experience, Schleiermacher had failed to do justice to its nature or significance.[4] However, through the impact of Romanticism, the dry intellectualism of the previous generation had begun to give way to a wider conception of religious truth that embraced the head and the heart. This theological step forward was appreciated by Kierkegaard just as much as any of the Romantics.

Like Kant before him, Kierkegaard recognized the necessity of setting a limit to the ambitions of the 'pure', or speculative reason in theological matters. In a sense he sought to continue Kant's critique further, making a radical departure from the rationalist agenda of the *Aufklärung* whilst devoutly adhering to a more traditional Lutheran theology. Unfortunately, the nature and level of his criticism have led some to categorize him as an 'irrationalist' who denigrated the use of reason in theology.[5] Others, in supposed defence of his position, choose to define him as an 'anti-intellectualist'.[6] Unfortunately this term is just as problematic, with its connotations lending themselves to the hostile interpretations that one had hoped to avoid. Although less familiar, the term 'anti-rationalist' could also be applied, mindful that this must be done in the context that Kierkegaard self-consciously set himself against theological 'rationalism' in its various manifestations. So, clearly care must be taken in order to refute these charges of irrationalism and anti-intellectualism successfully and show instead that Kierkegaard's intention was to define the limitations of reason precisely

---

[3] James Collins, *The Mind of Kierkegaard* (Princeton: Princeton University Press, 1983), p. 101.

[4] Consider for instance Schleiermacher's famous discussion of 'the feeling of absolute dependence' in *The Christian Faith* (Edinburgh: TandT Clark, 1989), pp. 131ff.

[5] See for instance Christopher Hamilton's article 'Kierkegaard on Truth as Subjectivity: Christianity, Ethics and Asceticism', *Religious Studies*. Vol. 34, 1998, p. 61. The irrationalist interpretation is also put forward by Isaiah Berlin in *Against the Current, Essays in the History of Ideas*, although this is done in the context of a discussion of Hamann and his influence on 'German irrationalism'. (Isaiah Berlin, *Against the Current, Essays in the History of Ideas* (Oxford: OUP, 1981), p. 19.) However, Kierkegaard's harshest critic has probably been the American Idealist philosopher Brand Blandshard. (Cf., Brand Blandshard, *Reason and Belief* (London: Allen and Unwin, 1974), p. 241.)

[6] This term is adopted by one of Kierkegaard's earliest interpreters David Swenson. However, Swenson does so with the reservation that it is only employed in order to enable modern readers new to Kierkegaard's ideas to understand him more in the context of more contemporary movements. (Swenson, *Something About Kierkegaard*, pp. 135ff). Cf. David Gouwens *Kierkegaard as Religious Thinker* for a careful description of the nature of Kierkegaard's 'anti-intellectualism' in the face of some common misunderstandings that have arisen amongst his interpreters over the years. (Gouwens, *Kierkegaard as Religious Thinker*, p. 53.)

in an area that involves more than just the intellectual acceptance of metaphysical propositions. Therefore, it is perhaps more fitting to refer to him as a 'supraratonalist', as he held that both faith and revelation redeem reason by transforming its canons.[7]

Within this chapter I will begin to show how Kierkegaard, both directly and pseudonymously, offers his own contribution to the classic reason-revelation debate. A considerable amount of attention will be devoted to *Philosophical Fragments* ('by' Johannes Climacus), as this work does present us with a fascinating, though oblique, insight into his views on the matter. Supporting material will be taken from such texts as the *Concluding Unscientific Postscript to Philosophical Fragments*, *The Sickness Unto Death* ('by' Anti-Climacus) and Kierkegaard's *Journals*. The first section will relate how Kierkegaard uses his pseudonym to raise the problem of how we might acquire religious knowledge in *Philosophical Fragments*. In the second section I will discuss how he posits the existence of human sin as being the decisive factor in preventing our knowledge of God. Then, finally, I will examine how he posits 'the moment in time', the Incarnation, as the decisive revelatory event and why this is intrinsically linked to his soteriology.

1. On Learning the Truth

'Can the truth be learned? With this question we shall begin.' So reads the opening sentence of the first chapter of *Philosophical Fragments*. Climacus informs the reader that, 'It was a Socratic question or became that by way of the Socratic question whether virtue can be taught - for virtue in turn was defined as insight.'[8] In keeping with his penchant for indirection, Kierkegaard uses his pseudonym to refer to more than just the niceties of Socratic-Platonic philosophy. Although Climacus' direct references may be to antiquity, his allusions do in fact go way beyond this. I wish to begin by doing him the courtesy of enquiring into the nature of his 'Socratic question' by means of a brief excursion into two of Plato's Socratic dialogues: *Protagoras* and the *Meno*. Once this has been done, I wish to delve deeper into the matter and discern the real question implied within the text, namely, Kierkegaard's contribution towards solving 'the problem of the status and acquisition of religious truth'.[9] Yet this truth to which Climacus refers is of more than just theoretical, or intellectual interest, he refers to it as 'an eternal

[7] A term adopted by Stephen M. Emmanuel in his *Kierkegaard and the Concept of Revelation* (Albany: State University of New York Press, 1996), p. 44.
[8] *Fragments*, p. 9.
[9] Gardiner, *Kierkegaard*, p. 68.

happiness'.[10] It would instead be more appropriate to understand it to mean a person's salvation.[11] Considering this understanding, *Fragments* seems not so much a work of philosophy, but of evangelism. As Kierkegaard explains through the same pseudonym three years later in the *Postscript*, 'the issue in *Fragments* [is] an introductory issue, not to Christianity but to becoming a Christian.'[12]

A Socratic Question

In Plato's *Protagoras*, Socrates begins by claiming that virtue cannot be taught. Yet he follows this by professing his uncertainty and so invites his companion Protagoras to enlighten him.[13] This initiates a debate on the matter, at the end of which Socrates concludes,

> It seems to me that the present outcome of our talk is pointing at us, like a human adversary, the finger of accusation and scorn. If it had a voice it would say: 'What an absurd pair you are, Socrates and Protagoras. One of you, having said at the beginning that virtue is not teachable, now is bent upon contradicting himself by trying to demonstrate that everything is knowledge - justice, temperance and courage alike - which is the best way to prove that virtue is teachable. If virtue were something other than knowledge, as Protagoras tried to prove, obviously it could not be taught. But if it turns out to be, as a single whole, knowledge (which is what you are urging, Socrates), then it will be most surprising if it cannot be taught. Protagoras on the other hand, who at the beginning supposed it to be teachable, now on the contrary seems to be bent on showing that it is almost anything rather than knowledge; and this would make it least likely to be teachable.'[14]

In the *Meno*, relating an episode some thirty years later, the same topic arises and Socrates is asked, 'Is virtue something that can be taught? Or does it come by practice? Or is it neither teaching nor practice that gives it to a man but natural aptitude or something else?'[15] At this point his uncertainty covers not only whether virtue is teachable, but even how virtue may be defined in itself. The dialogue ends, however, with Socrates' somewhat incomplete conclusion, 'On our present reasoning then, whoever has virtue gets it by divine dispensation. But we shall not understand the truth of the matter until, before asking how men get virtue, we try to discover what virtue is in and by itself.'[16]

---

[10] *Fragments*, p. 1.
[11] Evans, *Passionate Reason*, p. 27.
[12] *Concluding Unscientific Postscript* 1:381
[13] Plato, *Protagoras and Meno*, trans. W.K.C. Guthrie (London: Penguin, 1968), p. 51.
[14] Ibid., p. 99.
[15] Ibid., p. 115.
[16] Ibid., p.157.

This profession of ignorance, customarily occurring as it does in various forms at the end of most of Plato's Socratic dialogues, is not an admission of defeat. Instead, it is an important part of Socrates' maieutic method, a literary tactic Kierkegaard admired and emulated throughout his aesthetic authorship.[17] The significance is that the reader, like the speakers in the dialogue, is compelled to examine the matter at hand in order to find an answer himself. In so doing he might be led to question whether his own life meets the standards implied.

The maieutic method used by Socrates attempts to draw out the answer to any given question by means of the principle of 'recollection'. Climacus refers to this principle as the Socratic, or A, hypothesis and later posits as an alternative to it, a B hypothesis, something that just happens to bear an uncanny resemblance to the Incarnation. The Socratic hypothesis holds, 'That all learning and seeking are but recollecting. Thus the ignorant person merely needs to be reminded in order, by himself, to call to mind what he knows. The truth is not introduced into him but was in him.'[18] The implications of this are used by Socrates in attempting to demonstrate the pre-existence and immortality of the soul. In the *Meno* he states:

> Thus the soul, since it is immortal and has been born many times, and has seen all things both here and in the other world, has learned everything that is. So we need not be surprised if it can recall the knowledge of virtue or anything else which, as we see, it once possessed. All nature is akin, and the soul has learned everything, so that when a man has recalled a single piece of knowledge - learned it, in ordinary language - there is no reason why he should not find out all the rest, if he keeps a stout heart and does not grow weary of the search, for seeking and learning are in fact nothing but recollection.[19]

The examples of truth recollected in this manner which occur in Plato's dialogues are normally such timeless, universal truths as those of mathematics and geometry.[20] Socratic-Platonic thought also places religious truth within this 'timeless' category. Against this position would be the thesis that religious truth could be particular, and/or

---

[17] See p. 16 above.
[18] *Fragments*, p. 9.
[19] Plato, *Protagoras and Meno*, pp. 129-30.
[20] See for instance the example of the slave's geometry lesson in the *Meno* (Ibid., pp. 130ff).

dependent upon a single, historical, revelatory event such as the Incarnation.[21]

Within the Socratic-Platonic framework the whole process of acquiring knowledge is not reliant upon any specific person to act as a teacher, instead, there is what Socrates calls the 'midwife'. The role of this midwife is to question the learner in such a manner that he may, after careful recollection and introspection, 'recover' all that is needed to be known by himself.[22] By Socrates' own admission there is no actual authority in this role, it is purely that of a catalyst. Returning to *Fragments*, Climacus comments on this: 'Viewed Socratically, any point of departure in time is *eo ipso* something accidental, a vanishing point, an occasion. Nor is the teacher anything more, and if he gives of himself and his erudition in any other way, he does not give but takes away.'[23] If anybody is capable of acting as a midwife in this context, with the principal requirement being that they do not actually attempt to *teach* the other anything, then the method begins to appear quite 'accidental' indeed. The importance lies not with how or when or why knowledge is recollected, but with the fact that it has been recollected at all. Climacus objects to this theory on the grounds that, 'If this is the case with regard to learning the truth, then the fact that I have learned from Socrates or from Prodicus or from a maidservant can concern me only historically'; and also, 'Neither can the fact that the teaching of Socrates or Prodicus was this or that have anything but historical interest for me, because the truth in which I rest was in me and emerged from me.'[24] The accidental role of the midwife fails to provide any certain authority for the resulting information. In addition to this one wonders to what extent the midwife can remain truly impartial in the process. It is often the case that questions are asked with something of

[21] This distinction is by no means confined to Platonism and its influence has permeated much of Western philosophical thought. Plato distinguished between two kinds of truth claim, those derived solely from reason and those derived from sense-experience. The former are deemed to be universal and necessary, the latter contingent (although not necessarily particular). Such epistemological dualism comes to the fore in Lessing's well-known saying, '*Accidental truths of history can never become the proof of necessary truths of reason* ... That ... is the ugly, broad ditch which I cannot cross, however often and however earnestly I have tried to make the leap.' Lessing's concern was over how vitally important moral and religious beliefs could be derived from historical events that are in principle uncertain. (Colin Gunton, *Yesterday and Today: A Study in the Continuities in Christology* (London: DLT, 1983), pp. 139f.) I offer a fuller explanation of this topic in chapter three within the context of Kierkegaard's Christology, where it comes to the fore. There I discuss his treatment of Lessing's philosophy in the *Concluding Unscientific Postscript* and show its relevance to the concept of 'the Absolute Paradox' of the Incarnation in the Climacus writings.

[22] Plato, *Protagoras and Meno*, p. 138.

[23] *Fragments*, p. 1.

[24] Ibid., p. 12.

the answer already being implied or presupposed. This can arise whether it is done by the phrasing of such a question, the context in which it occurs, or even the manner in which it is asked by another person. To a certain extent these and other factors can all serve to influence the outcome.

For Climacus then, the Socratic hypothesis appears at best ambiguous.

> With half-thoughts, with higgling and haggling, with claiming and disclaiming, as if the individual to a certain degree owed something to another person but then again to a certain degree did not, with vague words that explain anything except what is meant by this 'to a certain degree' - with all such things one does not go beyond Socrates or reach the concept of revelation, either, but simply remains in empty talk. In the Socratic view, every human being is himself the midpoint, and the whole world focuses only on him because this self-knowledge is God-knowledge.[25]

It is apparent that the personal subject holds the central role in acquiring knowledge and hence *I* am the most important item in the process ('the truth in which I rest was in me and emerged from me'). No ultimate significance can be given to the means whereby I became aware of anything, nor any to the occasion or even the purpose for it.

This also applies to the question of religious knowledge, something Climacus sees fit to refer to as 'eternal happiness'. He states that, 'My relation to Socrates or Prodicus cannot concern me with regard to my eternal happiness, for this is given retrogressively in the possession of the truth that I had from the beginning without knowing it.'[26] If the Socratic theory is to be held forth as being viable, then there will be definite implications for any concepts of revelation as the Socratic theory fails to allow for need of any external authority. The immortal, pre-existent soul knows all there is to know, only it cannot remember the occasion in which this first happened and is thereby lost in a timeless mist of imprecision.

> The temporal point of departure is a nothing, because in the same moment I discover that I have known the truth from eternity without knowing it, in the same instant that moment is hidden in the eternal, assimilated into it in such a way that I, so to speak, still cannot find it even if I were to look for it, because there is no Here and no There, but only an *ubique et nusquam* [everywhere and nowhere].[27]

---

[25] Ibid., p. 11.
[26] Ibid., p. 12.
[27] Ibid., p. 13.

So there can be no value in the events of the present. Likewise, there can be no revelation from an external source. Because of this, the exact origin of the matter recalled remains a mystery to the person who recalled it.

As I stated earlier, Kierkegaard's concerns were not confined to details of classical philosophy. From the material quoted from the text of *Fragments* so far it will be possible to discern the real subject of his interest. However, before moving on to detailing what that is, I ought first to clear up one potential misunderstanding that may have arisen from what has been written so far. I have just outlined some of the weaknesses inherent in the Socratic hypothesis which I then interpreted to be referring directly to Socrates' maieutic method. Yet, it will have been noted that this method was described in far more positive terms in my first chapter when discussing Kierkegaard's tactics for indirect communication. It would have been entirely contradictory for Kierkegaard to have used that very method himself as his most positive literary weapon, and yet allow it to be subjected to the harsh criticism of his pseudonyms at the same time. Although irony pervades the authorship at this stage, it cannot be claimed that it extended to this level of self-contradiction. What is actually being done is very different. On the one hand, the use of Socrates' maieutic method as a literary device was intended to provoke his readers into reflecting upon what it means to be a Christian. Addressing the educated upper and middle classes of Danish society, he would have been aware that by far the majority of his readers would have received the sacraments of baptism and confirmation into the Evangelical Lutheran Church. Yet for many this was simply a component part of good citizenship. In general he would not have been teaching them something entirely new, but was trying to present it in such a way that its truth would strike them with a renewed depth and sense of urgency. He was the Socratic 'midwife' attempting to breathe new life into a Christian faith that he believed many had forgotten or turned away from, or, to put it in his own words, 'to reintroduce Christianity ... into Christendom.'[28]

A Theological Question

The real theological target, or targets, behind the rhetorical facade of the Socratic hypothesis now remain to be unmasked. According to Alastair Hannay there exist under this heading,

> Both an ostensible and a covert theme. Ostensibly it sketches (in the form of a 'thought project', i.e., no more than an interesting hypothesis) a possible alternative to Platonic Idealism, an alternative which preserves a

[28] *The Point of View*, p. 23.

> Socratic element but dispenses with the Idealistic one. The Socratic element is the method of refutation, the so-called elenctic [maieutic] method, which proceeds not by establishing any thesis constructively but by destroying initial assumptions. The Idealist element is the principle that the process of eliminating falsity is tantamount to laying bare the truth, as if falsehood and illogicality were merely impediments to a pre-established capacity to grasp the ultimate nature of things. The latter element is archetypal immanentism and as such is Kierkegaard's most general target. More or less implicitly, however, the subject of the *Fragments* is the relation of philosophy to Christianity, and its immediate target the specifically Hegelian understanding of this relation.[29]

That is not to claim that Hegel himself is the target, but those Danish academics and churchmen who had embraced his philosophy and contributed to its popularity in that country. Most obviously, one of his favourite targets was Martensen. Not only was he at one time Kierkegaard's tutor at Copenhagen University, but he later rose to become Bishop Primate of the Evangelical Lutheran Church of Denmark and a theologian of international reputation.[30]

C. Stephen Evans agrees that philosophical Idealism provides the most obvious object of criticism in this context. Along with Hegelian Idealism, Evans would include that of the German Romanticist philosopher Schelling.[31] Kierkegaard would have been very familiar with his ideas. He had studied Schelling's philosophy under Martensen in 1838-9, and in addition to this, he attended a course of Schelling's lectures entitled 'Philosophy of Revelation' at the University of Berlin in 1841-2. Originally Kierkegaard had welcomed the opportunity to learn from an individual who had been hailed as Hegel's greatest critic, being hired by the university for the specific purpose of 'rooting up the dragon's teeth' of Hegelianism.[32] Unfortunately, as the series of lectures progressed, Kierkegaard became increasingly disillusioned and wrote a friend back home that 'Schelling talks endless nonsense'.[33]

However, the Socratic hypothesis need not be confined to just these two views. Evans broadens the list to include another near contemporary, Schleiermacher. With his emphasis placed so heavily upon the believer's personal experience, Schleiermacher 'considered that no man need look beyond his own self-consciousness for living

[29] Hannay, *Kierkegaard*, p. 93.
[30] Ibid., p. 94.
[31] Evans, *Passionate Reason*, p. 29.
[32] Bernard Reardon, *Religion in the Age of Romanticism* (Cambridge: CUP, 1989), p. 112.
[33] *Journals and Papers*, 5552, *Letters*, no. 69 February 27, 1842.

contact with the divine'.[34] Evans' interpretation is based on the premiss that Kierkegaard was referring to a trait widely present within European religious thought, and therefore it is possible to understand several developments falling within this category. As he explains,

> However, if it is an extension of his concept, it is only a small extension. What all these views ... have in common is a conviction that the capacity for achieving truly human existence is possessed by human beings and does not need to be brought to humans by a teacher who is a divine creator of the individual.[35]

Such a broad interpretation of the Socratic hypothesis does indeed seem to be warranted as being within the spirit of Kierkegaard. In fact, to limit Kierkegaard's polemic to one which deals almost exclusively with (Hegelian) Idealism is to fail to appreciate the breadth of his theological awareness and acumen. It also facilitates an awareness of the contemporary relevance of his thought. His prime concern was with refuting the theory of human existential autonomy in whatever form it was manifested in the philosophical and theological trends around him.

Alongside the contemporary enthusiasm for various Idealist philosophies, were the rationalism and empiricism that had developed during the Enlightenment. Neither of these two movements had by any means died out by the 1840s when Kierkegaard was writing. In fact the most significant Danish rationalist theologian of the time was Henrik Georg Clausen who died in 1840 and his son, Henrik Nicolaj Clausen, was a Professor of Theology at Copenhagen University. His thought, which was less rationalistic than his father's, had been influenced by Kant and Schleiermacher and Kierkegaard had attended his lectures on historical theology from 1833-34.[36] In some cases, an over-confidence in the capacity of human reason had lent itself to the development of Deism. Although this creed had largely died out by this time, there was still the influence of various 'natural' theologies in which the very concept of revelation had either been considerably modified, or even rejected out of hand.

---

[34] Reardon, *Religion in the Age of Romanticism*, p. 56. Cf. Schleiermacher, *The Christian Faith*, pp. 12f.

[35] Evans, *Passionate Reason*, p. 31.

[36] Watkin, *Kierkegaard*, p. 14 and Lee Barrett, 'Kierkegaard's "Anxiety" and the Augustinian Doctrine of Original Sin', in Robert L. Perkins (ed.), *International Kierkegaard Commentary: The Concept of Anxiety* (Macon., Georgia: Mercer University Press, 1985), p. 49.

2. The Problem of Sin

Now that the objects of Kierkegaard's criticism have been identified, it is appropriate to discover what he proposed in their stead. The Socratic hypothesis attributes no significance to the temporal event, or 'moment' of recollection, and holds that truth, including religious truth, is timeless and already within the learner, yet for the B hypothesis the situation is different. It commences with a contrasting presupposition: 'If the situation is to be different, then the moment in time must have such decisive significance that for no moment will I be able to forget it, neither in time nor in eternity, because the eternal, previously non-existent, came into existence in that moment.'[37] In this context 'existence' is used by Climacus in a technical sense, solely with reference to that which falls within the limitations of historical and empirical reality.[38] According to such specific terminology, a transcendent God without the limits of space and time does not actually 'exist' in this sense. Hence we read in the *Postscript* that 'God does not exist, He is eternal'.[39] It can be seen now that, through the concept of the 'eternal' coming 'into existence' Kierkegaard is introducing the Incarnation into the argument in *Fragments* under the guise of Climacus' allegedly tentative 'hypothesis'. However, the question still remains the same, 'Can the truth be learned?' and Climacus now attempts to lead us in search of an answer that will avoid the numerous pitfalls of the Socratic hypothesis. He chooses to begin by considering the state of the learner prior to his receiving the truth.

Sin as Ignorance

According to the Socratic hypothesis, the problem of acquiring and understanding the truth is purely epistemic, not existential. It is also maintained that nobody is totally without the truth, hence nothing can be excused on grounds of ignorance. This leads to the dilemma within the hypothesis, that, if truth is akin to knowledge, then either it is known, or it isn't - two logical alternatives: ignorance or knowledge. However, if we are to adhere to the theory of recollection, then it is to be held that the truth, as knowledge, is to be recollected from the hazy mists of an eternal memory and therefore is to a certain degree already known and so already within the learner.

With the B hypothesis the position is different because crucial importance is attributed to the temporal event, or 'the moment', at

---

[37] *Fragments*, p. 13.

[38] Thulstrup, *Commentary on Kierkegaard's Concluding Unscientific Postscript*, p. 100.

[39] *Concluding Unscientific Postscript*, vol 1, p. 332.

which the truth is discovered. It states that 'if the moment is to acquire decisive significance, then the seeker up until that moment must not have possessed the truth, not even in the form of ignorance, for in that case the moment becomes merely the moment of occasion'.[40] If this is the case, and truth is absent from the learner, they are not just ignorant, as ignorance is too weak a term. From this the learner's position begins to appear more complicated than was at first assumed,

> Indeed, he must not even be a seeker. This is the way we have to state the difficulty if we do not want to explain it Socratically. Consequently, he has to be defined as being outside the truth (not coming towards it like a proselyte, but going away from it) or as untruth. He is, then, untruth. But how, then, is he to be reminded, or what would be the use of reminding him of what he has not known and consequently cannot call to mind?[41]

So the learner is not really a learner after all, and so not in search of this truth, but opposed to it. This suggests an involvement of, not only the intellect, but of the will and through that of the whole person. This state, he admits, is that of sin.[42]

Sin as a Position

In order to clarify this point I now wish to turn to the later pseudonym, Anti-Climacus. His views are contrasted to Climacus, 'who said he was not a Christian. Anti-Climacus is the opposite extreme: a Christian on an extraordinary level.'[43] In *The Sickness Unto Death*, the use of a more obviously Christian terminology betrays the real identity of the B hypothesis. Within this text Anti-Climacus discusses the Socratic view that 'sin is ignorance', but it is evident that what is here referred to as 'sin' is in fact Climacus' concept of 'untruth'.[44] Anti-Climacus is unable to rest content with this Socratic definition, quickly finding fault with its inability to clarify the origin and extent of such 'ignorance'.

> The defect in the Socratic definition is its ambiguity as to how the ignorance itself is to be more definitely understood, its origin, etc. In other words, even if sin is ignorance (or what Christianity would rather call stupidity), which in one sense certainly cannot be denied - is this an original ignorance, is it therefore the state of someone who has not known

[40] *Fragments*, p. 13.
[41] Ibid., pp. 13-14.
[42] Ibid., p. 15; cf. also *Concluding Unscientific Postscript*, vol. 1, p. 208.
[43] *Journals and Papers* 6431, X 1 A 510 *n.d.*, 1849.
[44] *The Sickness Unto Death*, p. 87.

> and up until now has been capable of knowing anything about truth, or is it a resultant, a later ignorance?[45]

The issue here is whether ignorance is due to lack of ability, perhaps an innocent result of intelligence or circumstances, or, is it deliberate? Anti-Climacus opts for the latter, presupposing what he calls 'the dogma of hereditary sin',[46] or original sin in more familiar language. In this case sin cannot be confined to ignorance alone and so he argues instead that, 'it must lodge in a person's efforts to obscure his knowing.'[47]

In failing to see the will as contributing to sin, the Socratic hypothesis posits 'an intellectual categorical imperative'.[48] By this Anti-Climacus is saying that the Socratic hypothesis 'does not have the courage to declare that a person knowingly does wrong, knows what is right and does wrong; so it manages by saying: If a person does what is wrong, he has not understood what is right.'[49] The claim that we are responsible for our own sin is an unpleasant doctrine to the ears, especially if the listener is existing in an aesthetic or ethical life-view. Commenting on *The Sickness Unto Death* in his journal, Kierkegaard claims that the existence of sin has permeated human nature to such a degree that it has become 'hidden': 'Not merely that the one who has it, or that one who has it, may wish to hide it. No, the dreadfulness that it is so hidden that one may have it without knowing it.'[50] It is not difficult to understand why the Socratic view is all the more appealing to the vast majority of people.

> Absolutely right. And no human being can come further than that; no man of himself and by himself can declare what sin is, precisely because he is in sin; all his talk about sin is basically a glossing over of sin, an excuse, a sinful watering down. That is why Christianity begins in another way: man has to learn what sin is by a revelation from God; sin is not a matter of a person's not having understood what is right but of his being unwilling to understand it, of his not willing what is right.[51]

Anti-Climacus' argument is that the Socratic, in any of its varieties, fails to identify the real issue. When such beliefs occur within Christianity, 'sin is made out to be something merely negative - weakness, sensuousness, finitude, ignorance, etc.'; and as a result 'Christianity is

---

[45] Ibid., p. 88.
[46] Ibid., p. 89.
[47] Ibid., p. 88. Consider also Kierkegaard's claim in the *Journals* a year later that 'Sin is not to believe'. (*Journals and Papers*, 4020, X A 348 *n.d.*, 1849.)
[48] Ibid., p. 90.
[49] Ibid., p. 95.
[50] *Journals and Papers*, 6137, VIII 1 A 652 *n.d.*, 1848.
[51] *The Sickness Unto Death*, p. 95.

flabby and spineless'.[52] At this point Kierkegaard seems to be levelling his criticism against the Liberal Protestant teaching, largely derived from Schleiermacher, in which sin is really a product of our finitude and the lack of 'God consciousness' within us. On a more Platonic note, he may also have had in mind the doctrine that evil is non-being. Advocated by some Platonic and Neoplatonic thinkers this was the teaching that evil is in itself merely the absence of the good, a belief that found its way into Hegelian Idealism. Sin, for both Schleiermacher and Hegel, is a form of ignorance. By allowing for the fallen state of humanity, Anti-Climacus is clearly less ready to ascribe greatness and potential to a human reason that is contained within this fallenness. In itself reason is capable of grasping much of the truth, but it is bound by the will, which itself is affected by sin, and there lies its most significant drawback.

Under the effects of sin we exist in a state of 'despair' (the 'sickness unto death' itself) that prevents us from achieving our true nature.[53] The specific form of 'despair' varies considerably, whether it becomes manifest as desperation, hopelessness or just plain apathy. Indeed, knowing Kierkegaard's opinion on the state of the average churchgoer in 'Christendom', it comes as no surprise to read Anti-Climacus lament that: 'Most men are characterized by a dialectic of indifference and live a life so far from the good (faith) that it is almost too spiritless to be called sin - indeed, almost too spiritless to be called despair.'[54] Because of this and similar assertions, some have tended to see in Anti-Climacus nothing but 'a dry, humorless [sic], severe moralist'.[55] However this is certainly not the case as he cheerfully tells us that salvation is 'humanly speaking, utterly impossible'.[56] Kierkegaard's Christian pseudonym was not one to lapse into strict moralism, nor was he to advocate salvation by works. Sin is not something to be overcome by human effort, and on this point Anti-Climacus stands within the Augustinian-Lutheran tradition.[57] Sin's severity lies in the fact that it is 'before God'.[58] Sin is a 'position' that refers to the existence of humanity,[59] it creates the barrier between humanity and God and only God can remove it. Through Anti-Climacus, Kierkegaard introduces the doctrine of the Atonement, and in so doing, raises the subject of a 'paradox':

---

[52] Ibid., p. 96.
[53] Ibid.
[54] Ibid., p. 101.
[55] Mullen, *Kierkegaard's Philosophy*, p. 44.
[56] *The Sickness Unto Death*, p. 38.
[57] Cf. Vardy, *Kierkegaard*, p. 13.
[58] Ibid., p. 77.
[59] Ibid., p. 100.

> The paradox is the implicit consequence of the doctrine of the Atonement. First of all, Christianity proceeds to establish sin so firmly as a position that the human understanding can never comprehend it; and then it is this same Christian teaching that undertakes to eliminate this position in such a way that the human understanding can never comprehend it. Speculation, which talks itself out of the paradoxes, snips off a little bit from both sides and thereby gets along more easily - it does not make sin quite so positive - but nevertheless cannot get it through its head that sin is to be completely forgotten. But Christianity, which was the first to discover the paradoxes, is as paradoxical on this point as possible; it seems to be working against itself by establishing sin so firmly as a position that now it seems to be utterly impossible to eliminate it again - and then it is this very Christianity that by means of the Atonement wants to eliminate sin as completely as if it were drowned in the sea.[60]

The reasoning behind Kierkegaard's decision to refer to the Atonement, alongside other Christian doctrines, as a 'paradox' will be examined in some detail in the next chapter. For the moment, however, let us return to Climacus in order to see how he introduces the Incarnation into his B hypothesis.

3. The Moment in Time

Returning again to *Fragments*, Climacus develops the B hypothesis as an Incarnational theology of revelation. This Christocentric approach is the defining factor for Kierkegaard's theological position as a whole. To fail to give enough significance to the Incarnation as *the* decisive Christian revelation is to omit the central tenet of Kierkegaard's faith.

In keeping with his rhetorical style, Kierkegaard carefully omits any traditional Christological terminology in the texts attributed to Climacus. Instead, he permits his pseudonym casually to introduce the notion of 'the teacher' to solve the various inadequacies of the Socratic view.

> Now if the learner is to obtain the truth, the teacher must bring it to him, but not only that. Along with it, he must provide him with the condition for understanding it, for if the learner were himself the condition for understanding the truth, then he merely needs to recollect, because the condition for understanding the truth is like being able to ask about it - the condition and the question contain the conditioned and the answer.[61]

---

[60] Ibid.

[61] *Fragments*, p. 14.

This teacher is capable, not only of bringing truth to the learner, but also making him aware of his own untruth (or even his need for the truth). In addition he enables the learner to understand it by means of a 'condition' not already possessed. Yet this process of communication is far more extensive than mere teaching, otherwise we remain within the Socratic hypothesis.[62]

The B hypothesis begins to take on a greater resemblance of Christianity as Climacus clarifies the nature and role of the teacher:

> But the one who not only gives the learner the truth but provides the condition is not a teacher. Ultimately, all instruction depends upon the presence of the condition; if it is lacking, then a teacher is capable of nothing, because in the second case, the teacher, before beginning to teach, must transform, not reform the learner. But no human being is capable of doing this; if it is to take place, it must be done by the god himself.[63]

Kierkegaard sought to emphasize reliance upon divine transformation and the centrality of the Incarnation throughout his authorship, both indirectly (through the Climacus and the Anti-Climacus texts) and directly. Due to this it is possible to see that the problem of knowing God is not so much philosophical as existential as Kierkegaard takes the issue of the fallen learner as a whole, not that of reason viewed in isolation. This is supported by the fact that the learner's original state is one of sin, not just ignorance. There is therefore an intrinsic link between this subject and Kierkegaard's soteriology, and it is impossible to separate these two topics in his thought. Hence, 'the teacher, then, is the god himself, who, acting as the occasion, prompts the learner to be reminded that he is untruth and is that through his own fault. But this state - to be untruth and to be that through one's own fault - what can we call it? Let us call it *sin*.'[64] The power of sin is such that only the god as teacher can set the learner free from it. Climacus continues,

> What, then, should we call such a teacher who gives him the condition again and along with it the truth? Let us call him a *savior*, for he does indeed save the learner from unfreedom, saves him from himself. Let us call him a *deliverer*, for he does indeed deliver the person who had imprisoned himself, and no one is so dreadfully imprisoned, and no captivity is so impossible to break out of as that in which the individual holds himself captive! And yet, even this does not say enough, for by his unfreedom he had indeed become guilty of something, and if the teacher

[62] Ibid.
[63] Ibid., pp. 14-15.
[64] Ibid., p. 15.

> gives him the condition and the truth, then he is, of course, a *reconciler* who takes away the wrath that lay over the incurred guilt.[65]

Through the transforming presence of Christ, the learner is able to recognize his sin and begin a new life of repentance. As Murray Rae points out, in the New Testament such a transition is metanoia, the transformation of our minds in addition as our consciences.[66] Rae continues, stating that, 'In this moment of revelation and confession [the learner] is transformed. He experiences *metanoia*, which is to say that his understanding of Jesus is no longer to be shaped by his prior categories nor constrained by a prior paradigm. Rather, his understanding of everything else is now to be shaped by this Jesus who is also his Lord.'[67] Commenting on Climacus's argument, Evans observes, that, if any reader was in doubt as to the implicit Christianity behind the text, by now 'it is fair to say that the ironical character of the whole enterprise of "inventing" the B hypothesis begins to show through rather clearly'.[68]

The vital point at which this B hypothesis, or rather Christianity, differs radically from any Socratic view is that the historical actuality of Christ cannot in any way be 'accidental'. Kierkegaard's Incarnational Christianity stands in sharp contrast to any claim that there should be a humanistic religion of Jesus in which the historically real person of Christ is of passing interest in favour of the eternal value of his moral teaching. Several years later Kierkegaard was to clarify this through Anti-Climacus in *Practice in Christianity.*

> The teacher ... is inseparable from and more essential than the teaching ... But in our day everything is made abstract and everything personal is abolished: we take Christ's teaching - and abolish Christ. This is to abolish Christianity, for Christ is a person and is the teacher who is more important than the teaching. - Just as Christ's life, the fact that he has lived, is vastly more important than all the results of his life ... , so also is Christ infinitely more important than his teaching. It is true only of a human being that his teaching is more important than he himself; to apply

[65] Ibid., p. 17.

[66] Rae, *Kierkegaard's Vision of the Incarnation*, p. 142. Cf. Romans 12:2. Rae likens the transformation brought about through metanoia to that of a scientific paradigm shift in that: 'Human sinfulness is radical and renders the individual utterly dependent upon God. An inadequate paradigm in science may well be construed as a kind of bondage just as sin is described as bondage in *Philosophical Fragments*, but not least among the emphasis in [the] account of the structure of scientific revolutions is that scientists have the capacity to overcome such bondage ... Such capacity is denied in the Kierkegaardian account of Christian conversion for which the condition is a gift given by God.' (Ibid., p. 143.)

[67] Ibid., p. 149.

[68] Evans, *Passionate Reason*, p. 37.

> this to Christ is a blasphemy, inasmuch as it makes him into only a human being.[69]

The historical event of Christ's existence cannot be swept aside in order to retain only a few tenets of his teaching. Kierkegaard vigorously upholds a religion of the Incarnation in which the personal, active God takes the initiative with humanity.

If it is the case that it is primarily through God Incarnate that religious truth is revealed and comprehended (by means of this as yet unnamed 'condition'), is Kierkegaard prohibiting natural theology? It is generally agreed amongst Kierkegaard scholars that the divinely-given 'condition' for receiving and understanding religious truth is faith. According to Niels Thulstrupp in his commentary on *Fragments*, 'Here Kierkegaard clearly gives allegiance to the Evangelical-Reformed doctrine of *testimonium Spriritus Sancti internum*, the inner witness of the Holy Spirit.'[70] This therefore posits divine prevenience and an emphasis upon God as the subject of revelation suggests a reversal of the traditional process of human research and enquiry. In this situation God ceases to be an object anticipating our discovery and is instead both the origin and end of that search. To remove the prevenience of God is to prohibit the very process of enquiry itself - as without faith the learner would not begin. This suggests a composite nature of faith as the condition: through faith we are led to seek God, enabled to recognize him as the source of truth, and, to recognize that truth when revealed by him to us. Yet faith is given before we ask, as the very act of asking requires the presence of faith in the first place and so cannot be attributed to human agency. Kierkegaard is not implying that the learner is entirely passive, as will be shown later he suggests quite the reverse. Instead he constantly argues for a divine initiative, without which the reason is powerless. His concern is to dispel the myth of human autonomy and to assert the indispensability of a real faith in a God who acts for our salvation. However, a reliance upon faith in this context has led some to argue that for Kierkegaard faith is blind and hence it 'requires us to put logic aside'.[71] At first glance an examination of the text could appear to give support to this assertion, as Climacus gently introduces the term 'paradox' into the discussion.

> If a human being is to come truly to know something about the unknown (the god), he must first come to know that it is different from him, absolutely different from him. The understanding cannot come to know this by itself ... if it is going to know this, it must come to know this from

---

[69] *Practice in Christianity*, pp. 123-4.
[70] *Fragments* 1962, p. 190.
[71] Brand Blandshard, *Reason and Belief* (London: Allen and Unwin, 1974), p. 241.

> the god, and if it does come to know this, it cannot understand this and consequently cannot come to know this, for how could it understand the absolutely different? If this is not immediately clear, then it will become more clear from the corollary, for if the god is absolutely different from a human being, then a human being is absolutely different from the god - but how is the understanding to grasp this? At this point we seem to stand at a paradox. Just to come to know that the god is the different, man needs the god and then comes to know that the god is absolutely different from him. But if the god is to be absolutely different from a human being, this can have its basis not in that which man owes to the god ... but in that which he owes to himself or in that which he himself has committed. What, then, is the difference? Indeed, what else but sin, since the difference, the absolute difference, must have been caused by the individual himself.[72]

However, it can be seen that there is no claim that either the content or the revelation of religious knowledge is irrational. Instead what is asserted is that knowledge of God must be revealed by God. As Murray Rae puts it, Kierkegaard is showing the importance of 'a relational epistemology ... an epistemology, in other words, which finds the condition for learning the Truth, not within the self, but in that which is given by God'.[73] This is not a metaphysical dilemma resulting from a difference where the natural has no access to the supernatural. Kierkegaard has not alleged that humanity and the transcendent God are so far apart as to prohibit communication. Instead, 'we will not rightly interpret [Climacus'] account of reason and the paradox in the *Fragments* if we overlook that sin, and not finitude, lies at the crux of the issue.'[74] The acceptance of the noetic effects of sin forms the focal-point of Kierkegaard's critique of natural theology. As is shown in the next chapter, it provides pivotal information about one of his reasons for describing the Incarnation as, not only a paradox, but 'the Absolute Paradox'.

---

[72] *Fragments*, pp. 46-7.

[73] Murray Rae, *Kierkegaard's Vision of the Incarnation*, p. 147.

[74] Merold Westphal, *Kierkegaard's Critique of Reason and Society* (Pennsylvania: The Pennsylvania State University Press, 1991), p. 111; cf. also Mullen, *Kierkegaard's Philosophy*, p. 146.

Chapter Three

Kierkegaard's Christology I: The Absolute Paradox

It is now appropriate to investigate the most problematic term in Kierkegaard's writings. At the centre of Kierkegaard's theology stands the reality of the Incarnation of the God-man, 'the Absolute Paradox' of Jesus Christ.[1] I have already outlined how Kierkegaard denies the possibility of obtaining a real knowledge of God without the revelation of God incarnate, and that we cannot speak fully of Kierkegaard's Christology without incorporating his soteriology. However, his decision to adopt the meta-concept of 'the Absolute Paradox' for the Incarnation presents us with difficulties. It is sometimes said that the classical Chalcedonian doctrine of the Incarnation is a paradoxical attempt to link logical opposites together, such as time and eternity, or humanity and deity.[2] When Kierkegaard is heard to refer to Christ as 'the Absolute Paradox', he is usually interpreted as claiming that such opposites as these cannot be linked. We therefore appear to be faced with two alternatives: either, we are being invited to reject the classical doctrine of the Incarnation on grounds of its irrationality; or, we are being asked to embrace it whilst uttering Tertullian's 'I believe because it is absurd' in our defence.

I must admit that neither of these two options is very appealing and both are wholly against the spirit of what Kierkegaard himself wrote and believed in. We must be careful to see precisely why he referred to Christ as 'the Absolute Paradox'. In so doing, I will show how, contrary to the views of some of his more hostile critics, 'he both described an ancient tradition and set theology upon a new and promising path.'[3] To begin with I discuss some philosophical uses of the term 'paradox', in particular those as put forward by A.J. Ayer and Bertrand Russell. This

---

[1] *Journals and Papers*, 3074, IV C 84 *n.d.*, 1842-43; Ibid., 3077, IV A 116 *n.d.*, 1843.

[2] Cf. Macquarrie, *Jesus Christ in Modern Thought*, p. 164f.

[3] Alastair McKinnon, 'Søren Kierkegaard', in Smart et al. (eds), *Nineteenth Century Religious Thought in the West*, vol. 1 (Cambridge: Cambridge University Press, 1988), p. 181.

explains the philosophical presuppositions of British and American scholars who approach Kierkegaard's writings from the background of the Analytic tradition. In the second section I illustrate the context of Kierkegaard's own uses of 'paradox' with particular reference to the influence of Gotthold Lessing, then to that of German Idealism. The third section presents some treatment of the nature of the term 'mystery' as is found in some classical, patristic Christologies with examples are taken from Tertullian, Hilary of Poitiers, and Athanasius before moving on to consider the Chalcedonian Definition of Faith formulated in AD 451. The fourth section concludes the chapter by considering how Kierkegaard's use of 'paradox' is related to 'mystery' in the context of such early Christologies, and from this whether he remains within the framework of Chalcedonian orthodoxy on this point.

1. Paradoxes and Contradictions

The Oxford English Reference Dictionary, defines 'paradox' as: '*1 a* a seemingly absurd or contradictory statement, even if actually well-founded. *b* a self-contradictory or essentially absurd statement. *2* a person or thing conflicting with a preconceived notion of what is reasonable or possible. *3* a paradoxical quality or character.' Most often 'paradox' is interpreted as a logical (or formal) contradiction, or a self-contradiction and thereby taken to be a negative term, as a thing contrary to reason such as a square circle. If this is the case, a paradox, or contradiction, 'is by definition untrue; it differs from other falsehoods only in that it is something which never was, never will be, and never could be true.'[4] It is by definition necessarily self-contradictory and logically incoherent.

Formal Contradictions and Meaningless Statements

A famous example of a paradox as a formal contradiction is 'the Epimenides', also known as 'the Liar Paradox'. Bertrand Russell describes it as follows: 'Epimenides the Cretan said that all Cretans were liars, and all other statements made by Cretans were certainly lies. Was this a lie? The simplest form of this contradiction is afforded by the man who says "I am lying"; if he is lying, he is speaking the truth, and vice versa.'[5] This is a self-contradiction because it is self-referential: it

---

4 Richard Sturch, *The Word and the Christ, An Essay in Analytic Christology* (Oxford: Clarendon Press, 1991), pp. 17-18.

5 Bertrand Russell, 'Mathematical Logic as Based on The Theory of Types', in *Logic and Knowledge* (London: Routledge, 1992), p. 59.

claims to talk about itself, yet in doing so falsifies itself.[6] So, with a linguistic attempt to do the impossible, the result has been a statement that is found to be, not only contradictory, but meaningless.

Similar objections were made against theological statements by A.J. Ayer. According to Ayer, 'any transcendent truths of religion', (such as belief in God, the hope of eternal life, etc.) are meaningless. He made this damaging claim in *Language, Truth and Logic*, from which the following passage is also taken:

> For we are often told that the nature of God is a mystery which transcends the human understanding. But to say that something transcends the human understanding is to say that it is unintelligible, and what is unintelligible cannot significantly be described. Again, we are told that God is not an object of reason but an object of faith. This may be nothing more than an admission that the existence of God must be taken on trust, since it cannot be proved. But it may also be an assertion that God is the object of a purely mystical intuition, and cannot therefore be defined in terms which are intelligible to reason. And I think that there are many theists who would assert this. But if one allows that it is possible to define God in intelligible terms, then one is allowing that it is impossible for a sentence both to be significant and to be about God. If a mystic admits that the object of his vision is something which cannot be described, then he must also admit that he is bound to talk nonsense when he describes it.[7]

If this really is the case, then we are to view the vast majority of theological truth claims as self-contradictory and unintelligible. No sooner does any person, whether Christian believer or otherwise, begin to talk about God, than she must admit that such language is incoherent. God-talk becomes impossible leading us 'into paradox and incomprehensibility'.[8]

'Sublime Paradoxes'

Paradox, in the senses discussed so far, denotes an occasion where language has gone out of bounds. Such a paradox contravenes the rules of logic and runs straight into absurdity. If Ayer is to be taken at his word most religious language can be rejected for these very reasons. With such a hostile verdict in mind, we would naturally interpret Kierkegaard's writings as denying the logical possibility of the central doctrine of the Christian faith: the Incarnation. However, as the period of Kierkegaard's authorship pre-dates the rise of this particular form of

---

6 Ibid., pp. 61-62.

7 A.J. Ayer, *Language, Truth and Logic* (Harmondsworth: Penguin, 1980), p. 155.

8 Frederick Ferré, *Language, Logic and God* (New York: Harper & Row, 1961), p. 32.

philosophy by some time, it might be somewhat inappropriate to interpret his texts as if he shared the same, pseudo-scientific views about language. We cannot expect Kierkegaard to employ the manner of philosophical discourse and reasoning that developed out of British empiricism and into, say for instance, the Logical Positivism of the early twentieth century.

Instead, Kierkegaard's use of language arose largely out of Romanticism. As such it is highly rhetorical, being designed for anything but the precision and near mathematical accuracy that is demanded by Analytical philosophy. Like any figure in the history of ideas, it is important that his writings be considered as products of their times and hence be interpreted within context. Otherwise, unsympathetic attempts to force the terminology of the past into that of the present can confuse its meaning.[9] We ought therefore to be careful in such matters of interpretation. The meaning of theological statements is dependent upon the specific religious contexts in which they occur. Taking these particular statements out of their contexts and then attempting to turn them into general religious propositions can all too easily result in a loss of meaning.[10]

So, could we in fact understand 'paradox' in a less constrictive sense than has been described so far, or is it to remain merely a univocal term devoid of alternative meanings? 'When is a contradiction not a mere contradiction', asks R.W. Hepburn, 'but a sublime Paradox, a Mystery? How can we distinguish a viciously muddled confusion of concepts from an excusably stammering attempt to describe what has been glimpsed during some "raid on the inarticulate", an object too great for our comprehension, but none the less real for that?'[11] If we return to the dictionary definitions of paradox we can see that one of them is 'a seemingly absurd or contradictory statement, even if actually well-founded'. This includes statements which, although they may appear to be contradictory, are actually supported by logical grounds, however tenuous these may at first appear to be. Hepburn draws parallels with certain scientific theories, which, in their earlier formulations appeared to contain mutually exclusive principles. For instance, light had to be technically explained by both wave and particle movements, even though they at first seemed to be incompatible. Yet it is accepted in modern scientific thinking that both are required in order to construct a

[9] Ibid., p. 42.

[10] Gustav Aulén, *The Drama and the Symbols, A Book on Images of God and the Problems They Raise* (London: SPCK, 1970), p. 138. Cf. also T.F. Torrance's discussion of coherence-statements. (T.F. Torrance, *Theological Science* (Edinburgh: T&T Clark, 1996), p. 179).

[11] Ronald Hepburn, *Christianity and Paradox: Critical Studies in Twentieth Century Theology* (London: Watts, 1958), p. 17.

viable hypothesis. If we were to renounce either element 'in favour of conceptual tidiness and freedom from paradox', we would be denying a vital part of its composition. We never hear of anybody rejecting the factual existence of light because of the logical difficulties perceived in forming an all embracing theory![12]

The same claim can be made in defence of religious language, especially when attempting to describe the nature of God. In this context it is claimed that paradoxes arise from our attempts to explain various phenomena, or a greater reality, beyond our normal range of experience. It does not logically follow from this that the religious truth-claims in question become nonsensical as a result. Our knowledge might be incomplete at this stage of the enquiry, or our language found to be inadequate to the task assigned, yet this is because we are trying to grasp something standing beyond, and not against, the reaches of our intellects. The twentieth century Lutheran theologian Gustav Aulén cites the relationship between grace and works in the Lutheran doctrine of salvation as a prime theological example of this case. Although exhortations to do good works, to repent, etc., might easily make sense to humanity, the nature of divine grace and forgiveness is not so easily grasped. As he explains,

> It states that the action of divine love is not based on any performance from the side of man, that this love accepts man, unworthy as he is and fundamentally wholly unacceptable. This would entirely lose its religious meaning if it were subjected to rationalizing interpretations, whether they attempted to discover some human qualifications or to develop the idea that through Christ God was given some compensation or satisfaction. In either case God's *agape* would cease to be what it is for faith: wholly undeserved and therefore incomprehensible, a mystery.[13]

It is therefore important not to reject some apparently contradictory concepts out of hand. As he continues,

> When used in the context of a doctrine, the word [i.e. 'paradox'] means that this content cannot be rationally explained, and that we have not the ability to interpret it and give an adequate description of it. But this does not necessarily mean that the linguistic form in which the doctrine is clothed need be paradoxical in the sense of being logically contradictory. So the word 'paradox' occurs in two quite different senses, and it is the confusion of these two that gives it an ambiguous character.[14]

---

[12] Ibid., pp. 17ff.

[13] Ibid., p. 139; cf. also Ibid., p. 132.

[14] Ibid., p. 140.

The existence of paradoxes in this context must be embraced as a challenge to the intellect, not rejected as the objects of scorn.[15] In such situations we are forced to reconsider the strength of our methods and the validity of our presuppositions. Only by doing this can it be ascertained whether the paradox in question really is a paradox, or just a mistake.[16] This is a vital consideration to be born in mind when seeking to interpret Kierkegaard's use of the term. As he put it in an early entry into his journal, 'Paradox is the real pathos of the intellectual life, and just as only great souls are exposed to passions, so only great thinkers are exposed to what I call paradoxes, which are nothing other than rudimentary majestic thoughts.'[17]

2. The Incarnation as 'the Absolute Paradox'

The Scottish theologian Donald Baillie states that Kierkegaard's thought 'has been described as par excellence "the theology of paradox"'.[18] However, 'paradox' is a word used only rarely by Kierkegaard in his published, signed works, and it is entirely absent from the homiletic *Upbuilding Discourses*. Instead it is far more commonly found in the vocabulary of the early pseudonyms, the study of which still dominates Kierkegaard scholarship, to the frequent disregard of the later works which more accurately reflect his own theology. A careful read through the aesthetic literature would show that Kierkegaard employs 'paradox' in several contexts through different pseudonyms. For instance, in the lyrical *Fear and Trembling*, Johannes de Silentio stands aghast at Abraham's 'prodigious paradox of faith'.[19] But this is not a reference to the nature and subject of the Christian faith, but to 'the purely personal definition of existential faith', that is to say 'faith' in more general, broadly religious terms.[20] It is in the writings attributed to Johannes Climacus that we first encounter a pseudonym referring to paradox in the context of Christianity.

But who's is the real 'theology of paradox' - does it belong to Kierkegaard or Climacus, or is it to both of them? I have already tackled the problem of irony and the pseudonyms in the first chapter. There I came to the conclusion that, whilst we must take seriously such

---

15 Ferré, Language, *Logic and God*, pp. 46-47.

16 Cf. T.F. Torrance, *Theological Science*, pp. 179-180.

17 *Journals and Papers*, 3070, II A 755 *n.d.*, 1838.

18 D.M. Baillie, *God was in Christ, An Essay in Incarnation and Atonement* (London: Faber and Faber, 1963), p. 107.

19 *Fear and Trembling*, p. 53.

20 *Journals and Papers*, 11, X B 80 *n.d.*, 1850.

warnings as *The Point of View* and the disclaimer in the *Postscript* that 'in the pseudonymous books there is not a single word by me',[21] Kierkegaard's name does still appear on their title pages as the 'editor' of both of the Climacus texts. There is therefore something within them that he wishes to convey that is at least in some ways close to his own beliefs. Regarding the problem of 'paradox', Alastair McKinnon argues that, 'whereas the pseudonyms repeatedly use the terms absurd and paradox, Kierkegaard himself can write about Christian belief at length without ever using these terms.'[22] This is because these particular pseudonyms 'find Christianity absurd or paradoxical primarily because they are not themselves Christians. By the same token Kierkegaard has no use for these terms because in some sense he writes from within Christianity.'[23]

Although I do agree with him on the non-Christian perspectives of the pseudonyms, it is surprising that McKinnon refuses to give significant weight to the numerous occasions paradox occurs in a Christian context throughout the *Journals*. The entries are dated from the late 1830s till the last year of Kierkegaard's life and they provide numerous valuable insights into his theological development. We therefore cannot dismiss the existence of 'paradox' from Kierkegaard's thought on the grounds that it is merely to be attributed to the pseudonyms. Because of this, in order to find references to 'the Absolute Paradox' of the Incarnation we will not only turn our attention to Climacus' B hypothesis (referred to as Religiousness B in the *Postscript*), but also to relevant material from the *Journals*. I begin by offering some criticisms of the traditional interpretations of 'the Absolute Paradox' in which it is taken to be a formal contradiction. After that, I move on to offer a revisionist view in which I examine the alleged contradictions of Kierkegaard's two natures Christology, first with regard to time and eternity, and then as regards the concepts of humanity and deity. From this, it will be seen that, the issue in question is not so much one of finitude, but of human perspectives on sin and salvation.

On Whether the Absolute Paradox is a Formal Contradiction

In the *Concluding Unscientific Postscript* Climacus tells us that, 'the thesis that God has existed in human form, was born, grew up, etc. is certainly the paradox *sensu strictissimo*, the absolute paradox.'[24] Whilst

---

21 *Concluding Unscientific Postscript*, vol. 1, p. 626.
22 McKinnon, 'Søren Kierkegaard', p. 192.
23 Ibid.; cf. also Ibid., p. 214.
24 *Concluding Unscientific Postscript*, vol. 1, p. 217.

in *Fragments* he discusses 'the coming into existence of such a paradox, or, as you put it, in the god's planting himself in human form'.[25] According to the traditional interpretation of Kierkegaard's writings, the statement that God became an individual man presents us with a formal contradiction. For instance, it has been argued that 'Kierkegaard's expositions look like a thorough elaboration of Tertullian's famous saying: *Credo quia absurdum* [I believe because it is absurd]'.[26] This is on the grounds that we are being asked to believe in something impossible, that is to say that an eternal God could enter time and take the finite form of a single human being. In a similar vein, Alastair Hannay claims 'it is contradictory to talk of an eternal historical fact'.[27] Patrick Gardiner agrees, saying that:

> Such a conception is paradoxical. Indeed, according to Kierkegaard, it represents what he calls 'the Absolute Paradox'. For it requires us to believe that there is a moment at which the eternal enters the temporal sphere, taking on the limitations of finite existence, and this seems to involve a manifest impossibility, something that cannot be accommodated within the bounds of human thought and comprehension.[28]

The Incarnation is regarded as paradoxical on the grounds that 'eternity' is to be understood as 'timelessness' as opposed to 'everlasting duration'.[29] Similar arguments can be found across the breadth of Kierkegaard scholarship, making this the most widely accepted interpretation.[30] What these scholars have in common is the belief that Climacus' paradox revolves around the antithetical juxtapositioning of the concepts of time and eternity. This is taken as the most significant difference between humanity and deity, something which therefore constitutes the stumbling block that stands before any acceptance the doctrine of the Incarnation.

---

[25] *Fragments*, p. 107.

[26] Frithiof Brandt, *Søren Kierkegaard* (Copenhagen: Det Danske Selskab, 1966), p. 68.

[27] Hannay, *Kierkegaard*, p. 106.

[28] Gardiner, *Kierkegaard*, p. 71.

[29] Hannay, *Kierkegaard*, p. 107.

[30] Other notable examples include Louis Pojman *The Logic of Subjectivity: Kierkegaard's Philosophy of Religion*, pp. 89, 102, where he argues that 'the Absolute Paradox' is a self-contradiction. Focusing on the *Postscript*, Herbert Garelick's *The Anti-Christianity of Kierkegaard* (The Hague: Martinus Nijhoff, 1965) maintains that 'God-man' is a nonsensical statement resulting from the linking of man and not-man ($P = m + -m$) which violates both reason and common sense. (Garelick, *The Anti-Christianity of Kierkegaard*, pp. 28f). Further support is rendered to this interpretation by Ed. L. Miller 'At the Centre of Kierkegaard: An Objective Uncertainty', *Religious Studies* 33 (1997), pp. 433-441.

The Absolute Paradox as an Apparent Contradiction

Contrary to the above interpretations, a closer reading of the Climacus texts will reveal an altogether different understanding of 'the Absolute Paradox'. According to *Fragments*, the Incarnation is held to be paradoxical on two separate accounts:

> In order for the teacher to be able to give the condition, he must be the god, and in order to put the learner in possession of it, he must be man. This contradiction is in turn the object of faith and is the paradox, the moment. That the god once and for all has given man the condition is the eternal Socratic presupposition, which does not clash inimically with time but is incommensurable with the categories of temporality. But the contradiction is that he receives the condition in the moment, and, since it is a condition for the understanding of eternal truth, it is *eo ipso* the eternal condition. If this is not the structure, then we are left with Socratic recollection.[31]

This passage echoes the earlier claim that the paradox results from the unity of humanity and deity, but, it adds to it the second, also 'paradoxical' fact that the 'eternal condition' is received in 'the moment'. I now wish to examine both of these reasons in some detail and show how the traditional interpretation is mistaken.

(a) Humanity and Deity On the alleged paradox of God becoming man, the first task is to deny the charge that Kierkegaard's use of the term 'paradox' implies a formal contradiction as explained at the beginning of the chapter. In his recent study of Kierkegaard's *Fragments* entitled *Passionate Reason*, C. Stephen Evans argues that Climacus is in fact referring to an apparent contradiction. Evans identifies the major weakness in the traditional interpretation, namely, that in order for Climacus to claim convincingly that the proposition 'God became a human being' is a logical contradiction, he must be able to show that 'God' and 'human being' are mutually exclusive predicates.[32] However, Climacus never attempts to offer such clarification. Chapter Three of *Fragments*, 'The Absolute Paradox', begins by describing Socrates' ignorance of human nature, and it then moves on to show how Climacus believes that his contemporaries are, to a certain extent, just as

---

[31] *Fragments*, p. 62.

[32] Evans, *Passionate Reason*, p. 103.

ignorant.[33] Although he gladly remarks on this ignorance in others, there is no indication from the text that he is able to furnish a philosophically credible definition himself, and so it appears that Climacus is just as ignorant as they. This might come as a surprise when we consider that Kierkegaard's thought offers many deep and penetrating insights into human nature. As the author of two great psychological works (*The Concept of Anxiety* and *The Sickness Unto Death*) we could be forgiven for expecting something more detailed. However, Climacus is only being used as a means to convey the fact that, however much we do know, we do not possess perfect knowledge, hence some aspects of human nature could well remain a permanent mystery to us.[34]

Added to this, Climacus' theism in *Fragments* is at best imprecise. On the question of God's nature he is largely agnostic, at times referring to God as 'the god', and at other times simply as 'the unknown'.[35] In fact, Kierkegaard purposefully leaves Climacus' theism largely undeveloped in *Fragments* as an indication of the allegedly experimental nature of the argument and of Climacus' non-Christian, aesthetic stance. Those in search of Kierkegaard's own beliefs regarding the nature of God would be better directed towards the *Journals*, the *Upbuilding Discourses* or *Practice in Christianity*, all of which illustrate a traditional Christian theism, (although this is normally implicit within the content of what is said rather than forming the main subject under discussion).[36]

---

[33] *Fragments*, pp. 37f. Climacus 'bold proposition' in this passage: 'let us assume that we all know what a human being is', is quite ironic in that he is only confident that his readers can differentiate human beings from other animals or inanimate objects! See for instance his comments in the footnote: 'I still wonder if in our age the matter has been clarified in such a way that it does not need to feel a bit uneasy about itself at the thought of poor Socrates and his awkward position.' (Ibid., p. 38fn.)

[34] Some insights from Kierkegaard's anthropology are quite useful here. In *The Sickness Unto Death* Anti-Climacus states that, 'A human being is a synthesis of the infinite and the finite, of the temporal and the eternal, of freedom and necessity, in short, a synthesis.' (*The Sickness Unto Death*, p. 13.) Likewise, in the *Journals* he puts it that, 'every man is a synthesis, is animal-spirit', and also, 'Man is a synthesis. He is an animal, but there is also a possibility of something divine in him.' (*Journals and Papers* 87, XI 1 A 408 *n.d.*, 1854; Ibid. 83, XI 1 A 358 *n.d.*, 1854.) In another journal entry Kierkegaard does suggest that spiritual and corporeal natures conflict, yet this is not within the context of metaphysics but of Christian living. (Ibid., 4354, XI 1 A 558 *n.d.*, 1854; Kierkegaard also refers to this as the 'complete qualitative difference between being spirit-man and animal-man.' Ibid., 81 XI 1 A 225 *n.d.*, 1854). In view of this, would it not seem that human nature is just as mysterious as the God-man?

[35] Ibid., p. 39.

[36] Cf. Chapter 5 below for treatment of Kierkegaard's theism in more detail. Evans describes Kierkegaard's position regarding the extent of our knowledge of God and human nature as one of 'modest agnosticism'. (C. Stephen Evans, *The Historical Christ and The Jesus of Faith* (Oxford: Clarendon Press, 1996), p. 123.)

Although Kierkegaard did not share the agnosticism of Climacus, he uses this pseudonym to illustrate the impossibility of human attempts to know the essential nature of God apart from that revealed by the Incarnation. Even with this revelation we can only know in part. It can therefore be seen that Evans makes a valid objection, and this can stand as the first point against the traditional interpretation.

A further objection may be derived from this point, namely the fact that, by definition, a formal contradiction is composed of elements that are within reason.[37] However, as God is 'the unknown' in Climacus' eyes, he admits that he is confronted with a subject beyond the scope of his understanding, and so in a sense above reason. He is therefore unable to make confident assertions regarding the nature of God as he lacks both the faith and the knowledge to do so with any sense of certainty. The 'paradox' occurs when this unknown God chooses to make Himself known in and through the Incarnation.[38] Such a revelation contradicts Climacus' previous assumptions regarding the nature and existence of God. He prefers to keep a certain distance between himself and what he discusses, and in so doing we are reminded that 'he is engaged not in theological reflection but in a thought experiment. His fundamental presuppositions exclude the possibility that his position can be Christian.' Because of this, 'the mystery of the Incarnation, of divine grace, eludes him.'[39] The Incarnation appears to be paradoxical, partly because Climacus does not understand it, and partly because he does not want to understand it. It is ironic that Climacus' very comments betray the fact that he is in the same position as the learner in his own hypothesis, who is 'untruth', and so by virtue of this Climacus too is 'polemical against the truth'.[40]

Additional support is rendered to the 'apparent paradox' interpretation by Merold Westphal in *Kierkegaard's Critique of Reason and Society*:

> The affirmation of the Incarnation as a contradiction is embedded in a context that forbids us to take this in a formal sense. The only possible ground for another understanding of Kierkegaard here is that what becomes historical in the Incarnation does so 'against its nature'. But when the iron axe head floated for Elisha and when Lazarus rose from the dead at the command of Jesus, they certainly did so against their nature, though I do not formally contradict myself if I affirm these events, nor utter a tautology

---

[37] Stephen M. Emmanuel, *Kierkegaard and the Concept of Revelation*, p. 45.

[38] Ibid., p. 49. Cf. also Kierkegaard's comment in the *Journals* that 'In relation to everything divine there is always the paradox'. (*Journals and Papers* 3217, X 1 A 628 *n.d.*, 1849.)

[39] Holmes Hartshorne, *Kierkegaard Godly Deceiver*, pp. 43, 42.

[40] *Fragments*, p. 15.

> if I deny them. The impossibility of things behaving contrary to their nature is not a logical impossibility.[41]

Westphal therefore sees the paradox of the Incarnation in the same sense as a miracle. There is good textual evidence to be found in the *Postscript* that fits in well with Westphal's argument: 'The historical is that the god, the eternal, has come into existence at a specific moment in time as an individual human being. The special nature of the historical in this case, [is] that it is not something historical in the ordinary sense but the historical that has been able to become historical only against its nature.'[42] The Incarnation arises from the action of an omnipotent, personal God who shatters our preconceptions and self-defined limits of reality. The charge of 'paradox' does not result from a contradiction of the immutable laws of logic, but betrays the human reaction to the unexpected power of God. Climacus calls this reaction 'offense', which in turn is 'the erroneous accounting' and 'the conclusion of untruth' and 'a misunderstanding of the moment'.[43]

To the Christian believer, the situation is different. In an *Upbuilding Discourse* of 1844 entitled 'He Must Increase; I Must Decrease', Kierkegaard compares the birth of John the Baptist with that of Christ: 'His origin was as marvelous as the one whose coming he proclaimed, but the difference here again was the same as the difference between the marvel that an aged woman becomes pregnant, which is contrary to the order of nature, and that a pure virgin bears a child by the power of God, which is above the order of nature.'[44] Speaking directly in this instance, Kierkegaard makes no attempt to rationalize the doctrine of the Incarnation, nor does he wish to dismiss it as a logical contradiction. It is interesting to observe that he states here that it is the birth of John the Baptist that is contrary to nature, thereby something going against our expectations of what is deemed to be normal. It does not then follow that he rejects it on the grounds of its being a self-contradiction, but instead it is accepted as a 'marvel', or miracle. The virgin birth, on the other hand, is in a higher category as it is even more miraculous and therefore 'above the order of nature'.

---

41 Westphal, *Kierkegaard's Critique of Reason and Society*, p. 102.

42 *Concluding Unscientific Postscript*, vol. 1, p. 578.

43 *Fragments*, p. 51. In the following chapter I will argue that it is the notion of 'offense' (I have chosen to use the American spelling throughout the thesis as this will occur frequently in material quoted from the American translations of Kierkegaard's works), rather than 'paradox', which dominates much of Kierkegaard's later Christology.

44 *Eighteen Upbuilding Discourses*, p. 277.

An important point to be made regarding the 'apparent' nature of the paradox derives from the Germanic background to Kierkegaard's authorship. Both Evans and Westphal argue that we must understand 'paradox' to incorporate aspects of the use of 'contradiction' in the Hegelian sense, whereby it is used 'to designate situations of opposition, otherness, difference, and tension rather than in the narrow sense of formal logic'.[45] In Hegelian philosophy 'contradiction' became a very broad, even vague term. Evans therefore suggests that we may allow the term 'incongruity' to be viewed as an appropriate alternative designation, although he realizes that Climacus' form of argument could seem very sloppy to modern readers.[46]

Finally, being mindful of Ayer's earlier charge that theological statements can be shown to be meaningless, we can see that Kierkegaard's understanding of paradox by no means implies that something is nonsensical.[47] On this Kierkegaard unequivocally states 'the paradox is composed in such a way that reason has no power at all to dissolve it in nonsense and prove that it is nonsense; no, it is a symbol, a riddle, a compounded riddle about which reason must say: I cannot solve it, it cannot be understood, but it does not follow thereby that it is nonsense.'[48] This therefore helps to counter any suggestions that Kierkegaard wished to use the Climacus texts to argue that the classical doctrine of the Incarnation is incoherent.

(b) Time and Eternity In offering us his meta-concept of 'the Absolute Paradox', Kierkegaard was attempting to underline 'the absolute

---

[45] Westphal, *Kierkegaard's Critique of Reason and Society*, p. 125.

[46] Evans, *Passionate Reason*, p. 100. Evans provides a clear treatment of this topic in his earlier study *Kierkegaard's 'Fragments' and 'Postscript': The Religious Philosophy of Johannes Climacus* (Atlantic Highlands, NJ: Humanities Press, 1989). He argues that, 'Since the works are specifically aimed at Hegelians, particularly the Danish Hegelians, it is only to be expected that the linguistic usage is shaped by the customary meanings in the Hegelian world of discourse.' However, 'This by no means implies that Climacus slavishly accepts his language from the Hegelians; he generally takes this language and gives it his own special sense. But some of the Hegelian meaning usually still remains.' Evans continues, saying, 'For Hegel, any relation of opposition can be described as a contradiction ... Contradictions are the creative oppositions that when mediated by thought, lead to higher realizations of spirit. They are thus found in every element of the Hegelian system, including logic, nature and spirit itself.' Unlike Climacus'/Kierkegaard's 'paradox', Hegelian contradictions are only relative and so capable of being resolved by reason. In this case, the 'paradox' of the Incarnation can in fact be seen to be 'the Absolute Paradox' when compared to other such relative contradictions. (Evans, *Kierkegaard's 'Fragments' and 'Postscript'*, pp. 213-14.)

[47] Something implied in e.g. Garelick, *The Anti-Christianity of Kierkegaard*, p. 28.

[48] *Journals and Papers* 7, X 2 A 354 *n.d.*, 1850.

difference by which a human being differs from God'.[49] As I showed earlier in this section, those who follow the traditional line of interpretation tend to see this as a conflict arising out of the incompatibility between the timeless nature of God and the temporal finitude of humanity. With both of the Climacus texts being at times notoriously ambiguous, this claim of *finitum non capax infiniti* does at first appear to be the correct reading of certain passages. Consider the following statement from the *Postscript*, for instance, 'But the absolute difference between God and a human being is simply this, that a human being is an individual existing being ... [but] God, however, is the infinite one, who is eternal.'[50] However, the difference is not one of finitude. Instead, as Mullen argues, it can be shown that it is a difference in quality between, on the one hand the perfection of God and, on the other hand, 'human existence, characterized by a giant chasm separating the sublime and the mundane.'[51] As I explained in the previous chapter, the theologically defining limitation of human existence is that we are all in a state of sin. This fact is affirmed by Climacus in *Fragments*: 'What, then, is the difference? Indeed, what else but sin, since the difference, the absolute difference, must have been caused by the individual himself.'[52] The same point is later made in more detail by Anti-Climacus:

> The teaching about sin - that you and I are sinners - a teaching that unconditionally splits up 'the crowd', confirms the qualitative difference between God and man more radically than ever before, for again only God can do this; sin is indeed: *before God*. In no way is a man so different from god as in this, that he, and that means every man, is a sinner, and is that 'before God', whereby the opposites are kept together in a double sense: they are held together (*continentur*), they are not allowed to go away from each other, but by being held together in this way the differences show up all the more sharply, just as when two colors are held together, *opposita juxta se posita magis illucesunt* [the opposites appear more clearly by juxtaposition]. Sin is the one and only predication about a human being

---

[49] *Concluding Unscientific Postscript*, vol. 1, p. 217.
[50] Ibid.
[51] Mullen, *Kierkegaard's Philosophy*, p. 158.
[52] *Fragments*, p. 47.

that in no way, either *via negationis* or *via eminentiæ*, can be stated of God.[53]

As Anti-Climacus then goes on to explain, the situation becomes more 'paradoxical' by God's attitude to human sin:

> As a sinner, man is separated from God by the most chasmal qualitative abyss. In turn, of course, God is separated from man by the same chasmal qualitative abyss when He forgives sins. If by some kind of reverse adjustment the divine could be shifted over to the human, there is one way in which man could never in all eternity come to be like God: in forgiving sins.[54]

The paradox is produced by the fact that God chooses to forgive sins, something humanity would not do if the situation were in reverse as this contravenes our concepts of what is rightly deserved. Although we earnestly desire divine forgiveness when we are in the wrong, it is another thing when we are wronged by another. The reality of divine grace is beyond our expectations and we are not confronted with a metaphysical paradox pertaining to the nature of the Incarnation, but with the moral paradox of its purpose: the Atonement, whereby the 'absolute' difference of sin is undeservedly annulled.[55]

The paradox is 'absolute', not only because it cancels the absolute difference of sin, but because it is absolutely unique.[56] Whether this is portrayed as Climacus' B hypothesis, or later by Anti-Climacus, or by Kierkegaard himself directly, all importance is assigned to Christ in the process of humanity's salvation. In affirming the uniqueness and finality of the Incarnation, Kierkegaard was to a certain extent setting

---

[53] *The Sickness Unto Death*, pp. 121-2. See also the following journal entry: 'For this reason only is Christianity the absolute religion, because it conceives of men as sinners, for no other distinction can in this way recognize man in his difference from God.' (*Journals and Papers*, 46, V A 16 *n.d.*, 1844; cf. 'God cannot be the highest superlative of the human: he is qualitatively different.' Ibid., 77, X3 A 186 *n.d.*, 1850.) This point is also brought out, although in this instance it is referred to as 'an eternal difference', in *Gospel of Sufferings*. In one of the discourses in this text entitled 'The Joy in the Thought that before God a Man is always accounted Guilty', Kierkegaard affirms the sinlessness of Christ against the rest of humanity and states that Christ is the only one to have suffered before God in innocence. Therefore, 'With him none dare compare himself, or apply his measure to himself; between him and every man is an eternal difference: whence it is manifest now with fresh clearness, that before God a man suffers always as one who is guilty.' (*Gospel of Sufferings*, p. 91.)

[54] *The Sickness Unto Death*, p. 122.

[55] This is in fact the same as Gustav Aulén's example of a theological paradox (but not a formal contradiction) which I cited earlier in this chapter. (Cf. Aulén, *The Drama and the Symbols*, p. 139.)

[56] Evans, *Passionate Reason*, pp. 102f.

himself up against the theology of Schleiermacher's *On Religion: Speeches to its Cultured Despisers.* Here Schleiermacher posits Christ as only one possible mediator between God and humanity and allows for the fact that there may be more, and better, later.[57]

Kierkegaard was additionally, and more specifically, reacting against the ideas of Lessing, the well known literary and philosophical figure of the *Aufklärung* whom he admired yet still criticized.[58] The subject of Lessing brings us back to the title page of *Fragments.* Upon this we find Climacus' question, 'Can a historical point of departure be given for an eternal consciousness?' which was inspired by Lessing's theological work *On the Proof of the Spirit and of Power.* Lessing had followed the general trait of many in the *Aufklärung* who categorized religious truth as eternal and necessary. In so doing he comes under Climacus' broad umbrella term of a 'Socratic' thinker as was introduced in the first chapter of *Fragments.* In Lessing's thought, historical events came into an entirely different category from religious events, as he understood historical events to come into existence in freedom and not necessity, they were therefore contingent, even 'accidental'.[59] In the *Postscript* Climacus puts it this way: 'Everything that becomes historical is contingent, inasmuch as precisely by coming into existence, by becoming historical, it has its element of contingency, inasmuch as contingency is precisely the one factor in all coming into existence.'[60] Because of the implicit uncertainty regarding historical events, Lessing argued that 'contingent truths of history can never become the demonstration of necessary truths of reason'.[61] As Alister McGrath points out, according to Lessing's philosophy 'historically mediated knowledge of God must be regarded as a contradiction'.[62] Yet once the historical event of the Incarnation is held to be the decisive event of all religious significance, we are faced with an incongruity - how can something merely historical and contingent be of eternal and necessary

57 'Allow yourself to enjoy an old rejected concept [i.e. Christology], and seek out among all the holy men in whom humanity is immediately revealed one who could be the mediator between your limited way of thinking and the eternal limits of the world; and when you have found him, go through all of humanity and let everything that heretofore appeared to you differently be illuminated by the reflection of this new light.' (Schleiermacher, *On Religion, Speeches to its Cultured Despisers*, p. 124.)

58 Cf. Gouwens, *Kierkegaard as Religious Thinker*, p. 45.

59 As I mentioned in Chapter 2, the distinction between the contingent and necessary, as originally derived from the Platonic dualism of the sensible and intelligible realms, has permeated much of Western thought since antiquity. (Cf. Gunton, *Yesterday and Today*, pp. 139f; T.F. Torrance, *God and Rationality* (Edinburgh: T&T Clark,1997), p. 108).

60 *Concluding Unscientific Postscript*, vol. 1, p. 98.

61 Lessing, quoted in ibid. p. 97.

62 McGrath 1986, p. 14.

importance? It does not logically follow that it should be this way and presents a difficulty to anybody who tries to accept it: 'That, that is the ugly broad ditch that I cannot cross, however often and however earnestly I have tried to make the leap.'[63] There appears to be a movement between categories for which Lessing uses Aristotle's phrase a μεταβασις εις αλλο γενος (shifting from one genus to another).[64] This is the basis for the apparent paradox between time and eternity, as Climacus states, 'the basis of the paradox of Christianity is that it continually uses time and the historical in relation to the eternal.'[65] The Incarnation is therefore understood by Climacus to be the relative historical event of absolute meaning.[66] A similar sentiment is found in the *Journals* where Kierkegaard writes that 'the forgiveness of sin is indeed a paradox insofar as the eternal truth is related to an existing person; it is a paradox in so far as the eternal truth is related to the person botched up in time and by time ... but forgiveness of sins is really a paradox only when it is linked to the appearance of the god.'[67] To claim that the actual events occurring within the thirty or so years of Christ's earthly existence are decisive for all eternity contravenes the whole temper of Lessing's Deistic thought. Yet this 'paradox' was by no means confined to Lessing and other like-minded thinkers of that period. Such a 'paradox' has been produced by those throughout history who object to the exclusive claim of Christianity, and is more often referred to as 'the scandal of particularity'.[68]

3. Excursus: Christology and Mystery in the Church Fathers

In the above section I have shown that Kierkegaard's Absolute Paradox is not a formal contradiction, and additionally, that neither is it a charge of absurdity against the doctrine of the Incarnation. The traditional interpretation holds that the paradox is a formal contradiction between time and timelessness in the union of God and a human being. Against this I have argued the following: that although the paradox arises out of the joining of humanity and Deity, the problematic difference is not finitude but sin; that the Absolute Paradox is so called because of the overcoming of this 'absolute difference'; that the 'paradox' is not a

[63] Lessing, quoted in *Concluding Unscientific Postscript*, vol. 1, p. 98.

[64] Ibid.

[65] Ibid., p. 95. Cf. also *Journals and Papers*, 73 X2 A 406 *n.d.*, 1850.

[66] Cf. Holmes Hartshorne, *Kierkegaard Godly Deceiver*, p. 98n.

[67] *Journals and Papers*, 3085, VI B 45 *n.d.*, 1845.

[68] Cf. John Baillie, *The Sense of the Presence of God. Gifford Lectures 1961-2*, (London: OUP, 1962), p. 204.

formal contradiction that contravenes the rules of logic, but is an apparent contradiction; that it refers to something above the limitations of human reason, or contrary to nature as we perceive it; that Kierkegaard is employing 'paradox' in the broad Hegelian sense of contradiction; that Kierkegaard is also offering a critique of Lessing's dictum 'contingent truths of history can never become the necessary truths of reason'.

Now that I have clarified Kierkegaard's use of paradox in the context of 'the Absolute Paradox' of the Incarnation, I wish to consider how far his Christology is in tension with classical Chalcedonian orthodoxy. In order to do this I will examine some notable exponents of classical Christology among the Church Fathers in order to discover whether we may trace some continuity from them to Kierkegaard. This will begin with Tertullian, discussing the reasoning behind the *'credo quia absurdum'*. I will then discuss the concept of the Incarnation as 'to paradoxotaton' as found in Athanasius. Following this will be an examination the terms *incomprehensibilis* and *sacramentum* (or 'to mysterion') in Hilary of Poitiers. Finally, I will examine some of the implications of the term 'homoousios' in the Chalcedonian Definition.

Tertullian and De Carne Christi

The second century theologian Tertullian is often hailed as 'the father of Latin theology', and his numerous writings helped to shape the course of Christian thought in both East and West for several centuries.[69] Although Tertullian was from Latin-speaking North Africa, it is appropriate to consider him to have been the last Greek apologist for he was well versed in the details of pagan Greek philosophies (notably of Stoicism, his creed before conversion), and more fluent and able in the Greek language than most of the Latin theologians after him.[70] However, his links with the Montanist heresy have led some to discredit him in addition to denying his doctrinal orthodoxy (though it is disputed as to whether he actually left the Catholic church[71]). The most common charge levied against him is that he was an irrationalist, or at best an extreme fideist. His accusers derive their charge from the infamous phrase '*credo quia absurdum*' ('I believe because it is absurd') allegedly found in his Christological treatise *De Carne Christi* ('On the

[69] G.L. Prestige, *God in Patristic Thought* (London: SPCK, 1975), p. 97; see also A. Grillmeier, *Christ in Christian Tradition. Vol. 1: From the Apostolic Age to Chalcedon (451)*, trans. J. Bowden (London: Mowbrays, 1965), p. 140; J.N.D. Kelly, *Early Christian Doctrines* (London: Longmans, 1973), p. 149.

[70] Prestige, *God in Patristic Thought*, p. 97.

[71] Cf. Stuart Hall, *Doctrine and Practice in the Early Church* (London: SPCK, 1991), pp. 67ff.

Flesh of Christ') and which is held to reflect his theological outlook as a whole. Henry Chadwick claims that, for Tertullian, 'to reduce all to sweet reasonableness is to miss its supernatural character, and therefore his ultimate Christian confession is the grinding paradox "I believe because it is absurd".' Chadwick then continues by stating that, '[Tertullian's] notorious utterance is a milestone along a path in Christian thought which leads ... to Kierkegaard and his modern disciples.'[72]

It is easy to see some similarities between Tertullian and Kierkegaard if we interpret both of them in the manner prescribed by traditional scholarship. Kierkegaard had studied Tertullian and he often mentions him in his *Journals*, describing him as 'the unconditionally most consistent and most Christianly two-edged of all the Church fathers'.[73] He also refers to him a few times in his authorship, most famously when he cites the *quia absurdum* in *Fragments*, but also in *The Concept of Irony*, and *The Concept of Anxiety*.[74] Yet, I have sought to refute the charge that Kierkegaard's meta-concept of 'the Absolute Paradox' implies irrationalism. Therefore, if there really are similarities between the two thinkers they cannot (or must not) be attributed to the traditional, and often rather unfavourable, interpretation of either.[75] Therefore Tertullian's '*credo quia absurdum*' stands in sore need of a revisionist interpretation.

It would perhaps be easy to take literally the '*credo quia absurdum*' as Tertullian's motto if he were known to have been a man of no learning and narrow-mindedness. Yet despite his severity and almost legalistic moralism, his style and arguments betray a keen mind and (perhaps because of these factors), Christian tradition asserts that he was a professional lawyer.[76] He was certainly well educated and aware of the academic developments of his time. Was he really one to turn his back on reasoned discourse when it came to communicating the truth of his Christian faith? Regarding Tertullian's attitude towards philosophy, Eric Osbourne claims that 'while Tertullian distrusts philosophy because of its part in division and heresy, there is ample evidence for his use of it and other elements in classical culture. His mind is marked by classicism, a wide culture as well as his own distinctive way of

---

[72] Henry Chadwick, *Early Christian Thought and the Classical Tradition: Studies in Clement, Justin and Origen* (Oxford: Clarendon Press, 1966), p. 2.

[73] *Journals and Papers*, 542, X 5 A 98 *n.d.*, 1853.

[74] *Fragments*, pp. 52-3; *The Concept of Irony*, p. 329; *The Concept of Anxiety*, p. 27.

[75] Cf. Rae, *Kierkegaard's Vision of the Incarnation*, p. 111.

[76] Hall, *Doctrine and Practice in the Early Church*, p. 67.

thinking.'[77] This view is also supported in the detailed study of Tertullian by Timothy Barnes who points out the extent of Tertullian's knowledge of classical literature.[78]

It soon becomes apparent that an important contributing factor to this debate is the significant role played by rhetoric in Tertullian's writings. Like any other educated Roman citizen of the second century, Tertullian would have undergone rigorous training in the skills of oratory, a vital background for anybody destined for public service and the principal skill of a professional lawyer. Barnes states that,

> Philosophy and theology, it must be concluded, are subordinated to oratory - which accounts for the effectiveness of Tertullian's writings. 'What has Athens to do with Jerusalem?' he once exclaimed 'or what has the Academy in common with the Church?' Almost every word he wrote gave the lie to the answer he implies. Tertullian would have deplored the attempts of Justin, Clement and Origen to reconcile Christianity and pagan philosophy. He explicitly rejected a Stoic, Platonic or dialectical Christianity. But in a wider sense, he had himself reconciled Christianity and classical culture. For he used the benefits of a traditional education and the fruits of his pagan erudition to defend and to propagate what he considered to be the truth. The closing words of the *De Palio* resolve any conflict between the two cultures: the humble *pallium* of the pagan philosopher is ennobled once it is donned by a Christian. In Tertullian's hands, rhetoric too underwent a similar transformation.[79]

It appears in the light of this that, to a certain extent, we can see Tertullian as a Christian orator, a subtle combination of the content of strict Biblical preaching with the stratagems of classical rhetoric. If this is the case, then it would appear that secular and non-Christian learning were employed by Tertullian in support of his faith, but not to rationalize faith's content, nor to accommodate it with the various trends of his time. Secular, or non-Christian philosophy is therefore found to be useful to the extent that its theological limitations are kept in mind and its methods and preconceptions are not allowed to dominate the subject. Kierkegaard spotted this in Tertullian's thought, commenting that,

> Tertullian stresses the difference between faith and non-Christian wisdom. He declares that among other things the difference is in range. 'Christianity is the complete revelation and has a definite goal. We do not need to

[77] Eric Osbourne, *The Emergence of Christian Theology* (Oxford: Clarendon Press, 1993), p. 276.
[78] Timothy Barnes, *Tertullian: A Historical and Literary Study* (Oxford: Clarendon Press, 1971), p. 210.
[79] Ibid.

speculate further after we have found the gospel. Since we believe, we do not need to go further than to believe, for above all we believe that there is nothing more that we have to believe.' This is the boundary, otherwise we would have to go on seeking in the infinite. Philosophy, on the other hand, has no boundary and therefore goes on into the infinite.[80]

At this point we do, almost inadvertently, come across a parallel with Kierkegaard, as he too made use of the literary forms of his period (in his case those of the Romantic Ironists) in service of Christianity. Kierkegaard could not agree with the beliefs of the Romantic Ironists, but, it is only too apparent that for him their methods of communication had their uses. Likewise, whilst Tertullian might not agree with the religious beliefs of Latin culture, he was to employ its rhetorical devices with devastating effect.

Returning to the '*credo quia absurdum*' of such notoriety, we can begin to see how it fits into Tertullian's agenda. The *De Carne Christi* in which it occurs was written against Marcion, a contemporary of Tertullian's who rejected numerous orthodox Christian beliefs about the person of Christ. In particular he decried Christ's human birth as an absurdity even though he was prepared to accept the fact of the crucifixion. The question then arises why it is so that he could be willing to accept one and not the other. Both contravene the accepted doctrines of Graeco-Roman mythology, as well as the rival philosophical pagan beliefs concerning the nature of God - although adherents to the former were perfectly at ease with the thought of their deities taking on the forms of swans, bulls or showers of golden rain![81] Tertullian asks Marcion which is really to be the most shameful, be it intellectually or morally, the manner of Christ's death or the manner of His birth?

> The Son of God was crucified; I am not ashamed because men must needs be ashamed [of it]. And the Son of God died: it is by all means to be believed, because it is absurd. And He was buried, and rose again: the fact is certain because it is impossible ... Thus the nature of the two substances displayed him as man and as God, - in one respect born, in the other unborn; in one respect fleshly, in the other spiritual; in one sense weak, in

[80] *Journals and Papers*, 4767, X4 A 140 *n.d.*, 1851.

[81] Consider Tertullian's comments on this: 'These things certainly are not 'foolish'. Inquire again, then, of what things he spoke, and when you imagine that you have discovered what they are, will you find anything to be so 'foolish' as believing in a God that has been born, and that of a virgin, and of a fleshly nature too ... And yet, according to the world's wisdom, it is more easy to believe that Jupiter became a bull or a swan, than that Christ really became a man, if we listen to Marcion.' (Tertullian, *De Carne Christi*, in *The Writings of Tertullian Vol. II, Ante-Nicene Christian Library Vol. 15* (Edinburgh: T&T Clark, 1870), p. 172.)

> the other exceedingly strong; in one sense dying, in the other living. This property of the two states - the divine and the human - is distinctly asserted with equal truth of both natures alike, with the same belief both in respect of the Spirit and of the flesh. The powers of the Spirit proved Him to be God, His sufferings attested the flesh of man.[82]

From this passage the actual wording and true context of Tertullian's alleged dictum can be seen: 'And the Son of God died: it is by all means to be believed, because it is absurd', or '*et mortuus est dei filius; credibile est, quia ineptum est*'. For Tertullian, the facts of the Incarnation are not absurd, neither are they shameful. But Marcion claims that they are, and Tertullian's response is to turn his opponent's position on its head by adopting the following trick from Aristotle's *The Art of Rhetoric*:

> Another line of argument refers to things which were supposed to happen and yet seem incredible. We may argue that people could not have believed them, if they had not been true or nearly true: even that they are the more likely to be true because they are incredible. For the things which men believe are either facts or probabilities: if, therefore, a thing that is believed is improbable and even incredible, it must be true, since it is certainly not believed because it is at all probable or credible.[83]

So, when Tertullian proclaims '*credibile est, quia ineptum est*' he is applying Aristotle's tactic to his defence of the doctrine of the Incarnation. The most problematic area of debate within the Christology of that time, and the centuries that followed, focused upon the question of Christ's two natures. Numerous heterodox teachings arose that attempted to circumnavigate the problem by denying the validity of either Christ's humanity or of his Deity. Tertullian adhered to the orthodox teaching that Christ is both human and divine without attempting to deny the significance of one or the other. We are confronted by a mystery that cannot be explained away, but, is still central to the Christian faith.

Athanasius and De Incarnatione

Athanasius' Christology puts great stress on the concept of the unity of Christ's person, that although he possesses two natures, they are not to be understood as being side by side, nor are they in any way mingled together.[84] Utilizing the vocabulary of Greek philosophy, he defends a

---

[82] Ibid., pp. 173-4.
[83] Aristotle, *The Art of Rhetoric*, 1400 a 5ff.
[84] R.V. Sellers, *Two Ancient Christologies* (London: SPCK, 1940), p. 36.

Christology of the Word, in which the eternal Word or Logos, the Son of the Father, truly God and of one substance ('homoousios') with the Father, has become man.[85] The idea of the Logos, originally borrowed from Stoic thought, referred to the governing, animating principle of the whole universe, and something parallel albeit on a far greater scale to the rational human soul. There was a complication in his ideas in how to reconcile the fact that, whilst the Logos was in control of the whole universe, he was at the same time incarnate and thereby (it logically follows) limited to one location.[86] Athanasius develops and presents his Christology in *De Incarnatione* ('The Incarnation').

> The Word was not confined within His body; nor was He there and nowhere else; He did not activate that body and leave the universe emptied of His activity and guidance. Here is the supreme marvel ['to paradoxotaton']. He was the Word and nothing contained Him; rather He Himself contained all things. He is in the whole creation, yet in His essential being He is distinct from it all, while He is in all things in the activities of His power, ordering all things, extending over all things His universal providence, quickening each and every thing at once, containing the universe and not contained by it, but in His Father alone existing wholly and entirely. So also when He was in human body He Himself gave that body life, and at the same time He was of course giving life to the whole universe, and was present in all things; and yet distinct from and outside the universe.[87]

In the above passage 'to paradoxotaton' is translated as 'the supreme marvel', although it is also possible to translate it as 'paradox', it is usually and more appropriately translated as 'beyond reason' or 'miraculous'.[88] There is at no point any implications that Athanasius is referring to a logical contradiction. Like Tertullian, although less rhetorically, he is allowing for a certain level of mystery as forming an indispensable component within his Christology.

---

[85] Ibid., p. 34. However, it must be noted that Athanasius did not generally employ the term homousios till over twenty years after writing *De Incarnatione*. (cf. A. Heron, 'Homoousios with the Father', in *The Incarnation*, (ed.) Torrance (Edinburgh: Handsel Press, 1981), p. 65).

[86] Kelly, *Early Christian Doctrines*, p. 28.

[87] Athanasius, in Bettenson (ed.), *The Early Christian Fathers* (Oxford: OUP, 1969), p. 288.

[88] *Greek-English Lexicon* (Cambridge: CUP, 1961).

Hilary of Poitiers and De Trinitate

A younger contemporary of Athanasius was Hilary of Poitiers, described by some as 'the Athanasius of the West'.[89] He was the leading Latin (Western) theologian in the development of Christology in the fourth century, an area which at that time was heavily dominated by developments in the Greek East. To a large extent the West still followed the theological tradition of Tertullian, and it was not until Hilary that there was any real original or decisive development.[90] Exiled to the East from AD 356 till AD 359, he had used this time as an opportunity to become well acquainted with the theological ideas and debates of the East, a chance that would have been denied him had he remained in the theologically xenophobic West. In an informal way he stood as an ideological bridge between East and West, helping theologians from both sides to understand the ideas of the other.

Like Athanasius, Hilary allows for the fact that any intellectual inquiry into the nature of the Godhead will be bound to involve a certain element of mystery. This matter comes to the fore in the text of his *De Trinitate* ('The Trinity') during a discussion of the co-inherence of the Father and the Son (a passage similar to that of Athanasius on the Logos incarnate). Referring to John 14:11 where Jesus states that 'I am in the Father and the Father is in me' (NRSV), Hilary admits that this statement may well 'confuse many minds, and not unnaturally, for the powers of human reason cannot provide them with any intelligible meaning. It seems impossible that one object can be both within and without another.'[91] G.L. Prestige claims that this is an admission of a real impossibility, and hence is to be understood as an actual paradox in the formal sense of the term.[92] However, the accent in Hilary's statement falls on the fact that coinherence seems to be impossible, not that it actually is, so we are in fact faced with an apparent paradox. Hilary continues: 'This is a problem which the wit of man will never solve, nor will human research ever find an analogy for this condition of Divine existence. But what man cannot understand, God can be. I do not mean to say that the fact that this is an assertion made by God renders it at once intelligible to us.'[93] There can be no immediate recourse to some Divinely imparted higher knowledge in resolving this

---

[89] Bettenson, *The Later Christian Fathers*, p. 1970, 5; Hall, *Doctrine and Practice in the Early Church*, p. 200.

[90] Kelly, *Early Christian Doctrines*, pp. 280, 334.

[91] Hilary of Poitiers, *De Trinitate*, in *Nicene and Post-Nicene Fathers*, Vol. 9 (Edinburgh: T&T Clark, 1995), p. 62.

[92] Prestige, *God in Patristic Thought*, p. 285.

[93] Hilary, *De Trinitate*, p. 62.

matter. It is the task of the believer to come to understand what he can, as far as he is able considering the nature of the subject and the extent of our limitations. As Hilary later states, 'We must think for ourselves, and come to know the meaning of the words, "I in the Father and the Father in me": but this will depend upon our success in grasping the truth that reasoning based upon Divine verities can establish its conclusions, even though they seem to contradict the laws of the universe.'[94]

Like Kierkegaard over a thousand years later, Hilary is careful to affirm that the nature of God transcends our understanding and hence cannot be described without a certain number of apparent contradictions. That is not their only similarity, as for the means whereby God chooses to make Himself known to us, Hilary relies on a concept of revelation that is strictly Incarnational: 'For He, being invisible and bodiless and incomprehensible, as the Son of God, took upon Him such a measure of matter and lowliness as was needed to bring Him within the range of our understanding, and perception and contemplation.'[95] Regarding the description of God as being 'incomprehensible' (*incomprehensibilis*), we must be careful to deny any charges of irrationality. On this point I am in agreement with G.L. Prestige when he explains that, 'when God is called incomprehensible, it does not mean that He is irrational - a conception which the Greek Fathers would have considered purely self-contradictory - but it does imply that His wisdom ranges infinitely further than human wisdom can compass, just as His power infinitely excels human creative capacity.'[96] Such Divine incomprehensibility does not denote the existence of contradictions, neither does it suggest meaninglessness, but instead stands for the honest human description of the infinity and power of God.

> We must not repose so blind a confidence in the human intellect as to imagine that we have complete knowledge of the objects of our thought, or that the ultimate problem is solved as soon as we have formed a symmetrical and consistent theory. Finite minds cannot conceive the Infinite; a being dependent for its existence upon another cannot attain to perfect knowledge either of its Creator or of itself, for its consciousness of self is coloured by circumstances, and bounds are set which its perception cannot pass.[97]

[94] Ibid.
[95] Ibid.
[96] Prestige, *God in Patristic Thought*, p. 6.
[97] Hilary, *De Trinitate*, p. 69.

The Incarnation in particular may well appear to be 'contrary to our experience of nature'.[98] Hilary describes this as *sacramentum*, a rather vague Latin term that is similar to the Greek 'to mysterion', normally translated as 'mystery' (originally 'secret'). The term is applied in *De Trinitate* to the 'mystery' of Divine unity, Christ's divine nature, the Incarnation and the role of Christ as mediator between God and the world.[99] With regard to the Incarnation (and to the others) this is 'a mystery [*sacramentum*], not for Himself [i.e. God], but for us'.[100]

The Definition of Chalcedon

The Definition of the Faith as produced and ratified by the fourth Ecumenical Council of the Church at Chalcedon in AD 451 has remained the authoritative statement regarding the doctrine of the Person of Christ within the mainstream Christian traditions. Part of it reads as follows:

> Therefore, following the holy Fathers, we all with one accord teach men to acknowledge one and the same Son, our Lord Jesus Christ, at once complete in Godhead and complete in manhood, truly God and truly man, consisting also of a reasonable soul and body; of one substance ['homoousios'] with the Father as regards his Godhead, and at the same time of one substance ['homoousios'] with us as regards his manhood; like us in all respect, apart from sin; as regards his Godhead, begotten of the Father before the ages, but yet as regards his manhood begotten, for us men and for our salvation, of Mary the Virgin, the God-bearer ['theotokos']; one and the same Christ, Son, Lord, Only-begotten, recognized in two natures ['en duo fusein'], without confusion, without change, without division, without separation; the distinction of natures being in no way annulled by the union, but rather the characteristics of each nature being preserved and coming together to form one person ['prosopon'] and one subsistence ['hupostasis'], not as parted or separated into two persons, but one and the same Son and Only-begotten God the Word, Lord, Jesus Christ.[101]

Opinion is divided as to whether we are to view this as an exhaustive definition, or as a principle that provides the framework for further Christian reflection upon the nature of Christ. However, if we examine the Chalcedonian definition in its historical and doctrinal context it will quickly become clear that it arose, not out of any desire on the part of the Church Fathers to impose a straight-jacket upon theology, but as an

[98] Ibid., p. 156.
[99] Cf. Kelly, *Early Christian Doctrines*, p. 423.
[100] Hilary, *De Trinitate*, p. 156.
[101] Huw Parri Owen, *Christian Theism* (Edinburgh: T&T Clark, 1984), p. 40.

effort to safeguard the doctrine of the Incarnation from the doctrinal errors that were threatening to split the Catholic Church at the time.[102] In the light of this Eric Mascall argues that, 'it both needs and is patient of much more exploration and extension than it has in fact received. It may well be that the very authority which it has been accorded in Christendom has led to it being treated too often as a static and finished product and to its potentialities for development being ignored.'[103] The significance of the definition lies in its simplicity: 'It is that the Lord Jesus Christ is one person, and that He is truly and perfectly God and is truly and perfectly man. It is not denied that this is a great and wonderful mystery or that it raises deep and perhaps insoluble problems for the human mind; but the statement itself is brief and lucid.'[104]

By discovering the contents of the views which Chalcedon set itself against, it is possible to discern the importance and value of the technical Greek terms used within it. Against the Arian heresy Chalcedon followed the earlier Council of Nicaea in declaring Christ to be 'of one substance ['homoousios'] with the Father'. Where Apollinarianism denied Christ's full humanity, Chalcedon declares that Christ has 'a reasonable [i.e. human] soul and body'. Against Nestorianism it affirms that Mary is the 'God-bearer' ['theotokos'], and that Christ 'is to be acknowledged in two natures ['en duo fusein'] ... without separation', in 'one person ['prosopon'] and one subsistence ['hupostasis']'. Finally, in refuting the Eutychian teachings Chalcedon states that, Christ is 'of one substance ['homoousios'] with us as touching the manhood'.[105]

As to the lasting value of the Definition, T.F. Torrance comments that:

> Jesus Christ was disclosed and known in the first place to the New Testament witnesses as Son of the Father, himself God manifest in the flesh, without any detraction from the perfection of his creaturely and human nature among men. It was precisely this understanding that Nicene and Chalcedonian Christology sought to express in such a way that it did full justice to the intersection and overlapping of divine and human reality in Jesus Christ, yet in such a way as to reject any confusion or separation between them. Judged by modern scientific standards alone it was thus an exemplary model of unitary theory and of the way in which the languages of the observable and the non-observable are to be co-ordinated. Yet the

---

102 Cf. Gunton, *Yesterday and Today*, p. 168.

103 Eric Mascall, *Whatever Happened to the Human Mind?* (London: SPCK, 1980), p. 37.

104 Ibid., p. 29.

105 Cf. Owen, *Christian Theism*, pp. 38-46; Macquarrie, *Jesus Christ in Modern Thought*, pp. 160-4.

> Nicene-Chalcedonian Christology cannot be regarded as merely a theory so much as the organized form of apprehension and conceptualization forced upon the Church by the ontic necessity of the given reality of God in Jesus Christ, although admittedly it cannot be confined within the concepts and statements used. Doubtless it stands in need of restatement and modification in view of the fuller knowledge of Christ that it has helped to mediate, but the very fact all through the history of Christian thought its economic simplicity has proved so astonishingly fertile in deepening and enlightening our thought far beyond the range of its original application, can only command our profound respect.[106]

A similar view is upheld by Mascall: 'Chalcedon was not trying to write metaphysics but simply to preserve the truth of the Christian Gospel, and the formula "one person, two natures" requires no philosophical expertise for its understanding.'[107]

4. The Similarities Between Kierkegaard and the Fathers Considered

What is the relationship between Kierkegaard's Christology and the views discussed above? At the beginning of this chapter I referred to a statement made by Alastair McKinnon in which he claims that 'by treating the Incarnation as a paradox', Kierkegaard 'both described an ancient tradition and set theology upon a new and more promising path'.[108] As regards at least one 'ancient tradition', I have argued that there is a definite influence from Tertullian on Kierkegaard's thought. This can easily be shown by the existence of numerous direct references to him in several works and some material in the *Journals*, some of which I referred to when discussing Tertullian's Christology. However, the exact relationship between Kierkegaard and Tertullian is perhaps more subtle than has previously been allowed for. As was shown in the discussion of Tertullian, his theology is frequently misinterpreted and too much weight assigned to the dictum '*credo quia absurdum*'. Instead, he anticipates one of Kierkegaard's tactics in that, at times, his arguments involve a certain amount of rhetoric. Like Kierkegaard, his apparent rejection of the rationality of the Incarnation is in reality an ironic echo of the negative verdict on it passed by non-Christian

---

[106] T. F. Torrance, *Space, Time and Incarnation* (Edinburgh: T&T Clark, 1997), pp. 80-81.

[107] Mascall, *Whatever Happened to the Human Mind?*, p. 34. Similarly Colin Gunton likens the Chalcedonian Definition to a map that was designed to clarify a few central features of Christology, rather than to stand as an exhaustive definition. (Gunton, *Yesterday and Today*, p. 153.)

[108] McKinnon, 'Søren Kierkegaard', p. 181.

philosophy. So, for Tertullian the Incarnation is no more an absurdity than it is for Kierkegaard a logical contradiction. Instead, both aimed to illustrate the incompatibility between Christian faith and the presuppositions of its rivals.

As regards the influence of such important figures as Athanasius and Hilary of Poitiers, the matter is by no means as simple and I have yet to find a single direct reference to either's Christology throughout the authorship. Because of this, I have chosen to cite details from their Christologies as forming some interesting parallels with those of Kierkegaard, rather than go so far as to claim that he was placinghimself in any self-conscious continuity with them.[109] In this way, I have attempted to illustrate that Kierkegaard was by no means alone in his acceptance of the mystery of Christ's two natures as a genuine mystery, (but not as a contradiction).[110]

If, however, Kierkegaard had claimed that the classical formulation of the Incarnation is a self-contradiction, then he would not have been alone on this account either. The nineteenth century had witnessed three significant figures who deserve to be mentioned in this context. Schleiermacher had rejected the classical two-natures doctrine in *The Christian Faith.*[111] This was largely over the fact that he felt the phrase 'two natures in one person' to be a wholly inappropriate use of terms.[112] In a radical development from Hegel, D.F. Strauss argued that, 'In an individual, a God-man, the properties and functions which the church ascribes to Christ contradict themselves.'[113] Also deriving his original inspiration from Hegelianism, Ludwig Feuerbach delivered a far-

---

[109] However, according to J. Heywood Thomas, there is evidence that Kierkegaard's use of 'the Absolute Paradox' was derived directly from his studies of both Tertullian and Athanasius. It would appear though that Kierkegaard's knowledge of Athanasius' Christology came largely from secondary sources. He possessed three works on Athanasius in his library all dating from before the end of the 1830s. (Cf. *Journals and Papers*, 5321, II A 745 *n.d*, 1838; J. Heywood Thomas, *Subjectivity and Paradox* (New York: Macmillan, 1957), p. 108.) Although I agree regarding the extent of Tertullian's influence on Kierkegaard's thought, I am less willing to give too much importance to the direct influence of Athanasius due to the lack of clear evidence from Kierkegaard's writings. As Kierkegaard was not hesitant in referring to his major influences, particularly in his *Journals*, there would certainly exist some references if Athanasius fell into this category.

[110] Consider for example the following statement from the *Journals* that, 'The divine and the diabolic are the only genuine mysteries, but the mystery of God is *revealed* in Christ.' (*Journals and Papers*, 292, II A 767 *n.d.*, 1838; cf. also 288, II A 276 October 13, 1838.)

[111] Schleiermacher, *The Christian Faith*, pp. 391ff.

[112] Ibid., p. 393.

[113] D. F. Strauss, *The Life of Jesus Critically Examined* (London: SCM, 1973), p. 780.

reaching critique of Christian doctrine. In *The Essence of Christianity* he argued that:

> The divine nature, notwithstanding the position that Christ was at once God and man, is as much dissevered from the human nature *in* the incarnation as *before* it, since each nature excludes the conditions of the other, although both are united in one personality, in an incomprehensible, miraculous, *i.e.*, untrue manner, in contradiction with the relation which, according to their definition, they stand to each other.[114]

Yet, as I have attempted to show, Kierkegaard remains quite Chalcedonian regarding his treatment of the two natures doctrine. An early quotation from the *Journals* helps to illustrate this when he states that: 'At every moment Christ is God just as much as he is man - just as the sky seems to be as deep in the sea as it is high above the sea.'[115] As such, he is within the mainstream of the broad spectrum of Western theological development. Yet his choice of the threatening meta-concept of 'the Absolute Paradox' does, at first glance, serve to set him apart from by far the majority of theologians. It is only when this meta-concept is interpreted correctly that we can begin to appreciate the importance of Kierkegaard's Christology. I shall attempt to show this further in the next chapter by moving the discussion away from 'the Absolute Paradox' and on to an evaluation of Kierkegaard's later Christological concepts, such as 'the sign of offense' and 'the sign of contradiction'.

---

114 Ludwig Feuerbach, *The Essence of Christianity* (London: Harper and Row, 1957), pp. 333-4.

115 *Journals and Papers*, 284, II A 595 *n.d.*, 1837.

Chapter 4

Kierkegaard's Christology II: The Sign of Contradiction

The vast majority of Kierkegaard's interpreters havc chosen to devote their attentions to *Fragments* and the *Postscript*, something which has generally led to discussions devoted almost entirely to 'the Absolute Paradox' as being the definitive aspect of Kierkegaard's Christology. However, Kierkegaard was later to develop a far richer Christology in *Practice in Christianity* under the guise of Anti-Climacus. In this work he has little to say under the heading of 'paradox', and instead, he challenges his reader with such Christological titles as 'the possibility for offense' and 'the sign of contradiction'. In many ways Anti-Climacus' Christology builds upon the aesthetic-poetical foundations already laid by Johannes Climacus in the B hypothesis we found in *Fragments*. The distance between the Christology of Anti-Climacus and that of Kierkegaard himself is minimal. In fact, Anti-Climacus generally serves to present Kierkegaard's own thought on this topic. Therefore, *Practice* will be compared with certain signed works from the late 1840s to the 1850s and in this way illustrate the close link between them. For this purpose some of Kierkegaard's *Christian Discourses* (written at the same time as *Practice*) have been chosen, in addition to the signed works *For Self-Examination* and *Judge For Yourself!* which were published in 1851, and a few passages from the *Gospel of Sufferings*, published under his own name in 1847.

The first section explores the Christology presented in *Fragments*, with particular reference to the 'Parable of the King and the Maiden' found in its second chapter, which is a vivid illustration of Climacus' ideas. This parable rhetorically offers two hypothetical solutions to the problem of how divine revelation is to be communicated to a human subject. The first possibility is that the human subject might be raised to the level of divinity. The second is a dramatic reversal of the first, whereby the god descends to humanity as one of us. Within the second possibility (for, after all, we are allegedly still musing freely within the framework of the B hypothesis), there arises the problem of our being offended by the nature of this divine incarnation.

I then move on to show how the nature and problem of this offense are expounded in *Practice*. Anti-Climacus carries this out under three headings: offense at Christ when viewed merely as a human political figure; offense at the 'God' in 'God-man'; and lastly, offense at the earthly reality of Christ's humanity. This section ends with a discussion of the doctrine of 'Christ as Redeemer and prototype' as expounded within Kierkegaard's direct works and *Journals*, showing how this relates to Anti-Climacus' theology.

The third section questions whether Kierkegaard is putting forward a form of kenotic Christology, that is, whether he envisages Christ as really emptying himself of certain properties of his divinity. Finally, I compare Kierkegaard's views with Luther's *theologia crucis*, or theology of the cross, in which the believer encounters the reality of God primarily through the suffering Christ on the cross instead of the *theologia gloriae* of works, natural theology, or philosophical speculation. In the light of this it will be seen to what extent Kierkegaard is offering us his own version of the theology of the cross, and how this serves to determine his whole theological method.

1. Christology in *Philosophical Fragments*

In *Fragments* Climacus rejects the 'Socratic' hypothesis as inadequate and posits in its stead the B hypothesis, with its concept of the god as teacher, in answer to the question 'can the truth be learned?' Through his answer, Climacus was making an indirect reference to the doctrine of the Incarnation. He develops this theme further in the second chapter of *Fragments*, under the heading 'The God as Teacher and Saviour'. However, we must be careful not to take him too literally, as the chapter's subtitle, 'A Poetical Venture', helps to betray the aesthetic nature of the discourse that follows. Climacus is careful to remind the reader repeatedly that, after all, he is 'only a poet'. In addition to this he offers apologies for his efforts, because 'the reader may already have lost patience when he hears that our analogy begins like a fairy tale and is not at all systematic'.[1] At the end of the chapter, we come across the words of an apparently enraged reader who protests against Climacus' 'shabbiest plagiarism, since it is nothing more or less than what any child knows'.[2] The reader's complaint is representative of the reaction Kierkegaard expected from the average church-going Dane, someone Kierkegaard hoped would easily see through the allegedly hypothetical

[1] *Fragments*, p. 26.
[2] Ibid., p. 35.

nature of the text. Climacus responds to the charge by denying that he is a plagiarist, in fact, he admits that he is not referring to any human invention. So, he claims, 'perhaps it is not a poem at all, or in any case is not ascribable to any human being or to the race, either.'[3] This teaching did not originate in anyone's imagination. Behind the rhetorical hypothesizing there stands a matter far too important for mere poetic rendition alone.

> Is not the whole thing wondrous, does not this word come to my lips as a felicitously foreshadowing word, for do we not, as I in fact said and you yourself involuntarily say, stand here before *the wonder*. And since we both are now standing before this wonder, whose solemn silence cannot be disturbed by human wrangling about what is mine and what is yours, whose awe-inspiring words infinitely drown out human quarrelling about mine and thine, forgive me my curious mistaken notion of having composed it myself. It was a mistaken notion, and the poem was so different from every human poem that it was no poem at all but *the wonder*.[4]

It could well be that, as Evans suggests, Kierkegaard's own Christian faith slips past the pseudonymity at this point in the discussion.[5] However, this seriousness only really applies to the closing passage of the chapter, for the most part we are left to delve beneath Climacus' aesthetic ponderings in order to discover Kierkegaard's own theology.

Unhappy Love

The parable (Climacus calls it an 'analogy') of the King and the Maiden is introduced within the context of a discussion of 'unhappy love'. Climacus explains that the god is motivated to reveal himself out of love for the human learner, yet this love appears to be considerably stronger on one side than on the other. First, although the god certainly loves the learner, the learner might not actually be very desirable according to human criteria. There is no evidence that the learner does in any way merit the god's love.[6] Second, the god is eternal, and by virtue of this we may safely conclude that his love is also eternal. Yet this love is fulfilled in time, during 'the moment', and so this appears to be a predominantly one-sided relationship. Climacus describes this as

---

[3] Ibid.
[4] Ibid., p. 36. Climacus' use of 'the wonder' with reference to the Incarnation is somewhat reminiscent of the use of 'mystery' (whether *sacramentum* or to musterion) as was found in the Patristic theologians cited in the previous chapter.
[5] Cf. Evans, *Passionate Reason*, p. 55.
[6] A similar theme is later taken up in *Gospel of Sufferings*, p. 67.

'the relation of the eternal resolution to the unequal occasion'.[7] This of course stands in stark contrast to the 'Socratic' hypothesis, where the relationship between teacher and learner is posited as being one of equals.[8] For Climacus, the existence of such inequality between the god and the learner seems to present us with a problem in need of his resolution, for what can be the god's motivation for revealing himself to such an undeserving subject?

> Out of love, therefore, the god must be eternally resolved in this way, but just as his love is the basis, so also must love be the goal, for it would indeed be a contradiction for the god to have a basis of movement and a goal that do not correspond to this. The love, then, must be for the learner, and the goal must be to win him, for only in love is the different made equal, and only in equality or in unity is there understanding. Without perfect understanding, the teacher is not the god, unless the basic reason is to be sought in the learner, who rejected what was made possible for him.[9]

Climacus' dilemma concerns how the god will be able to reveal himself appropriately to the capacity of the human subject: 'this love is basically unhappy, for they are very unequal, and what seems so easy - namely, that the god must be able to make himself understood - is not so easy if he is not to destroy that which is different.'[10] So, we are confronted with the problem. On the one hand, the god, who is self-existent, motivated wholly out of selfless love and sinless, desires to reveal himself to humanity, which is sinful, totally dependent upon the god (although blissfully unaware of this need as yet), and, in comparison with the god, extremely fragile. Climacus considers the possibility of communication between the two to be difficult, to say the least. Unable to explain the situation literally, Climacus metaphorically compares it to two types of unhappy love. The first arises because the two lovers cannot be together, the second arises because they are unable to understand each other. In the latter situation, 'this infinitely deeper sorrow is identified essentially with the superior person, for he alone also understands the misunderstanding. It is identified essentially only with the god, because no human situation can provide a valid analogy, even though we shall suggest one here in order to awaken the mind to an understanding of the divine.'[11] In this way Climacus introduces the 'Parable of the King and the Maiden'.

---

[7] *Fragments*, p. 25.
[8] Ibid., p. 24.
[9] Ibid., p. 25.
[10] Ibid.
[11] Ibid.

The Parable of the King and the Maiden

Climacus relates his analogy, or parable, very much in the manner of a fairy tale. This is perhaps not all that surprising when we realise that he was an acquaintance of the novelist Hans Christian Andersen, and that he wrote his first book, *From the Papers of One Still Living*, as a satirical attack upon Andersen's work *Only a Fiddler*.[12] However, rather than branching out his expertise into the writing of fairy tales, it is possible that Kierkegaard is adopting this method as a minor ironic jibe at the Romantic fascination with folklore. This fascination had been inaugurated, on the cultural level, by Johann Gottfried Herder towards the end of the eighteenth century. It was then carried on after him in a more political vein by Clemens Brentano and Achim von Arnim.[13] Although this movement is now best remembered in Britain through the works of the Brothers Grimm, the interest in national folklore contributed in some ways to the growth of nationalist feelings and 'culture Protestantism' amongst German intellectuals that Kierkegaard despised. In lightly presenting his hypothesis as a fairy tale, the very form of Climacus' parable was in ironic mimicry of the Romantic genre, in some ways being in anticipation of his polemical, satirical verdict upon his contemporaries.

Passing swiftly on from form to content, the parable relates how there was a king who had fallen deeply in love with 'a maiden of lowly station in life'. Yet this particular king terrified all those around him, hence,

> His resolution was easy to carry out, for every politician feared his wrath and dared not even to hint at anything. Every foreign country trembled before his power and dared not to refrain from sending a congratulatory delegation to the wedding. And no cringing courtier, grovelling before him, dared to hurt his feelings lest his own head be crushed.[14]

Yet the king could not ever let her know of his feelings, for how could it be possible for such a king as this to tell the maiden of his love for her? There would be no way that she could respond to his love freely. Instead, in this fairy tale medieval world, there would always be the fact that he was the king, and she but a commoner, to prevent them from feeling as equals in each other's company. 'Alone he grappled with the sorrow in his heart: whether the girl would be made happy by this, whether she would acquire the bold confidence never to remember what

---

[12] Cf. Collins, *The Mind of Kierkegaard*, p. 8.
[13] Cranston, *The Romantic Movement*, p. 45.
[14] *Fragments*, pp. 26-7.

the king only wished to forget - that he was the king and she had been a lowly maiden.'[15]

Climacus breaks from the story a moment in order to relate the analogy back to the rest of the argument in *Fragments*.

> Now if the moment is to have decisive significance (and without this we return to the Socratic ...), the learner is in untruth, indeed, is there through his own fault - and yet he is the object of the god's love. The god wants to be his teacher, and the god's concern is to bring about equality. If this cannot be brought about, the love becomes unhappy and the instruction meaningless, for they were unable to understand each other. We probably think that this may be a matter of indifference to the god, since he does not need the learner, but we forget - or rather, alas, we demonstrate - how far we are from understanding him; we forget that he does indeed love the learner.[16]

If Climacus is to be taken at all seriously, it is actually the god who is in difficulty and in need of some help to overcome this problem! Just as the king wonders how he could approach the maiden he loves without frightening her into terrified submission, so the god 'knows how nearly impossible it is to maintain the learner's bold confidence, without which understanding and equality disappear and the love is unhappy'.[17] We find that the god is at a loss, and who can offer assistance but the poet? Climacus graciously comes to his aid. After all, 'the poet's task is to find a solution, a point of unity where there is in truth love's understanding, where the god's concern has overcome its pain, for this is the unfathomable love that is not satisfied with what the object of love might foolishly consider himself blissfully happy to have.'[18]

According to M. Holmes Hartshorne, Climacus' apparently arrogant attitude in this context illustrates 'the aesthetical standpoint in its cold, cynical purity, barely disguised as religious concern'.[19] At first this might seem to be a harsh judgement. After all, this is but a fairy tale and every good fairy tale must have its narrator, be he a medieval bard or a Romantic poet. His is a pivotal role in making the story come alive for the reader, and the narrator is in a sense a part of the tale and yet, at the same time, he maintains a certain theatrical distance from the plot and the characters participating in the story which he brings to us. Yet, Climacus' parable is not a passion play but a fictional hypothesis, composed solely for his own intellectual amusement. He never asks to be taken seriously and in the book's preface he evens forbids it.

[15] Ibid., p. 27.
[16] Ibid., p. 28.
[17] Ibid.
[18] Ibid., pp. 28-29.
[19] Holmes Hartshorne, *Kierkegaard Godly Deceiver*, p. 34.

Towards the end of this chapter he admits to his 'plagiarism', thereby further absolving himself from any responsibility for the book's contents.[20] The god of his deliberations might not necessarily be the Christian God,[21] and Climacus cannot recognize the seriousness of the subject he tackles as the religious life-view is beyond him. Holmes Hartshorne's interpretation fails to realise that Climacus does not wish to deceive us into believing that he really exists within the religious life view. Instead Climacus just, quite casually, presents some possibilities for our consideration.

Possibility A

As Climacus explains his two possibilities, he constantly alternates, almost as if at random, from talking about the king and the maiden in the fairy tale, to talking about the god and the learner in the B Hypothesis of the main argument of *Fragments* itself. In this way the analogy and the hypothesis are closely intertwined. He places his two possibilities under the headings of A and B. In so doing he leaves the reader to wonder whether these are in any way to be referred back to certain themes within the 'Socratic', or A Hypothesis, and the B Hypothesis (of which this chapter is a part). As I discuss the possibilities, it will become apparent whether or not this is an appropriate link to be made.

Within possibility A there are two options. The first of these is that the god and the learner are to be made equal through the learner being elevated to the same state as that of the god. As Climacus explains,

> The god would then draw the learner up toward himself, exalt him, divert him with joy lasting a thousand years (for to him a thousand years are as one day), let the learner forget the misunderstanding in his tumult of joy. Yes, the learner would perhaps be very much inclined to consider himself blissfully happy because of this. And would it not be glorious suddenly to score a great success because the god's eye fell on him, just as it would be for that lowly maiden; would it not be glorious to be of assistance to him in taking the whole thing in vain, deceived by his own heart![22]

This is, however, not an effective solution and it actually turns out to be nothing more than a hollow deception. Instead of dealing with that most important and limiting difference between humanity and deity, namely, that caused by human sin, this possibility can only make the god forget all about the learner's sin. In possibility A it is not suggested that the problem of sin is first cancelled out by the outworking of divine

[20] *Fragments*, p. 35.
[21] See Chapter 5 below where I discuss Climacus' theism.
[22] Ibid., p. 29.

grace, after which the now perfect learner is deified. Instead, it implies that the still sinful learner becomes an immortal. There is no question of repentance. Neither is it even mentioned that the learner is at all aware of his sin, nor whether sin is construed as forming any sort of barrier between humanity and the god. This possibility is reminiscent of the Socratic Hypothesis that we encountered earlier, as here too the problem of sin is disregarded. As Stephen Dunning puts it,

> In both cases, the opposition between the human and the divine is denied by divinizing the human. It is salvation by apotheosis. The learner simply forgets his error and sin; they are shown to be of no more consequence for the relation with the divine teacher than were the historical occasions or the Socratic learner. In short, apotheosis begs the question; it denies the very problem that the possibility of revelation poses.[23]

Quite understandably, Climacus does not even pretend to support this option, yet not because of the problem of sin. To him the first option of possibility A is but a deception because, 'one is most terribly deceived when one does not even suspect it but remains as if spellbound by a change of costume.'[24] Once the learner is deified by the god, or, to return to the fairy tale, once the maiden is granted the status of royalty, each one faces the following personal dilemma: have I been exalted because I am loved, or am I loved because of my recent exaltation? Unsure whether they were equally precious in their original, humble state, they are unsure of their standing in the new situation. After all, if someone were to take away the maiden's regal costume, would she still be a queen in her rags? So then, Climacus needs to find an option in which the learner, and the maiden, can be genuinely loved without being inappropriately transformed into something that they are not. In this way Kierkegaard allows his pseudonym to begin to affirm the intrinsic dignity of human persons.

The second option within possibility A is that, 'the unity could be brought about by the god's appearing to the learner, accepting his adoration, and thereby making him forget himself. Likewise, the king could have appeared before the lowly maiden in all his splendor, could have let the sun of his glory rise over her hut, shine on the spot where he appeared to her, and let her forget herself in adoring admiration.'[25] Yet here again we are faced with the problem of deception. Climacus continues,

> This would perhaps have satisfied the girl, but it could not satisfy the king, for he did not want his own glorification but the girl's, and his sorrow

[23] Dunning, *Kierkegaard's Dialectic of Inwardness*, p. 170.
[24] *Fragments*, p. 29.
[25] Ibid.

> would be very grievous because she would not understand him; but for him it would be still more grievous to deceive her. In his own eyes, just to express his love incompletely would be a deception, even if no one understood him, even if reproach sought to vex his soul.[26]

What involves the pomp and splendour of a royal visit in the fairy tale, becomes the direct self-revelation of the god in the Hypothesis. In both cases the problem is the same: how can either the maiden, or the learner, freely respond to the offer of love? The maiden would be totally overawed by the mighty king's personal visit and any chance of him discovering her real feelings for him would be denied. Likewise, if the god chose to appear to the learner in the manner of, say an Old Testament theophany, then it seems highly likely that the learner would fall on his knees in front of him just as much out of fear as out of any other motive. This reaction is especially pertinent if we remember that the learner is 'untruth' in that he is orientated against the truth.[27] In this case he could just as easily recoil in horror if the god in whom he had never believed suddenly turned up in front of him! Thoughts of selfless love, mutual equality and intimate divine-human relationships would probably be the last things to cross his troubled mind on such an auspicious occasion.

Yet the fact remains that the god earnestly desires to express his love in a way appropriate to the learner, and he cannot rest content until this has been done. What has become apparent is that, however this may be done, the god must allow the learner the genuine freedom to respond with whatever love he is able. There must be no reaction out of fear or any other negative motive. Such a response would be one of misunderstanding, creating a vast distance between the god and the learner, and that is exactly what Climacus' poetic solution is trying to avoid.

Stephen Dunning argues that through the above discussion it is shown that 'the god is ... totally other and cannot be revealed to mere humans. With the logical rigour of an Apollinarius, Climacus asserts the incapacity of human nature to host the divine.'[28] Dunning's position denies, not only the possibility of a real divine self-revelation, but also prohibits any orthodox understanding of the Incarnation. There can therefore be no 'point of unity' and Climacus' search for a solution to the god's problem is in vain. To agree with Dunning here would mean to subvert the very theological principles that motivated Kierkegaard to write *Fragments* in the first place. Namely, that God has chosen to reveal himself to humanity, and, that this has been accomplished to the

[26] Ibid.
[27] Ibid., pp. 13f.
[28] Dunning, *Kierkegaard's Dialectic of Inwardness*, p. 170.

greatest possible extent in and through the historically real event of the Incarnation. As I have constantly argued in the previous two chapters, Kierkegaard understood the greatest problematic difference between God and humanity to be sin, not finitude (which almost pales into insignificance by comparison), and hence because of this, 'God is at one and the same time infinitely close to man and infinitely far away.'[29] There is never at any point, either through Climacus, or through Kierkegaard himself when writing 'directly', the assertion that the divine cannot assume human nature.

Instead, we find that what is said in the passage is that: 'not to disclose itself is the death of love; to disclose itself is the death of the beloved.'[30] By this Climacus is stating that the god's love must be expressed. Otherwise it is as if it were 'dead', but, as we have seen, the direct, theophanous manner would render the learner insignificant in the process as they lose themselves in the reality of the divine, and hence contribute to their apparent 'death'. True, the learner would be deified, and the maiden would be a queen, but they would no longer be the free individuals they once were, and this is what is so important to the god and to the king.

'The human mind so often aspires to might and power', he continues,

> And in its constant preoccupation with this thought, as if achieving it would transfigure everything, it does not suspect that there is not only joy in heaven but sorrow also: how grievous it is to have to deny the learner that to which he aspires with his whole soul and to have to deny it precisely because he is the beloved.'[31]

The learner would gladly welcome the god's love and deification, but if this is simply handed out in obvious splendour and in full view of others, would the learner really value it, would he really love the god? The situation is the same with the maiden. It would be easy for her to feign love when accepting an offer of marriage from the most powerful king on earth, and so the king is loved for the power and position he brings. But what if the same offer came from somebody at the bottom of the social pile? This leads us to possibility B.

Possibility B

So, Climacus' concern is to find a way to the truth that, whilst allowing the learner to have significance, manages to avoid the failings of the

---

[29] *Journals and Papers*, 1451, X A 171 *n.d.*, 1854.
[30] *Fragments*, p. 30.
[31] Ibid.

'Socratic'. Previously it was seen that the learner becomes the midpoint, and that the teacher finds himself dismissed as being unimportantly 'accidental'.

> If, however, the moment is to have decisive significance ... then this [i.e. the 'Socratic'] is certainly not the truth, for the learner owes the teacher everything. Just as the teacher's love, Socratically understood, would be a deceiver's love if he let the pupil go on thinking that he actually owed him something, whereas the teacher was supposed to assist him to become sufficient unto himself, so the god's love - if he wants to be a teacher - must be not only an assisting love but also a procreative love by which he gives birth to the learner, or, as we have called him, one born again, meaning the transition from 'not to be' to 'to be'.[32]

In possibility B there can be no question of the god's role being accidental, in fact Climacus accentuates the god's role to the highest degree as 'the learner owes the teacher everything'. Because of this, we can see that possibility B is already beginning to resemble the B Hypothesis of the previous chapter. Yet, the god's love requires that the learner cannot in any way be disregarded in this process, despite the inequality that stands between them. Possibility A offered us two options whereby, in effect, the learner is 'annihilated'. Through the god's actions, according to possibility B, the learner is enabled to be himself to a far higher degree than he was before. Yet, things are not so clear-cut as in the previous options, and it is not long before we find ourselves being confronted with some 'paradoxes'. Climacus tells us that,

> The truth then is that the learner owes him everything, but that which makes understanding so difficult is precisely this: that he becomes nothing and yet is not annihilated; that he owes him everything and yet becomes boldly confident; that he understands the truth, but the truth makes him free; that he grasps the guilt of untruth, and then again bold confidence triumphs in the truth.[33]

There exists here a dialectical relationship between god and learner, as the learner, though still confined to the limitations of finite, sinful humanity, is enabled to be himself as he recognises the truth and reality of his state before the god.

However, how does Climacus suggest that this is possible? If it is not appropriate to elevate the learner to the status of divinity, nor for the god to appear to the same learner in a triumphant blaze of glory, then what other option remains for the god?

---

[32] Ibid., p. 30.
[33] Ibid., pp. 30-31.

> If, then, the unity could not be brought about by an ascent, then it must be attempted by a descent. Let the learner be *X*, and this *X* must also include the lowliest, for even Socrates did not keep company solely with brilliant minds, how then could the god make distinctions! In order for unity to be effected, the god must become like this one. He will appear, therefore, as the equal of the lowliest of persons. But the lowliest of all is one who must serve others - consequently, the god will appear in the form of a servant.[34]

In a radical reversal of roles, the god adopts a most unlikely appearance in order to communicate his love to the learner effectively: the master becomes the servant.

For the king, such an action would involve dressing up as a peasant and acting the relevant part until the maiden came to love him in that state. The weak point in the argument is that in the fairy tale the king must himself hide behind a facade. On this point the analogy really begins to break down, for, on this level possibility B falls into the same trap of requiring the king to deceive the maiden. Once she falls in love with the king as a peasant, he will at some point have to come clean and admit his true identity - that all the time he was really the king and it was only a costume act that had made him out to be otherwise. Where she had previously thought she loved her equal, the maiden now finds herself with her tyrannical overlord. Where is the equality in their situation now? The maiden remains a servant girl and the king remains a king. The difference is still there between them and the moment that the king shows his true nature it is as if we are in the royal visit suggested in possibility A. What is there to prevent the maiden from feeling deceived? There is of course the possibility that her love for the king would overcome such feelings, but the king runs a serious risk that this may not be the case.

Returning to the B Hypothesis, the situation between the god and the learner is different and such deception is painstakingly avoided. Climacus explains,

> But this form of a servant is not something put on like the king's plebeian cloak, which just by flapping open would betray the king . . . - but is his true form. For this is the boundlessness of love, that in earnestness and in truth and not in jest it wills to be the equal of the beloved, and it is the omnipotence of resolving love to be capable of that of which neither the king nor Socrates was capable, which is why their assumed characters were still a kind of deceit.[35]

---

[34] Ibid., p. 31.

[35] Ibid., pp. 31-2.

From this passage onwards we leave the fairy tale behind, and the rest of Climacus' discussion refers solely to the B Hypothesis itself. However, the aesthetic-poetical banter of Climacus' earlier deliberations now gives way to a more serious reflection upon the surprising nature of the god's incarnation.

Climacus' main concern is to illustrate the actuality of the god's human nature. Alongside this he is careful to stress throughout the hypothesis that the god is acting out of unconditional love for the learner. Apart from these two concerns, much of what would be demanded for a comprehensive, systematic Christology is omitted. Rather than interpret this as a doctrinal failing on Kierkegaard's part, we must be careful to remember that *Fragments* is intended to be an introduction, not to Christian doctrine, 'but to becoming a Christian.'[36] Catechetical instruction can follow conversion, and it is the task of the various *Discourses* and later works such as *Practice in Christianity* to expound upon some of the finer theological details of his Christology.

Regarding the god's human nature, Climacus asserts that 'it is his true form', and that there can be no deception. So, clearly Climacus is no docetist, for the god does not *appear* to be human, he *is* human. Neither is his argument suggestive of monophysitism. We must remember that he is only stressing certain aspects of the Incarnation and because of that, Kierkegaard purposefully prohibits Climacus from embarking upon the subtleties of wider Christological and Trinitarian theology. All we need to know here is that God ('the god' for Climacus) loves us and comes to us as the historical person of Christ. He stresses the human nature in phrase with obvious Biblical allusions: 'therefore the god must suffer all things, endure all things, be tried in all things, hunger in the desert, thirst in his agonies, be forsaken in death, absolutely the equal of the lowliest of human beings - look, behold the man!'[37]

With this '*Ecce homo!*' Climacus' god is seen to be the lowest common denominator, and in that way he is able to reach out to the learner, whatever the learner's status may be. 'For love', he explains,

> Any other revelation would be a deception, because either it would first have had to accomplish a change in the learner (love, however, does not change the beloved but changes itself) and conceal from him that this was needed, or in superficiality it would have had to remain ignorant that the whole understanding between them was a delusion (this is the untruth of paganism). For the god's love any other revelation would be a deception.[38]

[36] *Concluding Unscientific Postscript* vol. 1, pp. 381ff.
[37] Ibid., pp. 32-3
[38] Ibid., p. 33.

However, there is no delusion on the god's side that the learner will automatically respond with anything like the love that he has offered him. In adopting the reality of a human nature the god makes himself vulnerable, not only to physical suffering and death, but to the possibility of being rejected by the learner he came to save. The lowly manner of his manifestation would seem absurd, almost as if he were inferior to us, but,

> If I pleaded with him to change his resolution, to manifest himself in some other way, to spare himself, then he would look at me and say: Man, what have you to do with me; go away, for you are of Satan, even if you yourself do not understand it! Or, if he just once stretched out his hand to bid it happen, and if I were to think that I understood him better or loved him more, I would then very likely see him weep also for me and hear him say: To think that you could become so unfaithful to me and grieve love in this way; so you love only the omnipotent one who performs miracles, not him who humbled himself in equality with you.[39]

The notion of the god becoming like this all for the sake of the learner is something that is difficult to comprehend. In this way the god's incarnation serves to challenge all previously held concepts of divinity.

> And the situation of the understanding - in its frailty, how close it is at every moment to the border of misunderstanding when the anxieties of guilt disturb the peace of love. And the situation of understanding - how terrifying, for indeed it is less terrifying to fall upon one's face while the mountains tremble at the god's voice than to sit with him as his equal, and yet the god's concern is precisely to sit this way.[40]

Such a notion of equality stands in stark contrast to human hopes of glorification and worldly power. In this way our whole process of making theological value judgements is itself judged and found to be wanting. The god's entry into our form of existence calls into question our very ability to recognise the truth at all. 'Look, there he stands - the god. Where? There. Can you not see him? He is the god, and yet he has no place where he can lay his head, and he does not dare to turn to any person lest that person be offended at him.'[41] So, the god becomes one of us, but we do not like what we see and find him offensive. Or, unable to penetrate the divine *incognito*, we are offended that our own abilities are inadequate without his assistance. With the possibility of offense it becomes appropriate to turn to the Christology

[39] Ibid.
[40] Ibid., pp. 34-5.
[41] Ibid., p. 32.

of *Practice in Christianity*. In this Anti-Climacus presents Kierkegaard's theology in greater detail, and, in a manner that is more overtly within the Christian tradition. From this it will be seen that the possibility of offense, not paradox, stands as the hallmark of Kierkegaard's Christology.

2. Christology in the Later Writings

We encounter several different pictures of Christ in Kierkegaard's later writings. Kierkegaard chose to offer much of his own Christology through the mouthpiece of Anti-Climacus in *Practice in Christianity* and in addition to this he presented it as more noticeably his own in some of the signed works from 1848 onwards. To support this assertion, I will use material from some of these signed works such as *Christian Discourses*, *Gospel of Sufferings*, *For Self-Examination* and *Judge For Yourself!* at certain points in the following text where the connection is most obvious. The Christology of these later works builds upon the foundations already laid through Climacus in *Fragments*, although it does, quite understandably, lack his aesthetical-poetical approach to the subject. However, there are some differences between the two, a factor that may be attributed to the different perspectives of Climacus and Anti-Climacus/Kierkegaard rather than any conscious shift in doctrine on Kierkegaard's part. For instance, where in *Fragments* Climacus talks impersonally of 'the paradox', Anti-Climacus, in the second part of *Practice in Christianity*, chooses instead to refer to Christ as 'the possibility of offense'. It is largely under this somewhat threatening heading that I have chosen to examine his Christology. Anti-Climacus considers Christ to be 'the possibility of offense' in three different senses. In the first section I discuss 'the possibility of offense that is not related Christ as Christ (the God-man) but to him simply as an individual human being who comes into collision with an established order'.[42] Second, and more important, is 'the possibility of essential offense in relation to loftiness, that an individual human being speaks or acts as if he were God, declares himself to be God, therefore in relation to the qualification "God" in the composition God-man'.[43] Third, which is the key to Kierkegaard's Christology as a whole, comes 'the possibility of essential offense in relation to lowliness, that the one who passes himself off as God proves to be the lowly, poor, suffering, and finally powerless human being'.[44] In the following three sections each of these categories of offense will be discussed in turn, with reference to

---

[42] *Practice in Christianity*, p. 85.
[43] Ibid., p. 94.
[44] Ibid., p. 102.

the signed works and *Journals* as well as to *Practice*. After these I examine Kierkegaard's doctrine of Christ as Redeemer and prototype as it is found in the later writings. This theme follows on directly from the last possibility of offense and forms a more traditionally recognisable Christological discussion within his thought. In this way it will be possible to explain and evaluate the details of Kierkegaard's doctrine of the person of Christ.

Offense at the Christ Who Comes into Collision with an Established Order

Anti-Climacus cites two New Testament passages in support of this first category of offense. Matthew 15:1-12 relates how Christ and the disciples clashed with scribes and Pharisees over a matter of ritual cleanliness. Then in Matthew 17:24-27 tax collectors question Peter on Jesus' payment of the temple tax. In neither case is the dispute over whether Jesus is God, nor does it arise over whether he is the hoped for Messiah. Instead the matter is quite mundane: will an individual human being respect the norms of his society? The concern is not over a matter of mere etiquette however, and the real question underlying the words of Christ's contemporaries is this: 'Is the single individual higher than the established order? With this question or, more correctly, with this protest, the established order wants to force him either to come back again or to state categorically that he is more than human - and then the offense is present.'[45]

The offense arises out of Christ's seeming to place himself in the position of being able to pass judgement upon the order and traditions of his surrounding society. In taking such an elevated stance does he consider himself to be more than human? However, there is nothing distinctively Christological in this situation and Anti-Climacus argues that it is possible for any individual person to find himself in this position.

> Here Christ is in the more ordinary sense a teacher, a teacher of godliness, of inwardness, who with originality (without any question of his claim to be God) emphasises inwardness in contrast to empty outwardness, a teacher who transforms outwardness into inwardness. This is the collision, a collision that appears again and again in Christendom; to put it briefly, it is the collision of pietism with the established order.[46]

Where Christianity had become 'Christendom', that most despised of Kierkegaard's objects of attack, he saw only an impersonal institution, a

---

[45] Ibid., p. 85.
[46] Ibid.

faceless crowd. Kierkegaard believed that the individual Christian possesses the inalienable right to stand up for the truth of his or her beliefs, even when this entailed contradicting those of the majority. It is at such a moment of collision that the believer's choice to follow Christ is made manifest in his life, and through it is the truth of the gospel proclaimed. In his later years Kierkegaard was again to associate this form of Christianity with pietism:

> Yes, indeed, pietism (properly understood, not simply in the sense of abstaining from dancing and such externals, no, in the sense of witnessing for the truth and suffering for it, together with the understanding, together with the understanding that suffering in this world belongs to being a Christian, and that a shrewd and secular conformity with this world is unchristian) - yes, indeed, pietism is the one and only consequence of Christianity.[47]

It follows therefore that real Christianity cannot avoid this collision, and so he declares that, 'to be a Christian in Christendom in plain and simple conformity is just as impossible as doing gymnastics in a straightjacket.'[48] It is interesting to observe that there are similarities between this form of offense at Christ and the reaction of the early pseudonym Johannes de Silentio to Abraham in *Fear and Trembling*. Johannes de Silentio has difficulties accepting the religious faith of Abraham, specifically at the point when Abraham is called by God to sacrifice his only son Isaac as recounted in Genesis 22. Such a calling clearly contravenes the genteel morality of Johannes' bourgeois society and he cannot conceive of how God could possibly require such an action. To Johannes the demands of the religious life, in order to be reasonable, must be in conformity with the accepted moral standards of the society in which one lives: the 'universal', or the ethical life-view. Abraham, however, bases his life upon the revealed will of God, without recourse to the approval of his contemporaries, thereby positing a higher authority than the 'universal'. On this Johannes de Silentio begins to sound a little like his namesake, Johannes Climacus: 'Now we are face to face with the paradox. Either the single individual as the single individual can stand in an absolute relation to the absolute, and consequently the ethical is not the highest, or Abraham is lost.'[49] For Abraham, God is the absolute measure of all things, whereas society (or the state, the establishment, etc.) provides but a relative standard. In this case the object of true faith must be something, or rather someone, who transcends the immanent surroundings of the individual. Otherwise

---

[47] *Journals and Papers*, 3318, X 3 A 437 *n.d.*, 1850.
[48] Ibid., 409, XI 2 A 349 *n.d.*, 1854.
[49] *Fear and Trembling*, p. 113.

faith becomes acceptance of the norm, whatever the norm might be, and hence faith becomes something that is neither distinctive nor valued. As Silentio chooses to put it:

> Therefore, either there is an absolute duty to God - and if there is such a thing, it is the paradox just described, that the single individual as the single individual is higher than the universal and as the single individual stands in an absolute relation to the absolute - or else faith has never existed, or else Abraham is lost.[50]

The reaction of Silentio is that of the universal, or the established order. He is the one offended by Abraham, the man of faith, and he is also likely to be offended by Christ for similar reasons. Kierkegaard uses Anti-Climacus to speak from the other side of the relationship. Through the myth of Christendom the established order becomes deified. In *Practice* this is somewhat unsurprisingly attributed to Hegel, although we need not consider him the only culprit as this is a modern example of a tendency that has often occurred in world history. It follows from such a deification that any protest against the established order is then seen as rebellion against God, with the assumption that whoever rebels is somehow claiming divinity. When deity is understood entirely in terms of what is embodied by the established order this leads to the secularization of everything, even the believer's relationship with God.[51] When nothing higher than this established order can be visualised by those who are within it, it becomes the object of ultimate loyalty and devotion, the immanent god made in our own image. As Anti-Climacus puts it: 'so holy do people always become when they deify the established order that their worship makes a fool of God: under the guise of worshipping and adoring God, they worship and adore their own invention.'[52] This distorted image becomes the criterion for all that is true. Such an image is threatened by the Christ who calls their very presuppositions into question. He posits in their stead a different kind of piety, one that is defined through relationship with the transcendent God who is distinct from the established order. Anti-Climacus' Christ does this with the simple authority of a teacher with no claim to divinity, yet the reaction of the established order is to charge him with blasphemy. In reality, the situation is reversed as it is the self-deified establishment which is found to be blasphemous.[53]

---

[50] Ibid., p. 81.
[51] *Practice in Christianity*, p. 87.
[52] Ibid., p. 92.
[53] Cf. *Journals and Papers*, 3034, X 2 A 117 *n.d.*, 1849. Cf. also: 'established Christendom's orthodoxy has actually transformed Christianity into paganism.' (Ibid., 3035, X 2 A 389 *n.d.*, 1850.)

The vision of Christ as the champion of individual rights, of unorthodoxy and of protest against an unjust establishment may well be a popular one today. It fits in well with the political theologies that have arisen out of the dissatisfactions permeating many levels of contemporary society. To a certain degree there were similar feelings in the mid nineteenth century. It witnessed the composition of the *Communist Manifesto*, plus the violent outbreak and aftermath of the 1848 revolutions that occurred throughout much of mainland Europe. Yet it will be seen that Kierkegaard was not limiting his Christology to the confines of secular protest and liberation, however important both of these might be. If he were to do this there would be little distance between his theology and those in the Enlightenment who wished to portray Christ as a merely human teacher. In this way Christ-the-teacher was often conceived along similar lines to Socrates, namely, as the innocent individual condemned by a society that failed to understand him. Although there are differences in that, unlike the first view, the later portrayal tended to be little more than a defence of Enlightenment values, in both versions the result is that the Gospel message is confined to ethics and the Kingdom of God does not transcend the boundaries of this earth.

Such a humanistic Christology would fail to do justice to Christ's divinity and to the extent of his saving work. Besides which it goes against the whole tenor of Kierkegaard's affirmation of Christ's humanity and deity through his proclamation of 'the Absolute Paradox' as discussed in the previous chapter. In *Practice*, any purely human Christology is considered to be an 'aberration', or 'a fallacy with respect to the God-man' of which Ebionitism is cited as the prime example.[54] For that reason, the offense against Christ in this category is not what Anti-Climacus terms 'essential' offense, for it 'does not relate specifically to Christ as Christ, as the God-man'.[55] To discover what this entails we must move on to discuss the next category of offense.

Essential Offense against Loftiness

The second form of offense is in essence the opposite of the first. Where previously Christ was envisaged as a purely human figure, an offense to 'respectable' society due to his priorities, in the second category the case is regarding 'the possibility of essential offense in relation to loftiness, that an individual human being speaks or acts as if he were God, declares himself to be God, therefore in relation to the qualification "God" in the composition God-man'.[56] Anti-Climacus

[54] *Practice in Christianity*, p. 123.
[55] Ibid., p. 83.
[56] Ibid., p. 94.

further explains that on this occasion 'the contradiction in which the possibility of offense lies is to be an individual human being, a lowly human being - and then to act in the character of being God'.[57] Passages used to illustrate this category of offense at Christ are Matthew 11:3-6 and John 6:51-61. Both of these episodes relate how people are faced with the situation where Jesus challenges them to accept who he really is, something which seems to be wholly incompatible with his human nature. In the passage from Matthew's Gospel, John the Baptist sends a messenger to ask Jesus if he is the Messiah. Jesus' reply is to point to his actions and then state 'and blessed is he who is not offended at me',[58] thereby leaving John to decide the answer for himself. This surely begs the question that, if not even John the Baptist was immediately able to recognise Jesus for who he is, then what about the rest of his contemporaries? Through this passage, and Anti-Climacus' discussion of it, it becomes clear that he was by no means directly recognizable as the Son of God. 'Pay attention to the situation of contemporaneity', Anti-Climacus warns the reader, 'if you do not pay attention to that, then you deceive yourself into a delusion. The point is that in Christendom one has only a fantasy picture of Christ, a fantasy God-figure, directly related to performing miracles. But this is an untruth: Christ never looked like that.'[59]

Over the centuries it has become easy for Christian apologists to stress the significance of the miraculous events in Christ's life and so use them as seemingly conclusive evidence for his divinity. In this way it appears pure madness for those around him not to recognise him. But through the Gospel passages it is brought home to us that this was not necessarily the case. It is important to remember that there existed a constant contradiction between Christ's outward appearance and the fact that he performed miracles. Many people would have had little trouble in revering him as a great teacher, even as one chosen by God, but the idea of him actually being divine was another matter entirely - in Anti-Climacus' terms, one that was liable to cause offense.

If this level of offense is omitted it becomes possible to believe that Christ's divinity was directly visible, something Anti-Climacus is at great pains to deny wholeheartedly.[60] Yet it remains quite a common practice to treat the miracles in particular as providing direct and conclusive demonstrations of this fact:

> In Christendom ... every demonstration and every folio end with: ergo, Christ was the one he claimed to be. By means of the demonstrations it is

[57] Ibid., p. 97.
[58] Ibid., p. 94.
[59] Ibid., p. 97.
[60] Ibid.

> just as certain as 2 + 2 = 4 and as easy as putting one's foot into a sock. With this irrefutable 'ergo', which *directly* clarifies the matter, the assistant professor and preacher bid defiance, and the missionary confidently goes forth to convert the heathen with this 'ergo'.[61]

This leads to a rationalist form of apologetics that is unfaithful to the Biblical witness. There will be a discussion of Kierkegaard's approach to Christian apologetics alongside consideration of his treatment of the traditional proofs of God's existence in the next chapter. However, at this point it is pertinent to consider the Christological implications of Anti-Climacus' discussion. In this context, the claim that Christ's divinity was directly visible may be seen to lend itself to a form of docetism. This would claim that Christ's humanity is but an appearance, and hence, 'Jesus the man is the transparent cloak for God.'[62] Although docetism formed one of the most ancient of Christological heresies in the early Christian period, arising out of Gnosticism, similar ideas have persisted into the modern age. John Macquarrie cites Kant's humanistic Christology as an example as his Jesus is merely the temporal personification of the eternal moral archetype ('the personified idea of the good principle'), an archetype that is recognizable to all rational beings through its conformity with an eternal ideal that is already present in their minds.[63]

The second passage used to illustrate 'the possibility of essential offense at loftiness'[64] is the 'Bread of Life' discourse in John 6:51-62, where many followers found Christ's teaching about himself hard to bear. But, nearly two thousand years later, the original difficulty of this passage can easily be overlooked. 'These words have now been placed in the context of Holy Communion; a doctrine of the ubiquity of Christ's body has been advanced, and because one has in Christendom a fantastic Christ-figure, all this is not incomprehensible and in no way does it contain the possibility of offense.'[65] On the reference to the ubiquity of Christ's body it would seem very likely that Kierkegaard is implying the Lutheran doctrine of the *genus majestaticum* which occurs within the framework of the *communicatio idiomatum* (communication of attributes). Through this it is claimed that whatever is said of Christ's

---

[61] Ibid., p. 95-6.
[62] Dietrich Bonhoeffer, *Christology* (London: Fontana, 1980), p. 76.
[63] Macquarrie, *Jesus Christ in Modern Thought*, p. 185; cf. Immanuel Kant, *Religion Within the Limits of Reason Alone* (New York: Harper & Row, 1960), pp. 54, 57. According to Kant, because of the moral archetype already present to human reason, any historical manifestation serves little real value. In fact, by demanding such a historical figure we only confess our unbelief. Instead, he believes that we each ought to serve as our own moral archetypes.
[64] *Practice in Christianity*, p. 94.
[65] Ibid., p. 99.

deity may be said of his humanity and vice versa.[66] Care must be taken in interpreting this passage. There is no evidence to suggest that Kierkegaard was attempting to refute this doctrine, particularly as it is one that stands at the heart of classical Lutheran Christology. Instead, just as with the previous passage, his main concern is to use Anti-Climacus to draw attention to the situation of contemporaneity. As the pseudonym explains to his readers:

> It is in the situation of contemporaneity with an individual human being, a human being like others - and he speaks about himself in such a manner! He defines himself as superhuman, spiritual in such a way that he speaks of eating his flesh and drinking his blood as fantastically as possible in the direction of a divine quality, omnipresence, and yet the next time as paradoxically as possible, that it is his flesh and blood. He says that he will rise on the last day only the person who eats his body and drinks his blood - certainly defining himself as God in the most decisive terms. He says he is the bread that comes down from heaven another striking expression in the direction of the divine. And since he knew that his followers grumbled about this and found it a hard saying, he says, 'Does this offend you?'[67]

So, the point being made is the same as with the first passage. To his contemporaries Christ was just another man, unremarkable in appearance to the extent that few would have recognised him as the Son of God. If what has been termed the 'fantasy figure' of Christ is put forward then this is obscured and the possibility of offense removed. The danger with the highly developed Christologies of Christian tradition is that this can happen and thereby create such a distance between the modern believer and the details of the Biblical witness.

Essential Offense against Lowliness

This is the final and most important of Anti-Climacus' three categories of offense. He describes it as 'the possibility of essential offense in relation to lowliness, that the one who passes himself off as God proves to be the lowly, poor, suffering, and finally powerless human being'.[68] This is a radical change from the previous category of offense where it is the divinity of Christ that is being questioned. In the final category it is not the possibility of the Incarnation that gives rise to offense, but instead it is the specific nature of Christ's humanity: 'Here a person brought to a halt by the possibility of offense says: Assuming for a

---

[66] Cf. Bonhoeffer, *Christology*, pp. 91ff.
[67] *Practice in Christianity*, p. 100.
[68] Ibid., p. 102.

moment that you are God, what foolishness and madness that you are this lowly, poor, powerless man!'[69]

To appreciate the significance of this category of offense it is appropriate to remind ourselves of the ideological background to Kierkegaard's theological reflection. It can hardly come as any surprise to hear that this category of offense, like so much of Kierkegaard's thought, implies a reaction against the influence of Hegelianism. To Hegelian Idealism the very fact that God had chosen to become incarnate in an individual human being at all ran counter to its presuppositions. Consider the following passage from *Practice*:

> In the first period of Christendom, when even aberrations bore an unmistakable mark of one's nevertheless knowing what the issue was, the fallacy with respect to the God-man was either that in one way or another the term 'God' was taken away (Ebionitism and the like) or the term 'man' was taken away (Gnosticism). In the entire modern age, which so unmistakably bears the mark that it does not even know what the issue is, the confusion is something different and far more dangerous. By way of didacticism, the God-man has been made into that speculative unity of God and man *sub specie aeterni* or made visible in that nowhere-to-be-found medium of pure being, rather than that the God-man is the unity of being God and an individual human being in a historically actual situation.[70]

As the first two possibilities of offense related to Ebionitism and Gnosticism, it is quite fitting that the final category now takes on this 'speculative unity of God and man'. Ever one to champion the particular over the general, Kierkegaard wholeheartedly rejects any abandonment of Christ's individual human nature. Hegel's Christology understood Christ to be a manifestation of the divine-human unity that was an immanent possibility for the entire human race by virtue of its own historic evolution towards the Absolute.[71] So, in this case Christ is the illustration of what we all might become quite naturally, not the incarnate Son of God of classical Christology.

Such an understanding of the Incarnation can be seen as a contribution to the secularization of Christianity. This is on the grounds that, if it is true that humanity is naturally progressing towards God through the evolutionary development of history, then it follows that 'to be God becomes a direct superlative of what it is to be a human being'.[72] Because of this it becomes easy to believe that to be a good

---

[69] Ibid., p. 103.

[70] Ibid., p. 123.

[71] Reardon, *Religion in the Age of Romanticism*, p. 84. Nowhere was this concept to be developed more fully in Kierkegaard's lifetime than by David Strauss in *The Life of Jesus Critically Examined* (London: SCM, 1973), cf. e.g. pp. 779-80.

[72] *Practice in Christianity*, p. 104; *Journals and Papers*, 3102, X I 2 A 212 *n.d.*, 1854.

Christian entails nothing other than what it is to be a good citizen. If this is the case civic norms serve to dictate Christian behaviour instead of vice versa.[73] In this scenario we can only return to the previously rejected 'ethical' life-views of pseudonyms such as Judge William or Johannes de Silentio in *Either/Or* and *Fear and Trembling* respectively.

Because of the discrepancy between the Hegelian and the orthodox Chalcedonian understanding of the Incarnation, on one occasion Anti-Climacus goes so far as to describe the nature of the Incarnation as a 'self-contradiction'. In this context the term is employed in its literal sense. However, it does not refer to the linking of God and a human being *per se*, but to the lowly nature of the human being in question. It therefore concerns precisely 'this boundless self-contradiction: that God should be a mortal man like this'.[74] Kierkegaard develops the same theme in his *Journals*: 'He is this very paradox, the compounding of God and a socially insignificant man . . . Jesus Christ is the sign of offense and the object of faith. Only in eternity is he in his glory. Here upon earth he must never be presented in any other way than in his social insignificance - so that everyone can be offended or believe.'[75] One wonders how much Kierkegaard would have agreed with Dostoyevsky's similarly radical vision of Christ as presented in the character of Prince Myshkin in (and as) *The Idiot*.

> He does not separate himself, but clumsily causes offense everywhere. He does not go around with the great ones, but with children. He is laughed at and loved. He is the fool and the wise man. He bears everything and he forgives everything. He is revolutionary and yet he conforms. He does not want to - but he does - call attention to himself just by his existence. Who are you? Idiot or Christ?[76]

Although he might not agree with the concept of Christ 'clumsily' causing offense, Kierkegaard holds that Christ draws attention to himself by what he is, and in this way he demands a response from those who encounter him: whether to be offended, or to believe in him.[77]

In support of this argument Anti-Climacus refers to Paul's description of Christ in 1 Corinthians 1:23 as being 'an offense to the Jews, and foolishness to the Greeks'.[78] Kierkegaard illustrated the significance of this verse in his *Journals* a couple of years before publishing *Practice* when he argued that,

---

[73] *Practice in Christianity*, p. 111; *Judge For Yourself!* p. 166.
[74] *Practice in Christianity*, p. 102.
[75] *Journals and Papers*, 321, IX A 57 *n.d.*, 1848.
[76] Bonhoeffer, *Christology*, p. 35.
[77] *Practice in Christianity*, p. 126.
[78] Ibid., p. 135 cf. also *Judge For Yourself!* p. 201.

> Christianity must be foolishness to the Greeks, because God's revelation of himself in suffering was precisely the paradox; suffering is abnormality, weakness, and yet it is the negative form of the highest - the direct form is beauty, power, glory, etc., but for the highest to have its adequate form in the direct form shows thereby that the highest is not extraordinarily the highest.[79]

The Greek word 'moria', translated as 'foolishness' in 1 Corinthians, implies a note of madness. This is appropriate because the details of Christ's earthly life openly conflicted with the expectations of educated Greek society. As Martin Hengel explains,

> To believe that the one pre-existent Son of the one true God, the mediator at creation and the redeemer of the world, had appeared in very recent times in out-of-the-way Galilee as a member of the obscure people of the Jews, and even worse, had died the death of a common criminal on the cross, could only be regarded as a sign of madness.[80]

Kierkegaard was not alone in employing Paul's motif of Christ as foolishness. Probably the most famous use of this theme can be found in Erasmus' wonderfully satirical *Praise of Folly*, from which the following is taken:

> All mortals are fools, even the pious. Christ too, though he is the wisdom of the father, was made something of a fool himself in order to help the folly of mankind, when he assumed the nature of a man and was seen in man's form; just as he was made sin so that he could redeem sinners. Nor did he wish to redeem them in any other way save by the folly of the cross and through his simple, ignorant apostles, to whom he unfailingly preached folly.[81]

One of the most frequent problems with satirical works is that their readers often forget to recognise the satire. Erasmus had to compose the *Letter to Martin Dorp* in order to explain the real significance of *Praise of Folly* to a Catholic theologian of that name. Just as Kierkegaard employed his pseudonyms, so Erasmus' satirical mouthpiece is the female personification of *Folly* herself. Her words are not always to be taken literally and serve to call attention to the misunderstandings of the world, hence,

> There is surely no danger of anyone's imagining that the apostles and Christ were fools in the literal sense. Yet in them too there is some sort of weakness due to human affections which in comparison with the pure

[79] *Journals and Papers*, 3087, VII 2 B 235, pp. 66-67 *n.d.*, 1846-47.
[80] Martin Hengel, *The Cross of the Son of God* (London: SCM, 1986), pp. 98f.
[81] Erasmus, *Praise of Folly* (London: Penguin, 1985), pp. 198-9.

> eternal wisdom can be seen to be not wholly wise. This is the folly which triumphs over the whole world ... Thus, in showing a folly which is wise, I also showed an insanity which is sane and a madness which retains its senses.[82]

Both Erasmus and Kierkegaard use 'foolishness' with caution, mindful that the world's charges of foolishness soon rebound back to where they came.

Yet if Christ is to be foolishness to the Greeks, then there are to be reasons why he is an offense to the Jews. In the passage from 1 Corinthians the Greek word translated in Kierkegaard's works as 'offense' is 'scandalon', from which we get 'scandal', and is normally rendered 'stumbling block'.[83] The original use of 'scandalon' in classical Greek literature was in the sense of 'an enticement' to trap an opponent, but in the LXX and New Testament both senses are found.[84] In the context of 1 Corinthians 23 it is universally agreed that 'stumbling block' is appropriate, denoting 'something which stops a man's progress, something which trips him up, something which bars the way to him. That something may come from the malicious action of others, or it may come from the prejudice and the pride of a man's own heart'.[85] The latter certainly calls to mind Kierkegaard's 'possibility of offense at lowliness'.[86] First century Judaism found it very difficult to stomach the concept of a suffering Messiah, despite the words of Isaiah 53 concerning the suffering servant. Instead, it was generally expected that the true Messiah would come doing signs and wonders in order to prove his divine calling, something several individuals had already tried that century.[87] Another contributive factor to the 'offensiveness' of Christ to the Jews was the manner of his death, as according to Deuteronomy 21:23 'anyone who is hung on a tree is under God's

---

[82] Ibid., p. 233.

[83] Kierkegaard offers some illustration of the synonymity of 'offense' and 'scandal' in a journal entry written in 1849, a year before the publication of *Practice in Christianity*. (*Journals and Papers*, 3034, X2 A 117 *n.d.*, 1849).

[84] William Barclay, *New Testament Words* (London: SCM, 1964), pp. 255-6.

[85] Ibid., p. 257.

[86] It is important that both the intellectual and the moral factors are taken into consideration when interpreting Kierkegaard's use of Christ as 'offense' in this context. Otherwise, to perceive the nature of offense in Kierkegaard's Christology as applying solely to the intellectual acceptance of the historical figure of Jesus would be to confuse Kierkegaard with the speculative philosophy he wished to refute. Although Emil Brunner's general discussion of the 'stumbling block' in *The Mediator* (London: Lutterworth, 1963), p. 42, brings both factors to the fore, it is unfortunate that he makes the mistake of criticizing Kierkegaard's concept to be of intellectual significance alone.

[87] William Barclay, *The Daily Study Bible: Letters to the Corinthians* (Edinburgh: The Saint Andrew Press, 1965), p. 20.

curse'.[88] So, clearly the doctrine of a lowly, crucified Messiah ran counter to the expectations of the age.

Christ as Redeemer and Prototype

Although the categories of offense in *Practice* do present us with elements of Kierkegaard's own Christology, they do not contain a complete exposition of his ideas. Notoriously unsystematic as he was, Kierkegaard leaves the reader to piece together numerous details from several different works. Apart from the categories of offense in *Practice in Christianity*, Kierkegaard's Christology in his later works employs a terminology that is more in keeping with traditional Christological discourse. In these writings his Christology is dominated by the doctrine of Christ as Redeemer and prototype.

It is obvious from the start that Kierkegaard remains clearly within Christian orthodoxy by accentuating the completeness and uniqueness of Christ's saving work.[89] Likewise, in true Lutheran fashion he is careful to stress that the Atonement is an act of God, not a human reward for deeds done, and hence it is entirely a gift of grace. However much Kierkegaard sought to uphold the doctrine of Christ as the Redeemer, he also wished to give a special emphasis to the doctrine of Christ as the prototype, where, 'looking at his life, we shall see the unconditional requirement and see it fulfilled.'[90] Where some see only foolishness and offense, the dedicated believer sees his goal. In this way the radical disjunction between the values of Christ and those of the world are brought out, and 'according to Christian doctrine, there is only one loftiness, that of being a Christian; everything else is lowly, lowliness and loftiness'.[91] True loftiness is defined by existing wholly before God, that is to say that the believer's life is determined entirely by her God-relationship through Christ instead of by her relationship with others. She strives to be herself in truth before God. The reasoning behind this is simple enough to understand, even if it is difficult to put into practice. 'There is only one who completely knows himself, who in himself knows what he himself is - that is God,' explains Kierkegaard. 'And he also knows what each human being is in himself, because he is that only by being before God.'[92] But only the prototype was able to do this, and

[88] Cf. Galations 3:13.

[89] *Judge For Yourself!*, p. 147; *Gospel Of Sufferings*, p. 52; *Christian Discourses*, p. 298-9; cf. Rae, *Kierkegaard's Vision of the Incarnation*, pp. 237ff.

[90] *Judge For Yourself!*, p. 159. See also *Practice*: 'Christ's life here on earth is the paradigm; I and every Christian are to strive to model our lives in likeness to it'; and, 'every generation must begin from the beginning with Christ and then set forth his life as the paradigm.' (*Practice in Christianity*, p. 107.)

[91] *Christian Discourses*, p. 47.

[92] Ibid., p. 40.

so it follows that Christ is the only real criterion for a full human existence.[93]

However, the importance of Christ as prototype must not be stressed to the level that it obscures his role as Redeemer. In fact, Kierkegaard posits a fundamental link between these two functions, with each one being dependent upon the other. A passage from his *Journals* remarks on this:

> Galatians 2:19 (for I through the law died to the law) corresponds to the presentation I usually give of our relationship to 'the prototype'. 'The prototype' must be presented as the requirement, and then it crushes you. 'The prototype', which is Christ, then changes into something else, to grace and compassion, and it is he himself who reaches out to support you.[94]

The same point is also clearly shown in the prayer introducing the discussion of Christ as prototype in *Judge For Yourself!*:

> Help us all, each one of us, you who both will and can, you who are both the prototype and the Redeemer, and in turn both the Redeemer and the prototype, so that when the striving one droops under the prototype, crushed, almost despairing, the Redeemer raises him up again; but at the same moment you are again the prototype so that he may be kept in the striving.[95]

Kierkegaard's reasons for choosing to maintain this particular balance are explained in the following two passages from the *Journals*:

> Since the Middle Ages had gone farther and farther astray in accentuating the aspect of Christ as the prototype - Luther came along and accentuated the other side, that he is a gift and this gift is to be received in faith ... But now in our time it is clear that what must come to the fore is the aspect of Christ as prototype. The main point is to have learned from the Middle Ages to avoid the errors of this approach. But it is this side which must come to the fore, because the Lutheran emphasis on faith has now become a fig leaf for the most unchristian shirking.[96]

---

[93] *Judge For Yourself!*, p. 198. Kierkegaard's argument for this point also serves to counter the interpretation of 'the Absolute Paradox' as arising out of the metaphysical incompatibility between humanity and deity. In a journal entry of 1848 he states that: 'Because Christ simply expresses that he was a human being like everybody else, he is truly the prototype, but he also constitutes the eternal strenuousness in what it means to be a human being. He makes the divine commensurable with being a completely ordinary human being.' (*Journals and Papers*, 1848, IX A 101 *n.d.*, 1848.)

[94] Ibid., 349, X 2 A 170 *n.d.*, 1849.

[95] *Judge For Yourself!* 147; cf. also *Journals and Papers*, 1863, X 6 B 241 *n.d.*, 1849-51.

[96] Ibid., 2481, X 1 A 154 *n.d.*, 1849.

> Luther is entirely right in what he says in the preface to his sermons about the distinction between Christ as pattern and as gift. I am quite conscious of the fact that I have moved in the direction of Christ as pattern. But something must be kept in mind in this regard. Luther was confronted by the exaggerated misuse of Christ as pattern; therefore he accentuates the opposite. But Luther has long since been victorious in Protestantism and Christ has been completely forgotten as the pattern, and the whole thing actually has become pretence in hidden inwardness.[97]

Therefore it can be seen that, as may be expected, Kierkegaard was attempting to correct perceived errors within his own tradition. He is not attempting to level criticism at Luther's abandonment of the doctrine of the *imitatio Christi* as some have argued.[98] Instead, with the classical Lutheran emphasis upon salvation by faith alone taken to extremes in more recent developments in Danish Lutheranism, Kierkegaard now felt himself compelled to propose his exemplarist Christology as a corrective.[99] Yet it is with the difference that now 'Christ as the pattern ought to jack up the price so enormously that the prototype itself teaches men to resort to grace', and thus avoid the danger of suggesting salvation by works.[100]

3. Kierkegaard and Kenotic Christologies

I have just shown that through both *Fragments* and his later works, Kierkegaard lays exceptional stress upon the lowliness of Christ's humanity. Whether in Climacus' poetic parable of the god and the maiden, or in the directness of Kierkegaard's discourses, it is affirmed that Christ has become 'absolutely the equal of the lowliest of human beings'.[101] Due to this and his emphasis upon the actuality of Christ's sufferings, it has been claimed by a variety of scholars that Kierkegaard is putting forward a kenotic Christology.[102] Such a view proposes that the Son of God was compelled to empty himself of certain divine properties in order to become incarnate. However, supporters of kenotic Christology differ according to both the extent and the necessity of this divine self-emptying.

---

[97] Ibid., 2503, X2 A 30 *n.d.*, 1849.

[98] Gouwens, *Kierkegaard as Religious Thinker*, p. 128.

[99] *Journals and Papers*, 1877, X3 A 409 *n.d.*, 1850.

[100] Ibid., 2503, X2 A 30 *n.d.*, 1949. The following passages from the *Journals* expand upon this: 692, IX A 153 *n.d.*, 1848 and 693, X 1 A 132 *n.d.*, 1849.

[101] *Fragments*, p. 33.

[102] For some of the most interesting theological discussions in which this view is put forward see: Gouwens, *Kierkegaard as Religious Thinker*, p. 169, n59; Law, *Kierkegaard as Negative Theologian*, pp. 183-8; Macquarrie, *Jesus Christ in Modern Thought*, p. 242.

It is therefore appropriate to begin by determining what is generally contained within the doctrine of kenosis as found in kenotic Christology. This will primarily involve some examination and evaluation of kenotic theories as developed within Lutheranism, although it will also be necessary to compare these briefly with a few relevant developments outside of that tradition. After this I will then move on to discuss whether, in view of this, Kierkegaard's Christology may genuinely be classed as a kenotic Christology, or whether some alternative classification is required.

Kenosis

As I have already stated above, kenotic Christology holds that the Son of God was forced to empty himself of certain powers and attributes in order to become incarnate as Jesus Christ. The actual term 'kenotic' is derived from the Greek verb meaning 'to empty' and refers to the kenosis, or self-emptying, of the Son of God. The New Testament passage most often cited in support of kenoticism is in the second chapter of Philippians where Paul states that, 'Christ Jesus, who, though he was in the form of God, did not regard equality with God as something to be exploited, but emptied ('ekenosen') himself, taking the form of a slave, being born in human likeness.'[103] Another passage, sometimes used as additional support, is 2 Corinthians 8:9: 'For you know the generous act of our Lord Jesus Christ, that though he was rich, yet for your sakes he became poor, so that by his poverty you might become rich.'[104]

The classical exponent of kenotic Christology was the nineteenth century German Lutheran theologian Gottfried Thomasius. He held that humanity was naturally capable of receiving and being penetrated by God. In addition to this, Thomasius also held that during the Incarnation the whole of the Son of God was present in Christ and so nothing of the divine Logos existed outside him during this event. This latter point is in complete accord with traditional Lutheran Christology, although it is in opposition to the Reformed teaching that the Logos also existed outside of Christ during the period of the Incarnation (dubbed the *illud extra Calvinisticum* by the Lutherans).[105] Thomasius' problem was to discern how the Son of God could be so compressed (as it were) whilst still permitting full divine self-revelation in and through the Incarnation.

In his *Christ's Person and Work* Thomasius attempts to find an answer to this when he states that it is the nature of God's love 'to

[103] Philippians 2: 5-7, NRSV.
[104] NRSV.
[105] Macquarrie, *Jesus Christ in Modern Thought*, p. 246.

accept every limitation ... What seems to be the alienation or finitization of deity is the deepest internalization of deity itself, the concentration of its energies on one point which, in its significance far outweighs the most inclusive manifestation of omnipotence'.[106] In order to relate to the world on terms that it could comprehend the Son of God abandons attributes such as omnipotence, omniscience and omnipresence. Such attributes are considered by Thomasius to be but 'relative attributes', as opposed to the Son of God's 'essential attributes'. The latter, also called the 'immanent attributes', define the essence of God and include absolute power, truth and love. In view of this, Thomasius argues that Christ 'exercised no other lordship at all than the ethical one of truth and love'.[107]

The question arises whether the Son of God actually remains truly divine when incarnate if the kenosis is as Thomasius describes. Clearly, if his ideas are to be taken as true then we are faced with a very humanistic conception of the Incarnation at the expense of Christ's deity. In this case, such a kenotic Christology is not in accord with the principles of the Chalcedonian Definition and therefore cannot be accepted as it stands. Thomasius appears to be guilty of confusing the humility of the Logos ensarkos with the renunciation of the Logos asarkos.[108] This confusion was carried further by another nineteenth century Lutheran, W.F. Gess. According to Gess, Christ possessed only a human consciousness and so the Logos literally ceases to be divine at all during the Incarnation. Somewhat unsurprisingly, this form of kenoticism has been labelled 'incarnation by divine suicide'.[109]

Kenoticism has appeared in other theologies apart from that of the Lutheranism of Thomasius and Gess. British theology has witnessed several developments in this area. These have mostly occurred within Anglicanism, and begin with the work of Charles Gore in the nineteenth century. However, these have not always been as drastic as Thomasius' contribution and they vary considerably as to the nature and extent of Christ's abandoning his divine attributes. Gore, for instance, held that the abandonment only applied to the Logos within his human activity. This seems to place Gore within Chalcedonian orthodoxy, thereby

---

106 Ibid., p. 247.
107 Ibid.
108 Cf. Bonhoeffer, *Christology*, p. 96.
109 Louis Berkhof, *Systematic Theology* (Edinburgh: Banner of Truth Trust, 1994), p. 327. It is also the case that kenotic Christology can be criticised from the opposite perspective. That is to say, that if the renunciation of certain divine properties by the Logos during the Incarnation is on the grounds that these divine and human properties are incompatible; then it could be suggested that at the end of Christ's earthly life, he likewise sets aside his humanity. In this way the Incarnation becomes a temporary event as Christ is first God, then man, then God again successively, but not as 'the God-man' in hypostatic union. (Cf. D.M. Baillie, *God Was in Christ*, p. 97.)

raising the question whether his Christology really is kenotic,[110] or whether kenoticism need be redefined. Due to the variety of allegedly kenotic theories, the latter option would appear to be necessary. Although Brian Hebblethwaite describes any Christology that takes Christ's humanity 'absolutely seriously' as kenotic, this is too broad an employment of the term. Instead Richard Sturch offers the following definition:

> It might be best to restrict the use of the word to theories which assert that the Son no longer possesses, or no longer uses, some of his divine attributes during the Incarnation - neither on earth nor in heaven. If, however, it is preferred to use it also for views which see the knowledge and power of Jesus as limited, but not those of God the Son, even during the earthly life of Jesus, well, that too is acceptable.[111]

If this wide definition is to be accepted then it is possible to trace elements of kenoticism within many Christologies from the Patristic period. Sturch cites both Gregory of Nyssa and Athanasius on the grounds that their Christologies allowed for Christ's ignorance when on earth. Later theologians rejected this because of the belief that ignorance is a product of the fall and not temporality.[112] Within the Western Patristic tradition it is possible to consider Hilary of Poitiers as a proponent of this form of Christology as he likened the incarnate state of the Son of God to a kenosis. Hilary manages to avoid the problem of verging on to a purely humanistic Christology. As Grillmeier explains, 'this kenosis or *evacuatio*, which consists in the renunciation of the forma *Dei* and the acceptance of the *forma servi*, presupposes in Hilary's writing that in fact the subject remains in his divine nature.'[113] However, Hilary also states that Christ chooses not to show himself completely and retains his divine attributes, therefore miracles come quite naturally to him and he was unable to suffer.[114] On these grounds it appears that his Christology, quite unlike that of kenoticists such as Thomasius, is veering close to docetism. On the subject of Christ possessing all the divine attributes, yet choosing not to employ them, we move from kenoticism to crypticism, a theory which alleges that Christ merely concealed his powers (from 'krypsis chreseos'

[110] Richard Swinburne uses an argument along these lines to deny that Gore's Christology is actually kenotic in the traditionally accepted use of the term. (Richard Swinburne, *The Christian God* (Oxford: Clarendon Press, 1994), p. 230n.)

[111] Richard Sturch, *The Word and the Christ: An Essay in Analytic Christology* (Oxford: Clarendon Press, 1991), pp. 255-6.

[112] Ibid., p. 256.

[113] Grillmeier, *Christ in Christian Tradition*, p. 308.

[114] Ibid., p. 309.

'hidden power'[115]). Crypticism argued that Christ merely pretended to suffer, something also put forward by the docetists. So, like Thomasius' kenoticism, this too moves away from Chalcedon.

The Abasement of Christ in Kierkegaard's Theology

The first difficulty with ascribing a kenotic Christology to Kierkegaard is that the term does not occur in any of his writings, whether direct or pseudonymous. Neither does he mention any of the known German exponents of the theory, even though both Thomasius and Gess were near contemporaries. Kierkegaard kept a watchful eye on theological developments in Germany. He would surely have cited such theologians if he was in accord with their views, especially as Thomasius purposefully developed his ideas in opposition to Hegelianism. It is of course possible that he would have come across other exponents of kenoticism, yet the direct evidence is still lacking from his writings. Considering all this, it is interesting to note that Kierkegaard owned and studied one work by a kenoticist: Martensen's *Christian Dogmatics*. Martensen's discussion of the kenotic theory is brief but clear, being similar to Gore in that Martensen talks more of the limitations of the human Christ rather than of the Logos.[116] Although Kierkegaard often attacks Martensen on several issues, he fails to raise the subject of kenosis. From all of the above evidence it would seem that, unless he was totally unaware of it (which seems somewhat unlikely), Kierkegaard either largely ignored traditional kenoticism, or he developed a similar theory independently without the traditional terminology. It is now appropriate to consider what evidence may be cited from his works to support one or other of these theories.

From the fact that I have chosen to discuss the question of Kierkegaard's kenoticism under the title of Christ's abasement, rather than kenosis, may be taken to suggest from the outset that I do not consider Kierkegaard's Christology to be truly kenotic. This is on the grounds that Kierkegaard limits his discussion to the abasement of Christ on earth, rather than considering a metaphysical abandonment by the eternal Logos. Various passages from his works illustrate this clearly, for instance:

> He lived in actual earthly lowliness ... he did not choose to be an eminent person and yet a lowly one in his innermost being. No, he literally was the lowly person, and in an entirely different way than when a king

---

[115] Bonhoeffer, *Christology*, p. 94.

[116] Hans Martensen, *Christian Dogmatics: A Compendium of the Doctrines of Christianity* (Edinburgh: T&T Clark, 1878), pp. 265f, 269. See also Berkhof where the Martensen-Gore link is made. (Berkhof, *Systematic Theology*, p. 328.)

> momentarily sets aside his rank and is known by the courtiers, consequently all the more honored - for his humility.[117]

Taken from *Christian Discourses*, this passage is set within Kierkegaard's doctrine of Christ as the prototype. In this context the emphasis is upon asserting two things: first, that contrary to docetism, Christ was genuinely human and hence can be the true prototype for the believer. This is reminiscent of the difference between the king who, in the parable of the king and the maiden in *Fragments*, merely puts on a 'plebeian cloak', and the reality of the god's form of a servant, adopted in order to teach the learner.[118] The second point is that, as the prototype, Christ shows genuine faith and humility within the lowliness of his social condition.

Christ's lowly status in society is constantly stressed by Kierkegaard as a means to underline the radical nature of his commitment to the Father. The most interesting discussion of this theme comes in the section 'Christ as the prototype, or no one can serve two masters' in *Judge For Yourself!* He states that Christ 'allows himself to be born in poverty and lowliness, and not only that, but in disrepute, to a betrothed virgin ... That is how he came into the world, as if he were outside the world, ostracized by the world immediately on arrival.'[119] The significance of these humble origins is that, through them 'from the very beginning his life was designed to make it possible to serve only one master', for, as Kierkegaard continues, 'birth is a tie that immediately binds a human being in closer alliance with other human beings; an alliance with the world and what is of the world, and thus an alliance with other human beings, is what makes it so difficult to serve only one master.'[120]

However, Kenotic elements do seem to spring to the fore on the question of Christ's suffering and the extent of what Kierkegaard calls the divine 'incognito'. In *Practice in Christianity* Anti-Climacus explains the difficulty of the situation:

> He is God but chooses to become this individual human being ... But it is his will, his free decision, and therefore it is an omnipotently maintained incognito. Indeed, by allowing himself to be born he has in a certain sense bound himself once and for all; his unrecognizability is so omnipotently maintained that in a way he himself is in the power of his own incognito, in which lies the literal actuality of his purely human suffering, that this is not merely appearance but in a certain sense is the assumed incognito's upper hand over him ... It is a strange kind of dialectic: that he,

---

[117] *Christian Discourses*, p. 54.
[118] *Fragments*, p. 31f.
[119] *Judge For Yourself!*, p. 160.
[120] Ibid., pp. 160-1.

> omnipotent, binds himself and does so omnipotently that he actually feels bound, suffers under the consequence of his loving and free decision to become an individual human being.[121]

Here the limitations of Christ are described, whilst at the same time the omnipotence of God the Son is preserved. There is therefore no abandonment of divine attributes as is found in Thomasius' Christology. What Kierkegaard is claiming is that the reality of Christ's humanity depends upon the exercising of his divine omnipotence.[122] Only in this way could Christ genuinely share in the grim reality of human suffering and weakness, and be for us the prototype. Kierkegaard clarifies this in the *Gospel of Sufferings*, a small, direct work he published the year before *Practice*:

> He who was and is the Truth, he who knew all, yet learned one thing, and nothing else, learned obedience by the things which he suffered. Were it possible that a man should learn obedience to God apart from sufferings, then Christ, as man, had not needed to learn it from sufferings. It was human obedience that he learned from sufferings, for the eternal accord of his will with that of the Father is certainly not obedience. Obedience belongs to his humiliation, as it is written; 'he humbled himself and became obedient' [Phil. 2:8]. But this, this obedience of his is just what it means to be a man, and so it is true of a man in relation to God that obedience is learned from sufferings; and if it is true of the pure how much more of a sinful man![123]

Both these passages would place Kierkegaard's Christology within the bounds of Sturch's somewhat broad definition of kenoticism,[124] but clearly not with that of Thomasius. David Gouwens interprets Kierkegaard as being within the kenotic tradition of the school of Geissen in that, although Christ retains his divine powers but chooses not to use them.[125] This would seem to be in accord with the material cited, but is it really kenoticism in the traditional sense of the term? I do not consider this to be genuinely kenotic, although it does fit in with Sturch's definition of kenoticism. However, Sturch freely admits that such a definition involves more of a taking up of a limited human nature by the Logos rather than it does a self-emptying. In the light of this he concludes that such a Christology could only really be called kenotic in

[121] *Practice in Christianity*, pp. 132-3.
[122] Cf. also *Judge ForYourself!*, p. 174.
[123] *Gospel of Sufferings*, pp. 63-4.
[124] Cf. Sturch, *The Word and the Christ*, pp. 255f.
[125] Gouwens, *Kierkegaard as Religious Thinker*, p. 169n.

order to avoid adding further to the wealth of titles and terms that can already be found in the theological vocabulary.[126]

4. A Theology of the Cross

In this final section I wish to argue that Kierkegaard's Christology may be more appropriately interpreted along the lines of another development in Lutheran theology: the theology of the cross. The theology of the cross played a pivotal role in the development of Martin Luther's theological position, affecting all aspects of his thought.[127] I will argue that Kierkegaard's whole theological approach is dominated by the same concerns that are found in this form of theology. The first section outlines the details of Luther's theology of the cross, in particular the doctrine of the hidden and revealed God (*Deus absconditus* and *Deus revelatus*). After this I will examine the importance of Kierkegaard's concept of Christ as 'the sign of contradiction'[128] and his statement that 'Christ cannot give a direct communication'.[129] Within this final section certain questions will be raised regarding the nature of such theological topics as the knowledge of God and the nature of faith, the answers to which will be the focus of the next two chapters in this thesis.

Luther's Theology of the Cross

'Christian faith stands and falls with the knowledge of the crucified Christ, that is, with the knowledge of God *in* the crucified Christ, or, to use Luther's even bolder phrase, with the knowledge of the "crucified God".'[130] So states Moltmann in his work *The Crucified God*. His statement may be used to introduce the central theme of Luther's *theologia crucis*. Luther developed his *theologia crucis* (theology of the cross) in clear opposition to what he referred to as the *theologia gloriae*

---

[126] Sturch, *The Word and the Christ*, p. 260. Sturch is not alone in adapting elements of kenoticism to allow for a Christology that falls safely within the boundaries of Chalcedonian orthodoxy. In *Christ and Creation* (Carlisle and Grand Rapids, Mich.: Paternoster and Eerdmans, 1992), Colin Gunton suggests that it is possible to employ the *concept* rather than theory of kenosis 'if the self-emptying is seen as the *expression* of the divine being rather than its *depotentiation*'. This avoids the faults of traditional kenoticism and so preserves the humanity and the deity of Christ. As Gunton explains, in this way kenosis of the Son of God is a plerosis. (Gunton, *Christ and Creation*, p. 84.)

[127] W. von Löwenich, *Luther's Theology of the Cross* (Belfast: Christian Journals, 1976), p. 18.

[128] Cf. *Practice in Christianity*, p. 125f.

[129] Ibid., p. 136.

[130] Jürgen Moltmann, *The Crucified God* (London: SCM, 1974), p. 65.

(theology of glory) of medieval scholasticism. This is well illustrated in the early stages of his theological development in the following theses from his *Heidelberg Disputation* (1518):

> 19. That person does not deserve to be called a theologian who looks upon the invisible things of God as though they were clearly perceptible in those things which have actually happened. 20. He deserves to be called a theologian, however, who comprehends the visible and manifest things of God seen through suffering and the cross. 21. A theology of glory calls evil good and good evil. A theology of the cross calls the thing what it actually is.[131]

For Luther Christian theology cannot do anything but begin with God's self-revelation in and through Christ. On this point he makes a radical break with the theological method of the Middle Ages, rejecting any attempts to furnish Christian theology with a philosophical metaphysic drawn from Platonic or Aristotelian thought. Christian theology is a theology of revelation, 'God has spoken, and therefore we are able to speak about God. God has shown himself, and therefore we know where we must look.'[132]

The word of God is the word of the cross. Not only does the believer see God revealed in the cross of Christ, she also comes to know God through taking up her own 'cross' of following the crucified Christ. Yet this revelation is not direct, as the figure of the suffering, dying Christ seems to proclaim anything but the love and mercy preached during his life. God reveals himself indirectly, being hidden in a revelation that conflicts with our natural expectations:

> God works in a paradoxical way *sub contrariis*: his strength lies hidden under apparent weakness [and] the future glory of the Christian under his present sufferings. It will therefore be clear that there is a radical discontinuity between the empirically perceived situation and the situation as perceived by faith. To the eye of reason all that can be seen in the cross is a man dying in apparent weakness and folly under the wrath of God.[133]

This revelation is addressed to faith, in which the believer has to admit with Isaiah 45:15 that: 'Truly you are a God who hides himself'.[134] McGrath observes that there are two different senses of Luther's phrase 'the hidden God', or *Deus absconditus*. There is the sense of the God hidden behind his revelation, the essence of God and those of his actions

---

[131] Martin Luther, *Heidelberg Disputation*, in *Career of the Reformer: Luther's Works*, vol. 31 (Philadelphia: Muhlenberg Press, 1957), p. 40.
[132] von Löwenich, *Luther's Theology of the Cross*, p. 19.
[133] Alister McGrath, *Luther's Theology of the Cross* (Oxford: Basil Blackwell, 1985), p. 167.
[134] NRSV.

which defy human comprehension. Second is the God who is hidden in his revelation, to which this discussion refers, where God reveals himself *sub contrariis.*[135] At the cross we are faced with the vital choice whether to take notice of its demands or to move away. Through the cross human pride in its own works is removed and the way to accepting God's revelation of himself opened.[136]

The Sign of Contradiction

Echoes of Luther's theology of the cross become apparent in *Practice in Christianity* where Anti-Climacus introduces the 'sign of contradiction'. 'To be a sign of contradiction is to be something else that stands in contrast to what one immediately is. So it is with the God-man. Immediately, he is an individual human being, just like others, a lowly, unimpressive human being, but now comes the contradiction - that he is God.'[137] The concept of the sign of contradiction arises out of the possibility of offense at lowliness. On this point Kierkegaard is unavowedly following in Luther's footsteps, for both theologians it is the harsh reality of the suffering figure of Christ which ultimately forces humanity to choose between faith or offense.

> And only the sign of contradiction can do this: it draws attention to itself and then presents a contradiction. There is a something that makes it impossible not to look - and look, as one is looking one sees as in a mirror, one comes to see oneself, or he who is the sign of contradiction looks straight into one's heart while one is staring into the contradiction ... It is a riddle, but as he is guessing the riddle, what dwells within him is disclosed by the way he guesses.[138]

Kierkegaard also follows Luther in his belief that God's revelation in Christ is indirect, and so 'the glory is not directly known as glory but, just the reverse, is known by inferiority, debasement'.[139] In fact, it is the very nature of the Incarnation that prohibits direct revelation, even if Christ were to declare his identity quite openly:

> If someone says directly: I am God; the Father and I are one, this is direct communication. But if the person who says it, the communicator, is this individual human being, an individual human being just like others, then this communication is not quite entirely direct, because it is not entirely direct that a human being should be God - whereas what he says is entirely

---

[135] McGrath, *Luther's Theology of the Cross*, p. 165.
[136] von Löwenich, *Luther's Theology of the Cross*, pp. 27; 30.
[137] *Practice in Christianity*, p. 125-126.
[138] Ibid., p. 127.
[139] *Judge For Yourself!*, p. 161.

> direct. Because of the communicator the communication contains a contradiction, it becomes indirect communication; it confronts you with a choice: whether you will believe him or not.[140]

The nature of God is such that it is impossible to recognise him directly.[141] Therefore, added to the lowliness of Christ, it would seem that the Incarnation is in itself the most unlikely of events. Turning to his *Journals* we hear Kierkegaard remark that, 'the least possible of all places or phenomena - one solitary, destitute, abandoned human being - this is the place for God; to such an extent does God relate negatively to appearance ... [that] he has to have as little appearance as possible.'[142] For Kierkegaard the Incarnation 'is a heartbreaking inversion of all human categories' through which God is revealed *sub contrariis.*[143]

These themes of contradiction and indirect communication are not confined to Kierkegaard's Christology alone. Just as the *theologia crucis* was largely to dominate Luther's own theological method, so these two themes reoccur throughout Kierkegaard's thought, making his theology a theology of the cross that is radical in its programme whilst remaining surprisingly faithful to his Reformation heritage. The following two chapters explain this further. In Chapter five I examine certain aspects of Kierkegaard's doctrine of God and illustrate his criticism of natural theology's claim to gain knowledge of God entirely independent from his revelation in Christ. In Chapter six, the final chapter, I discuss Kierkegaard's thoughts on the rationality of Christian faith.

---

[140] *Practice in Christianity*, p. 134.
[141] *Journals and Papers*, 3099, XI 2 A 51 *n.d.*; 1854.
[142] Ibid., 3100, XI 2 A 212 *n.d.*
[143] Ibid., 333, X 1 A 245 *n.d.*, 1849. Cf. also. 3102. XI 2 A 212 *n.d.*, 1854.

Chapter Five

The Doctrine of God and Natural Theology

Kierkegaard's theology is essentially a theology of the cross. Part of my present task is to determine to what extent this theology serves to prescribe his doctrine of God. There has been a strongly Christocentric emphasis dominating the discussion of Kierkegaard's religious thought so far, yet the subject of his Christian theism in general has yet to be dealt with. I therefore offer some treatment of the doctrine of God as contained within his writings, illustrating the significance of this doctrine for his times, and, to show how this led him to conflict with certain views of natural theology. It will also be pertinent to challenge what I consider to be some current misinterpretations of Kierkegaard's thought on this subject.

The first section of this chapter will focus on the concept of God in Kierkegaard's writings. This will begin by refuting the charge that his theism is more reminiscent of the deity of classical antiquity than it is faithful to the God of Christianity. I will then tackle the claim that Kierkegaard holds to an anti-realist doctrine of God. Following this will be an examination of his treatment of the themes of divine transcendence and divine immanence, showing how Kierkegaard came into conflict with the then popular tendencies towards pantheism found within Idealist philosophy. This section on the concept of God will conclude with a brief treatment of the subject of divine omnipotence in Kierkegaard's thought.

Moving on from the concept of God *per se*, the next section examines how Kierkegaard approaches the problem of the knowledge of God. This will begin with some discussion of the relevance of proofs and demonstrations for the Christian faith in general. I then examine Kierkegaard's treatment of two of the traditional arguments for God's existence: the ontological argument and the argument from design. Finally I will discuss the claim that Kierkegaard's thoughts in this area may be classed as negative (or apophatic) theology. Against this it will be argued that, just as with his Christology, Kierkegaard's thoughts on natural theology can instead be seen to illustrate his Lutheran heritage.

1. The Concept of God

Christian God or pagan deity?

It has been debated whether Kierkegaard's concept of God does in fact stem from Christianity. According to one writer this criticism maintains that, 'Because of his use of static metaphysical categories in describing God, the God of Kierkegaard's philosophical reflections was more like Aristotle's Unmoved Mover than like the God of the Bible.'[1] This criticism presupposes that there is a dichotomy between Christian, Biblical theism and that of classical Greek philosophy. If this is the case, and Kierkegaard does hold to a Greek, be it an Aristotelian, or even Platonic, doctrine of God over that of Christianity, how could this be recognized? A few elements will serve to illustrate what is contained in the first category. In *Existence and Analogy*, Eric Mascall outlines three leading theological conceptions in Greek thought. First, Greek theism generally held that the ultimate divine reality is understood to be identical with nature, and hence the distinction between world and deity was at best partial. Each and every natural occurrence was seen as a manifestation of divinity. Within this first point, it is also possible to discern the two orders of gods, both the heavenly bodies and the gods of classical mythology.[2] Second, the higher deity is impersonal and distant, and so,

> Aristotle's God, though admittedly transcendent, has no power over the world except that of originating motion, and even of motion he is only the final, and in no way the efficient, cause. Neither form nor matter in natural objects depends on him ... The only activity of which God is capable is the theoretical activity which terminates not upon the world but upon himself.[3]

Third, in the *Timaeus* Plato talks of the Demiurge, or Divine Craftsman, but this is no omnipotent Creator, 'His work is confined to bringing form and matter into union, but neither element owes its being to him.'[4] It may be seen then that traditional Christian theism differs from such beliefs in its rejection of pantheism, its clear affirmations of God's omnipotence and creation of the universe out of nothing, and

---

[1] M. Diamond, 'Kierkegaard and Apologetics', *Journal of Religion* 44 (1964), p. 123.
[2] Cf. Plato, *Timaeus* (London: Penguin, 1965), pp. 54-57.
[3] Eric Mascall, *Existence and Analogy* (London: Longmans, 1949), p. 5.
[4] Ibid., p. 6.

proclamation of God as Trinity. As I move on to explain Kierkegaard's beliefs it will become apparent that his certainly fall within the Christian category.

The concept of God found within the pages of *Philosophical Fragments* provides most of the ammunition used by Kierkegaard's critics. Instead of referring to 'God', the pseudonymous author Johannes Climacus prefers to talk of 'the god' (Danish *Guden* instead of the usual *Gud*). According to C. Stephen Evans this denotes a Platonic concept of deity, somewhat fitting perhaps for a work dealing with a Socratic lifeview and its alternatives.[5] However, rather than go so far as to claim this as being Kierkegaard's own vocabulary, Evans allows the pseudonym to stand on his own. Climacus never describes himself as a believer, instead he is content to remain an observer. He does not claim to represent full Christian doctrine on any point. Therefore it would be far more appropriate to interpret the use of 'the god' as being indicative of Climacus' speculative distance from the subject he seeks to discuss.[6]

The charges of this nature have also been produced by a reference to the Unmoved Mover of Aristotle's *Metaphysics*[7] found in Fragments: 'He must move himself and continue to be what Aristotle says of him, "ακινητος παντα κινει" [unmoved he moves all things].'[8] However, the context in which this occurs should be taken into consideration. In this case Aristotle's term is borrowed to illustrate the freedom of the god to become incarnate, against the thesis that he was compelled by force of human action, or other external forces. Climacus wishes to show that the god is entirely motivated by love, as opposed to being moved by obligation, or by need.[9]

The same phrase is also found in the *Postscript*. In this case Climacus is comparing the eternal reality of God against the fluctuations of human existence.

> Inasmuch as existence is motion, it holds true that there is indeed a continuity that holds the motion together, because otherwise there is no motion ... The motionless belongs to motion as motion's goal, both in the sense of τελος [end, goal] and μετρον [measure, criterion]; otherwise the statement that everything is in motion - if one takes away time and says that everything is always motion - is *eo ipso* stagnation. Aristotle, who in so many ways emphasizes motion, therefore says that God, himself unmoved, moves everything.[10]

[5] Evans, *Passionate Reason*, p. 185.
[6] Holmes Hartshorne, *Kierkegaard Godly Deceiver*, p. 33.
[7] Aristotle, *Metaphysics* (London and New York: J.M. Dent & Sons and E.P. Dalton & Co., 1956), pp. 345f.
[8] *Fragments*, p. 24.
[9] Ibid.
[10] *Concluding Unscientific Postscript*, vol. 1, p. 312.

Climacus is merely asserting the dependence of finite existence upon a transcendent God. His use of Aristotle here is in keeping with Western theology and follows Aquinas, so he cannot be taken as negatively as some would wish to assume. However, it is understood that Aristotle's concept of God, despite some valuable insights, is incomplete and abstract.[11] If this information may be taken into consideration, then the charge of Aristotelian theism may be seen to be unsupported.

Yet it is apparent that Kierkegaard does make frequent use of classical Greek terminology, both in the pseudonymous works and his *Journals*. Additionally it cannot be denied that he held many figures from classical thought and culture in high esteem. For instance in 1844 he wrote the following praise of antiquity in his *Journals*:

> It is a very strange experience for me to read the third chapter of the third book of Aristotle's *De Anima*. A year and a half ago I began a little essay, *De omnibus dubitandum*, in which I made my first attempt at a little speculative development. The motivating concept I used was: error. Aristotle does the same. At that time I had not read a bit of Aristotle but a good share of Plato. The Greeks still remain my consolation. The confounded mendacity which entered philosophy with Hegel, the endless insinuating and betraying, and the parading and spinning out of one or another single passage in Greek philosophy.[12]

Kierkegaard's admiration of classics and of Greek philosophy in particular cannot be overlooked. For instance, a fair proportion of Kierkegaard's attacks upon Hegelianism were inspired by the Aristotelian scholar and logician Adolf Trendelenburg.[13] A contemporary of Kierkegaard, Trendelenberg was professor of philosophy at Berlin and an opponent of Hegel. He sought to illustrate that, whilst Greek philosophy was in need of modification, it held many lasting insights.[14] It is not so surprising that Kierkegaard held Aristotle himself very highly, although, as the above quote states he did not begin reading him until the early 1840s, being far more a reader of Plato throughout his life. It is quotations and allusions to Plato's dialogues that so often adorn the pages of Kierkegaard's texts, yet they occur in reference to Socrates rather than Plato himself. Need we forget that his doctoral thesis was entitled *On the Concept of Irony, with Continual Reference to Socrates*? But may it be concluded from all this that his religious thought is dominated by Greek religious thought to the detriment of his Christian orthodoxy?

---

[11] Cf. *Journals and Papers*, 1332, IV A 157 *n.d.*, 1843.

[12] Ibid., 3300, V A 98 *n.d.*, 1844.

[13] Gardiner, *Kierkegaard*, p. 81; cf. *Concluding Unscientific Postscript*, vol. 1, p. 110.

[14] Frederick Copleston, *History of Philosophy, vol. VII Fichte to Nietsche* (London: Search Press, 1963), pp. 386f.

It is an unquestioned historical fact that both the Platonic and Aristotelian philosophies have played a most significant role in the development of Christian thought throughout the centuries. Despite the apparent antagonism between Greek philosophy and Biblical Christianity in the minds of some at that time, Platonic thought dominated the Christian theology of the Patristic period. This Neoplatonism as it was called (in fact a mixture of Platonic, Aristotelian and Stoic elements) became embedded in the thought of both the Western and Eastern traditions. Its topple from power in Europe only came with the resurgence of Aristotelianism in the Middle Ages (courtesy of Arabic translators, such was the lack of Greek expertise in the West!). Platonic thought made a little comeback, both during the Renaissance and in nineteenth century Romanticism, (although England produced the Cambridge Platonists in the seventeenth century, who owed more to the Neoplatonism of Plotinus than to Plato himself). However, Aristotelianism remained an intrinsic element of the European intellectual tradition until challenged by the rise of rationalism and empiricism from the seventeenth century. Its influence may have diminished, but it is by no means a spent force even in contemporary philosophy. Therefore, should it in any way be surprising then that Kierkegaard should exhibit some Greek influence in his writings? With much of both the school and university curricula of Kierkegaard's time being devoted to classics, it would be all the more startling if he were not to allow any mention of its contents to appear on his pages.

Is Kierkegaard an Anti-realist?

Not only have some interpreters argued for his holding to an impersonal Aristotelian concept of deity, but, others have detected the traits of an anti-realist (or non-realist) (a)theism from Kierkegaard's works. Probably the most notable contemporary proponent of this view is Don Cupitt, although another interesting variation of anti-realism has been put forward by D.Z. Phillips.[15] In *The Sea of Faith* Cupitt argues that, 'Kierkegaard is seeking to go beneath realist ideas of God to the primal meaning of God as my God, my life-aim, my spiritual task and goal; and "my God" is not a metaphysical being but the expression of my spiritual

---

[15] Phillips claims that 'Theology is the grammar of religious discourse' and as such does not relate to the objective reality of God as an independent being outside of the framework of a religious 'form of life'. In his view 'the grammatical parameters of our forms of discourse are *not descriptions of anything*. Rather, they determine what it *means* to offer a description or to make an existential claim in that context.' (D.Z. Phillips, *Wittgenstein and Religion* (London: Macmillan, 1993), pp. 4, 15.)

commitment to my life-aim.'[16] According to Patrick Gardiner this interpretation of Kierkegaard's theism claims that,

> Propositions concerning, for example, the nature of God or of personal immortality should not be treated as involving determinate truth-claims about a transcendent or supernatural reality; instead, they are best understood in a 'non-realist' and practically orientated way, and as playing a regulative rather than a descriptive or predicative role in religious contexts.[17]

Both Cupitt and Phillips are normally seen to represent a recent development in modern thought, with Phillips in particular drawing most of his inspiration from Wittgenstein's later philosophy. However, the attempt to ground theology wholly within the sphere of this worldly human existence has not been confined to the late twentieth century and may be seen in the writings of some of Kierkegaard's contemporaries.

Developments in Hegelian philosophy had led to the emergence of various splinter groups amongst his German followers in the mid-nineteenth century, one of the most radical of these was known as the 'Young Hegelians'. Like Kierkegaard they criticized the alliance of state Christianity with German culture. Unlike Kierkegaard they employed elements of Hegelian thought in their rejection of traditional theism in favour of atheism. The major figure of influence in the early development of this school was Ludwig Feuerbach, author of *The Essence of Christianity*.[18] In this radical work he claimed that,

> Religion, at least the Christian, is the relation of man to himself, or more correctly to his own nature (i.e., his subjective nature); but a relation to it, viewed as a nature apart from his own. The divine being is nothing else than the human being, or, rather, the human nature purified, freed from the limits of the individual man, made objective i.e., contemplated and revered as another, a distinct being. All the attributes of the divine nature are, therefore, attributes of the human nature.[19]

Rejecting belief in God as an objectively real, transcendent being, Feuerbach posited in its stead the concept of God as an 'objectification' ('projection' in some English translations) of human attributes. Religion is, for Feuerbach, a matter of feeling and a mark of humanity's infancy, something it will grow out of as it progresses. Where Hegel saw

---

[16] Don Cupitt, *The Sea of Faith* (London: BBC, 1984), p. 24.
[17] Gardiner, *Kierkegaard*, pp. 3-4.
[18] Some of the more famous members of the group at one time included Friedrich Engels, Karl Marx and Bruno Bauer.
[19] Feuerbach, *The Essence of Christianity*, p. 14.

the process of history as the unfolding of the self-consciousness of the Absolute, Feuerbach instead saw it as humanity's move to its own self-consciousness. Through this historical development theology will become anthropology as humanity realizes that 'in the origin of religion there is no qualitative or essential difference whatever between God and man'.[20]

This last point brings Feuerbach into conflict with Kierkegaard's constant assertion that 'there is an infinite, radical, qualitative difference between God and man'.[21] Kierkegaard was aware of Feuerbach's philosophy, he was one of the most talked about philosophers in Germany during the 1840s and Kierkegaard owned a copy of *The Essence of Christianity* which he read whilst writing *Philosophical Fragments*.[22] There are also a few direct references to Feuerbach in the *Journals*. In some ways they were similar in that through there criticism of him they both sought to 'stand Hegel on his head'.[23] Yet despite their shared animosity towards Hegel, Kierkegaard was to list Feuerbach amongst his opponents (alongside 'speculation' and 'Anabaptists'), thereby considering him to be a threat to the Christian faith as Kierkegaard saw it.[24] In fact, according to Murray Rae, Feuerbach is one of the prime targets of Kierkegaard's polemic in the first two chapters of Fragments.[25] This is on the grounds that his attempts to describe Christianity wholly in human terms do it a gross injustice and fall within the category of the Socratic hypothesis. In addition to this, further evidence may be found in the *Concluding Unscientific Postscript* where Climacus states,

> But that the by-nature eternal comes into existence in time, is born, grows up, and dies is a break with all thinking. If, however, the coming into existence of the eternal in time is supposed to be an eternal coming into existence, then Religiousness B is abolished, 'all theology is anthropology', Christianity is changed from an existence-communication into an ingenious metaphysical doctrine addressed to professors.[26]

Without the reality of the God-man there can be no full doctrine of God nor any Christianity. In the light of this, and of the general distance between Kierkegaard and Feuerbach, the anti-realist interpretation seems to be without foundation.

---

[20] Ibid., p. 17.
[21] *Journals and Papers*, 1383, X 1 A 59 *n.d.*, 1849.
[22] Cf. Rae, *Kierkegaard's Vision of the Incarnation*, p. 41.
[23] Hannay, *Kierkegaard*, p. 52.
[24] *Journals and Papers*, 3477, VIII 1 A 432 *n.d.*, 1847.
[25] Rae, *Kierkegaard's Vision of the Incarnation*, p. 41.
[26] *Concluding Unscientific Postscript*, vol. 1, p. 57.

Transcendence and Immanence

Having countered the previous two charges, I now wish to clarify more of what Kierkegaard did hold to. It is my contention that the majority of his assertions regarding the nature and attributes of God are intended to refute the pantheism he felt to be inherent within the then fashionable Idealist philosophy in particular. He sought instead to affirm a doctrine of God that included, not only such attributes as omnipotence and omnipresence, but especially transcendence. But of course, being who he was, Kierkegaard had to do so in no direct manner. Through the voice of Climacus he declares,

> What, then, is the unknown? It is the frontier that is continually arrived at ... Defined as the absolutely different, it seems to be at the point of being disclosed, but not so, because the understanding cannot even think the absolutely different ... It cannot absolutely transcend itself and therefore thinks as above itself only the sublimity that it thinks by itself. If the unknown (the god) is not solely the frontier, then the one idea about the different is confused with the many ideas about the different. The unknown is then in diaspora, and the understanding has an attractive selection from among what is available and what fantasy can think of (the prodigious, the ridiculous, etc.).[27]

He wishes to leave us in no doubt that God totally transcends our thoughts' abilities to attain him. Even for Climacus, the deity is 'absolutely different' from us, otherwise we remain within the realm of fantasy and our own 'prodigious' or 'ridiculous' creations.

Leaving the aesthetic texts behind we swap pseudonyms and encounter the later pseudonym Anti-Climacus. Within his writings the absolute difference becomes a qualitative difference:

> Let us never forget that Socrates' ignorance was a kind of fear and worship of God, that his ignorance was the Greek version of the Jewish saying: the fear of the Lord is the beginning of wisdom. Let us never forget that it was out of veneration for God that he was ignorant, that as far as it was possible for a pagan he was on guard duty as a judge on the frontier between God and man, keeping watch so that the deep gulf of qualitative difference between them was maintained, between God and man, that God and man did merge in some way, *philosophice*, *poetice*, etc., into one.[28]

As he goes to great lengths to explain in *The Sickness Unto Death*, from where this passage is taken, this qualitative difference is none other than original sin. It is an entirely Christian concept which makes it radically

[27] *Fragments*, pp. 44-45.
[28] *The Sickness Unto Death*, p. 99.

different from other religions. Without it, could humanity not better itself and claim divinity? This is not so much a metaphysical statement as it is an existential one, but with it the absolute difference between God and fallen creation is maintained. If that is not so, and sin is removed, there need be neither Incarnation nor atonement; humanity may then progress to its own autonomous fulfilment and 'the qualitative difference between God and man is pantheistically abolished'.[29]

In an entry in his journal two years earlier in 1847, Kierkegaard criticized pantheism as being 'an optical illusion, a vaporous image formed out of the fog of temporality or a mirage formed by its reflection, which claims to be the eternal'.[30] Kierkegaard's dissatisfaction with pantheism can be traced back at least to one of his earliest journal entries where he refers to 'the error in Schleiermacher's definition of religion as remaining in pantheism'.[31] In the case of Schleiermacher, Kierkegaard attributes his pantheism as being a throwback to Stoicism.[32] However, the main motivation behind the nineteenth century trend towards pantheism was a resurgence of interest in Spinoza's philosophy. This was brought about largely through the efforts of Schelling in his early philosophy, yet Schleiermacher also admired him.[33]

---

[29] Ibid., p. 117.

[30] *Journals and Papers*, 2004, VIII 1 A 482 *n.d.*, 1847.

[31] Ibid., 3849, II A 91 *n.d.*, 1837.

[32] Ibid., 3848, I A 305 *n.d.*, 1836.

[33] Traits of pantheism can be detected throughout Schelling's philosophy, even in his last years when he returned to Christianity (see J. Heywood Thomas, 'J.G. Fichte and F.W.J. Schelling', in (eds.) Smart et al, *Nineteenth Century Religious Thought in the West*, vol. 1 (Cambridge: CUP, 1988), p. 70). Schleiermacher, on the other hand, did not wish to accept this classification and frequently attempted to dispel the charges of pantheism made against him by his critics. At one point in *The Christian Faith* he claims that any appearance of pantheism in his theology arises out of the failings of philosophy to provide 'a generally accepted formula to express the relation of God and the world'. Because of this, theological discourse on this topic alternates between the two extremes of pantheism or of putting God and world in opposition to each other (Schleiermacher, *The Christian Faith*, p. 174). However, despite his attempts to disassociate himself from pantheism, Schleiermacher immensely admired Spinoza, and there is no denying that Spinozic echoes are frequently heard in his pages. To conceive of God as the unity correlative with the multiplicity phenomenally present as the world, or the equating of the divine omnipotence with the totality of natural causes, is a doctrine of radical immanence, a close parallel to the Spinozan *natura naturans* and *natura naturata*. (Reardon, *Religion in the Age of Romanticism*, p. 57.) Hegel is also frequently cited as a pantheist, yet he denied this in his writings. It is more accurate to refer to him as a 'panentheist' (Peter Hodgson, 'George William Friederick Hegel' in Smart et al (eds.), *Nineteenth Century Religious Thought in the West*, vol. 1 (Cambridge: CUP, 1988), p. 85; cf. Hegel, *The Christian Religion, Lectures on the Philosophy of Religion, Part III. The Revelatory, Absolute Religion* (Missoula: Scholars Press, 1979), pp. 110; 162, n7).

Kierkegaard in no way sought to deny God's omnipresence. As Anti-Climacus tells us in *Practice in Christianity*, God may be 'invisible on high, [but] he is also present everywhere'.[34] In his *Upbuilding Discourses* of 1844, Kierkegaard openly declares how God is always present with the believer, 'present as swiftly as only one can be who was already present.'[35] But he is always careful to prevent any interpretation of his words leaning towards pantheism. For instance, consider Climacus' words in the *Concluding Unscientific Postscript*, 'Nature, the totality of creation, is God's work, and yet God is not there, but within the individual human being there is a possibility (he is spirit according to his possibility) that in inwardness is awakened to a God-relationship, and then it is possible to see God everywhere.'[36] It would seem that God is to be understood as distinct from creation, but not to the extent that he is absent from it. Through Climacus, Kierkegaard is implying that God is not self evident to the casual observer, but his presence is discernible to the believer. 'Nature is certainly the work of God, but only the work is directly present, not God.'[37] This is an objective theism in opposition to God-concepts which, not only attribute divinity to the world, but the process of world history and development. Allowing for the belief that an omnipresent God is both transcendent and immanent, the polemical style of Climacus is used to deride a one-sided focus upon the latter: 'In the world-historical process, God is metaphysically laced in a half-metaphysical, half-esthetic-dramatic, conventional corset, which is immanence.'[38]

Divine Omnipotence

The doctrine of God's omnipotence also finds its way onto Kierkegaard's pages. It is God whose very power sustains the world's very existence at every moment. 'You ... see many forces stirring in nature around you, but the power that supports it all you do not see, you do not see God's omnipotence - and yet it is just as fully certain that he, too, is working, that one single moment without him and then the world is nothing.'[39] This makes an interesting comparison with two statements in the *Upbuilding Discourses*.

> But in heaven, my listener, there lives the God who is capable of all things, or, more correctly, he lives everywhere, even if people do not perceive it.[40]

[34] *Practice in Christianity*, p. 155.
[35] *Eighteen Upbuilding Discourses*, p. 322.
[36] *Concluding Unscientific Postscript*, vol 1, p. 246.
[37] Ibid., p. 243.
[38] Ibid., p. 156.
[39] *Practice in Christianity*, p. 155.
[40] *Eighteen Upbuilding Discourses*, p. 310.

> O Lord ... your very greatness makes you invisible, since in your wisdom you are much too far away from man's thoughts for him to be able to see you, and in your omnipresence you are too close for him to see you; in your goodness you conceal yourself from him, and your omnipotence makes it impossible for him to see you, since in that case he himself would become nothing! But God in heaven is capable of all things, and man of nothing at all.[41]

The latter statement in particular illustrates the core content of Kierkegaard's own Christian theism. Both of the above were written in 1844, close to the publication of *Philosophical Fragments*. Therefore it is interesting to note the absence of the aesthetic terminology that has given rise to the assumptions dealt with earlier. A brief scan of both the *Upbuilding Discourses* and his *Journals* shows how Kierkegaard's God is wholly consistent with the God of traditional Christianity. 'The god' of Climacus' speculations in *Philosophical Fragments* is absent, replaced by the 'Father in heaven'[42] of Kierkegaard's own experiences.

The Love of God and Love for God

The mention of God as Father brings us to the topic of the love of God. This topic arises in the discussion as it is a vital component in Kierkegaard's doctrine of God. An early illustration of the love of God in Kierkegaard's writings is in Climacus' analogy of the King and the Maiden in *Fragments* where we are told that love is the god's entire motive for making himself known to the learner. The god wishes both to love and to be loved.[43] Kierkegaard echoes these statements throughout the *Journals*, giving more explicitly theological discussions of Climacus' poetic musings. For instance, he states, 'Out of love God wants to be reconciled,' and, 'God is love. This is the thesis of Christianity. There is a twofoldness in it: God loves - and God wants to be loved. These two in equilibrium make true Christianity.'[44] On the subject of God as love and as wanting to be loved by us, Kierkegaard briefly returns to the style of the 'King and Maiden' analogy to explain the concept further:

> If someone were able to adhere on the greatest scale to the fact that God is love in the sense that God loves him and then suddenly come to see the other side, that God wants to be loved - he would certainly become anxious and afraid. Just as it can be grand and glorious for a poor girl to become the object of a very powerful man's love, who loves her with all his soul - but in another

---

[41] Ibid., p. 310; cf. also *Journals and Papers*, 1251, VII 1 A 181 *n.d.*, 1846.
[42] Ibid., p. 8.
[43] *Fragments*, pp. 24f.
[44] *Journals and Papers*, 532, X 4 A 212 *n.d.*, 1851 and Ibid., 1446, XI 2 A 99 n.d., 1854.

sense there is an enormous difference when she perceives the earnestness of his passionate desire to be loved - just so it is for the Christian. In one sense nothing is more blessed than this certainty that God loves him, and also the degree to which God is love, the fact that it is his essence - in another sense nothing is more dreadful than to be pulled up to this highest level of existence, where in one sense God's wanting to be loved is so frightfully earnest.[45]

It would appear then, that to be the object of God's love is a privilege, yet it is also a cause for consternation as the believer wonders if he could ever return such love appropriately.

At various times in the *Journals* Kierkegaard describes God as infinite love,[46] that he offers his love to all people equally,[47] and, that his love for us remains unchanged throughout eternity.[48] He even refers to God's love as being 'the one unshakeable thing in life, the true Archimedian point'.[49] Yet these are not glib platitudes and he frequently records in his *Journals* how difficult it can be for the believer to hold on to this when God seems distant or uncaring.

> This is spiritual trial, but it is entirely in order that it goes this way; even the apostles experienced this in relation to Christ. And yet God is infinite love, but he has only the spirit's conception of what constitutes your happiness and blessedness - alas, and you are flesh and blood. If you are to become blessed in your relationship to him, your conception must be transformed, and this transformation, this rebirth, is a very painful operation, and the in process there comes the moment when it seems to you as if God were like a superior sort of seducer.[50]

The concept of the transformation of our conceptions by God brings us back to the subject of metanoia that was mentioned in Chapter two. God, out of love, transforms the learner and thereby enables the learner to love him in return. Motivated by this love for God, the learner wishes to learn more, and so, in this sense, love is the true starting point

---

[45] Ibid., 1446, XI 2 A 99 *n.d.*, 1854.
[46] E.g. Ibid., 538, X 4 A 624 *n.d.*, 1852; 1409, X 3 A 359 *n.d.*, 1850; 1410, X 3 A 373 *n.d.*, 1850.
[47] E.g. Ibid., 1358, VIII 1 A 327 *n.d.*, 1847; 1368, IX A 77 *n.d.*, 1848.
[48] E.g. Ibid., 1379, IX A 374 *n.d.*, 1848.
[49] Ibid., 5468, III A 73 *n.d.*, 1840.
[50] Ibid., 1409, X 3 A 359 *n.d.*, 1850.

of theological enquiry.[51]

2. Demonstrations of God's Existence

Treatment of the traditional philosophical arguments for God's existence does not figure predominantly in any of Kierkegaard's writings. Throughout his authorship he appears to take God's existence to be the unqualified starting-point and presupposition for all that follows, assuming that by far the majority of his readers held to some form of belief in God. As I showed in the previous section, his principal concern was to proclaim that the God who exists is the Christian God, as opposed to any rival philosophical concepts. Commenting on the pseudonymous works, John Elrod writes, 'For Kierkegaard, the God question is an existential question, not an ontological one. Discussions of God appear in his descriptions of the ethico-religious stage of existence, not his ontology.'[52] Therefore, like all other topics of discussion, the context is that of personal relevance and appropriation, not that of detached philosophical speculation. With this in mind I wish to examine, first, Kierkegaard's thought regarding the validity of attempts to demonstrate the existence of God in general, followed by some comment upon the significance of 'proofs' for the Christian faith. It will then be appropriate to discuss his particular rejection of the ontological argument and of the argument from design, most of which is to be found presented through the mouth of Johannes Climacus in *Philosophical Fragments*.

Demonstrations and the Christian God

For Climacus, any attempt to demonstrate God's existence is found to be forlorn from the very beginning:

> It hardly occurs to the understanding to want to demonstrate that this unknown (the god) exists. If, namely, the god does not exist, then it is

---

[51] Consider the following passage from the *Journals*: 'Christ says: I will manifest myself to him who loves me. But it is generally true that something manifests itself to the one who loves it; truth manifests itself to the one who loves truth, etc. We usually think that the recipient is inactive and that the object manifesting itself communicates to the recipient, but the relationship is this: the recipient is the lover, and then the beloved becomes manifest to him, for he himself is transformed in the likeness of the beloved; the only fundamental basis for understanding is that one himself becomes what he understands and one only understands in proportion to becoming himself that which he understands.' (Ibid., 2299, IX A 438 *n.d.*, 1848.)

[52] John Elrod, *Being and Existence in Kierkegaard's Pseudonymous Works* (Princeton: Princeton University Press, 1975), p. 70n.

> foolishness to want to demonstrate it, since I, in the very moment the demonstration commences, would presuppose it not as doubtful - which a presupposition cannot be, inasmuch as it is a presupposition - but as decided, because otherwise I would not begin, easily perceiving that the whole thing would be impossible if he did not exist.[53]

The reason then, is that before any attempt at a demonstration begins, the person demonstrating would already be determined for a particular outcome. This would of course tend to be in the affirmative, since you cannot demonstrate the existence of what does not actually exist. The process is therefore circular as God's existence is actually serving as the presupposition of the argument, instcad of forming the long awaited conclusion. Because of this it is impossible to reach complete objectivity in such theological discourse. What in fact results is that the concept of God is given some explanation by means of the 'demonstration', and so: 'If, however, I interpret the expression "to demonstrate the existence of the god" to mean that I want to demonstrate that the unknown, which exists, is the god, then I do not express myself very felicitously, for then I demonstrate nothing, least of all existence, but I develop the definition of a concept.'[54] So God's existence is not proved at all. Instead his existence is taken as a given fact and it then follows that his nature is given a technical description in the process of the alleged demonstration. Climacus muses on this, saying that, 'Whether I am moving in the world of sensate palpability or in the world of thought, I never reason in conclusion to existence, but I reason in conclusion from existence. For example, I do not demonstrate that a stone exists, but that something which exists is a stone.'[55]

In a journal entry made in 1846 Kierkegaard claimed that 'God cannot be an object for man, since God is subject'.[56] This statement was made in the same year as he published the *Concluding Unscientific Postscript* where he allows Climacus to explain this further. Leaving the impersonal theism of *Fragments* behind, he criticizes demonstrations as turning God himself into some detached object of enquiry instead of relating to him as he really is.

> To demonstrate the existence of someone who exists is the most shameless assault, since it is an attempt to make him ludicrous, but the trouble is that one does not even suspect this, that in dead seriousness one regards it as a godly undertaking. How could it occur to anyone to demonstrate that he exists unless one has allowed oneself to ignore him; and now one does it in

---

[53] *Fragments*, p. 39.

[54] Ibid., p. 40.

[55] Ibid.

[56] *Journals and Papers*, 1349, VII 1 A 201 *n.d.*, 1846.

> an even more lunatic way by demonstrating his existence right in front of his nose.[57]

To omit the personal, relational aspect, is to misunderstand the nature of God and of religious faith entirely.[58] A faith that relies wholly on intellectual assent to what has been proved is not really faith, but rather knowledge. Plus, there could always be the possibility of its being disproved, and so it follows that if a man had belief in God merely because, 'he accepted it by virtue of a demonstration, he would be on the verge of abandoning his faith.'[59] In his typical polemical style Climacus is led to conclude: 'For whose sake is the demonstration conducted? Faith does not need it, indeed it must even consider it an enemy.'[60] For, as he sees it, true faith is strong enough without such aid. 'When faith begins to cease to be faith, then the demonstration is made necessary in order to enjoy general esteem from unbelief.'[61]

If Climacus is critical of alleged demonstrations, then more so is Kierkegaard in his *Journals*. In his opinion, how can it be that somebody can spend serious time and effort developing proofs and demonstrations if he or she already believes in the God they apparently wish to 'prove'? Special attention in this case is given to the Christian academic:

> The scientist and the scholar has his personal life in categories quite different from those of his professional life, but it is precisely the first which are the most important. He prays, for example - and then his entire effort is preoccupied with proving the existence of God. But how can he pray fervently in this way when his being is fragmented in this self-contradiction?[62]

On this then Kierkegaard's comments certainly appear to lend themselves open to the hostile charge of fideism:

> Away with all this world history and reasons and proofs for the truth of Christianity: there is only one proof - that of faith. If I actually have a firm conviction (and this, to be sure, is a qualification of intense inwardness orientated to spirit), then to me my firm conviction is higher than reasons; it is actually the conviction which sustains the reasons, not the reasons which sustain the conviction.[63]

---

[57] *Concluding Unscientific Postscript*, vol 1, p. 545.

[58] Anthony Rudd, *Kierkegaard and the Limits of the Ethical* (Oxford; OUP, 1993), p. 61; Law, *Kierkegaard as Negative Theologian*, p. 181.

[59] *Concluding Unscientific Postscript*, vol 1, p. 30.

[60] Ibid.

[61] Ibid., pp. 30-1.

[62] *Journals and Papers*, 928, VII 1 A 28 *n.d.*, 1846.

[63] Ibid., 3608, X 1 A 481 *n.d.*, 1849.

However, that is not to say that for him the intellectual defence of Christianity is disregarded *per se* as irreligious, as some interpreters wish to claim, nor is he arguing for the complete abandonment of 'the Christian metaphysical system'.[64] We must remember that Kierkegaard is not seeking to engage in the task of objective Christian apologetics for the benefit of those who have rejected Christianity, neither is he attempting to inform those who are unaware of the details of the Christian faith. Instead he is writing with the self-confessed believer in mind. In this context Kierkegaard does actually allow for demonstrations and the like to be valid, but only in that they may offer some limited help on the road to faith. What he rejects is the claim that they might lead directly to faith, or that faith ought to be grounded in such reasoning alone, as once God is encountered as living a reality all else becomes secondary. In a journal entry of 1849 we find the following,

> My development, or any man's development, proceeds in this way. Perhaps he does begin with a few reasons, but this is the lower stage. Then he chooses; under the weight of responsibility before God a conviction comes into existence in him through God ... Now he cannot defend or prove his conviction with reasons; it is a self-contradiction, since reasons are lower.[65]

It may therefore be seen that, according to Kierkegaard, reasons may be valid, but they can only serve a preparatory role to the conversion of an individual. They are neither certain, nor complete, nor sufficient in themselves.[66] In the words of Anti-Climacus, 'demonstrations can at best serve to make a person aware, so that made aware he can now come to the point: whether he will believe or he will be offended.'[67] Let us now consider how this is done, first with regard to the ontological argument, and then to the argument from design.

---

[64] Cf. Christopher Hamilton: 'For there can be no proof of the existence of God; . . . the only thing to do is to insist on the incomprehensibility of God and its total lack of defensibility in purely rational terms that is central to Christianity,' and, 'Kierkegaard says, then, that belief in God is essentially paradoxical.' (Christopher Hamilton, 'Kierkegaard on truth as subjectivity: Christianity, ethics and ascetism', *Religious Studies* 34 (1998), p. 63.) According to Hamilton 'Kierkegaard believed it was possible to defend a post-metaphysical conception of such belief by reflecting on its place in what one might call the spiritual economy of the life of the individual.' (Ibid., p. 61.) In such a view of religious belief the metaphysical question of God's existence is irrelevant to the Christian life. (Cf. Ibid., pp. 73, 75.)

[65] *Journals and Papers*, 3608, X 1 A 481 *n.d.*, 1849.

[66] Westphal, *Kierkegaard's Critique of Reason and Society*, p. 94.

[67] *Practice in Christianity*, p. 96.

The Ontological Argument

As I have already stated, Kierkegaard's specific treatment of the traditional arguments for God's existence is scarce. He briefly rejects the ontological and design arguments, but ignores the cosmological and moral arguments.[68] The ontological argument attempts to demonstrate God's existence a priori, in that it argues from the concept of God alone. According to Richard Swinburne it may be summarized as follows: 'God is by definition a most perfect being. A being which exists is more perfect than one which does not. Therefore God, being most perfect, exists.'[69] So it is claimed God necessarily exists, or alternatively his essence involves his existence, as Climacus puts it in *Fragments*: 'God is not a name but a concept, and perhaps because of that his *essentia involvit existentiam.*'[70]

Although this demonstration is most famous from its use first by Anselm, and then by Descartes,[71] Climacus chooses to focus instead to Spinoza's version of it. It would seem that, in keeping with the indirect nature of Kierkegaard's criticism Spinoza is not the main object of attack. Instead it would seem that Spinoza is used here to portray the pantheist tendencies in nineteenth century theology that were inspired by his philosophy.[72] Although Martensen swiftly rejected the ontological argument in his *Christian Dogmatics*,[73] it did receive

---

[68] Having said this, if we call to mind the few references to Aristotle's conception of God as the 'Unmoved Mover' in the *Postscript*, it can be seen that Kierkegaard had the cosmological argument in mind. However, he does not actually discuss it at length, nor does he even refer to this argument directly. Instead, it would seem that it is merely implicit in the discussion and therefore it would be safe to conclude that he did not consider it to be very important. Kierkegaard's reasons for choosing to focus on the ontological and design arguments were quite simple. Traditionally the argument from design has been the most preferred of the theistic arguments in Protestant theology, and interest in the ontological argument had recently been revived by Hegel. The cosmological argument featured far more in Roman Catholic apologetics and the moral argument was largely a Kantian innovation. As Kierkegaard generally had other targets in mind he would not have considered the last two arguments relevant to his argument.

[69] Richard Swinburne, *The Existence of God* (Oxford: Clarendon Press, 1993), p. 9n.

[70] *Fragments*, p. 41.

[71] Anselm's use of the argument differed greatly from that of Descartes. A 'text-book rationalist', Descartes sought to formulate a logical demonstration in a manner akin to that of a mathematical equation. Anselm, whilst not wishing to sacrifice any of his intellectual integrity, places his argument within the context of prayer and meditation. The central doctrines of Christianity are already presupposed and his intention is, not to 'prove' God's existence objectively, but to clarify certain aspects of God's nature and character. (Paul Helm, *Faith and Understanding* (Edinburgh: Edinburgh University Press, 1997), pp. 105ff.)

[72] Notable examples here would be Schelling and Schleiermacher, see Copleston, *History of Philosophy*, vol. VII, pp. 100 and 149 respectively.

[73] Martensen, *Christian Dogmatics*, p. 75.

lengthy and favourable treatment in Hegel's *Lectures on the Philosophy of Religion.*[74] In his *Ethics* Spinoza states that, 'God or a substance consisting of infinite attributes, each of which expresses eternal and infinite essence, necessarily exists.' Also, 'since ability to exist is power, it follows that the more reality anything in nature has, the more power it will have to exist; and accordingly a being absolutely infinite, or God, has an absolutely infinite power of existence from itself, and on that account absolutely exists.'[75] This is rejected by Climacus as being tautologous since it is impossible to conclude existence from perfection. To try to do so is an 'intrinsically unclear use of language', and 'with regard to factual being, to speak of more or less factual being is meaningless. A fly, when it is, has just as much being as the god'.[76]

Another of Climacus' objections to this theory centres around the idea that what might be appear necessary according to a hypothesis or rule of logic, might not correspond with what is actually the case - 'What is lacking here is a distinction between factual being and ideal being.'[77] He explains his particular criticisms at greater length in the *Concluding Unscientific Postscript,*

> When, for example, it is said: God must have all perfections, or the highest being must have all perfections, to be is also a perfection; ergo the highest being must be, or God must be - the whole movement is deceptive. That is, if in the first part of this statement God is actually not thought of as being, then the statement cannot come off at all. It will then run somewhat like this: A supreme being who, please note, does not exist, must be in possession of all perfections, among them also that of existing; ergo a supreme being who does not exist does exist. This would be a strange conclusion. The highest being must either not be in the beginning of the discourse in order to come into existence in the conclusion, and in that case it cannot come into existence; or the highest being was, and thus, of course, it cannot come into existence, in which case the conclusion is a fraudulent form of developing a predicate, a fraudulent paraphrase of a presupposition. In the other case the conclusion must be kept purely hypothetical: if a supreme being is assumed to be, this being must also be assumed to be in possession of all perfections; to be is a perfection, ergo this being must be - that is if this being is assumed to be. By concluding within a hypothesis, one can surely never conclude from the hypothesis. For example, if this or that person is a hypocrite, he will act like a hypocrite, a hypocrite will do this and do that; ergo this or that person has done this and that. It is the same with the conclusion about God. When the conclusion is finished,

---

[74] Hegel, *The Christian Religion*, pp. 45ff.

[75] Spinoza, *Ethics and On the Correction of the Understanding* (London and Melbourne: Everyman's Library, 1986), pp. 7, 9.

[76] *Fragments*, p. 41n.

[77] Ibid.

> God's being is just as hypothetical as it was, but inside there is advanced a conclusion-relation between a supreme being and being as perfection.[78]

So the end result is dependent upon a belief held prior to the demonstration. Even then though, everything may be seen to remain within the hypothetical and all that is accomplished is the elaboration of a God-concept.

In making his criticisms, Kierkegaard's pseudonym is closely following Kant's argument against Descartes and Leibniz as made in the *Critique of Pure Reason.* As part of his refutation of the ontological argument, Kant states that,

> It is absurd to introduce - under whatever term disguised - into the concept of a thing, which is to be thought solely in reference to its possibility, the concept of existence ... in reality [you] have enounced nothing but a tautology. I ask, is the proposition, *this* or *that thing* (which I am admitting to be possible) exists, an analytical or a synthetic proposition? If the former, there is no addition made to the subject of your thought by the affirmation of its existence; but either then the concept in your minds is identical with the thing itself, or you have supposed the existence of a thing to be possible, and then inferred its existence from its internal possibility - which is but a miserable tautology.[79]

In trying to deduce the existence of God through the concept of 'being' itself there results a general confusion of a logical with a real predicate. Hence Kant likens the ontological argument for God's existence with an attempt to increase someone's wealth by adding the mere concept of more money, or just by writing a few extra noughts on the balance sheet![80]

The Argument from Design

Climacus refers to the design argument by its Kantian title of the 'physico-teleological demonstration', but it will be seen that the similarities between Kierkegaard's pseudonym and this German philosopher do not end there. For both figures the rejection of the design argument is based upon some of the same premises as the ontological argument. Traditionally an argument from design may be described as 'one which argues from some general pattern of order in the universe or provision for the needs of conscious beings to a God responsible for these phenomena'.[81] Climacus' first point of

---

[78] *Concluding Unscientific Postscript*, vol. 1, p. 334.

[79] Immanuel Kant, *Critque of Pure Reason* (London: Everyman, 1996), p. 409.

[80] Ibid., pp. 411f.

[81] Swinburne, *The Existence of God*, p. 133.

contention is that there is no self-evident, or directly obvious, connection between God and the universe. The argument rests upon the presumption that there is a creator God. Like Kant before him, Climacus refuses to believe that it is appropriate to reason from visible causes to God. We are unable to perceive the totality of existence, hence the process of reasoning could never be completed and hence remain within an 'infinite chain of contingencies'.[82] This point echoes David Hume's criticism of such arguments that the connection between observable phenomena and the eternal God as a first cause 'is performed merely by an arbitrary act of the mind, and has no influence on the nature of things'.[83] As Climacus explains in the *Concluding Unscientific Postscript*, 'I observe nature in order to find God, and I do indeed see omnipotence and wisdom, but I also see much that troubles and disturbs. The *summa summarum* of this is an objective uncertainty.'[84] Similar thoughts are also found in *Fragments*:

> The works from which I want to demonstrate his existence do not immediately and directly exist, not at all. Or are the wisdom in nature and the goodness or wisdom in Governance right in front of our noses? . . . But I still do not demonstrate God's existence from such an order of things, and even if I began, I would never finish and would be obliged to live *in suspenso* lest something so terrible happen that my fragments of demonstration would be ruined. Therefore, from what works do I demonstrate it? From the works regarded ideally - that is, as they do not appear directly and immediately. But then I do not demonstrate it from the works, after all, but only develop the ideality I have presupposed.[85]

For both figures the rejection of the design argument is based upon some of the same premises as the ontological argument. Like the ontological argument, we are told that the validity of the physico-teleological demonstration is confined to the elucidation of a God-concept.[86] An objectively valid, real demonstration in this manner cannot be done, and attempts by those claiming to be capable of this are merely 'a superb theme for a crazy comedy'.[87] It is important then not to fall into the trap of giving it too much significance: 'At least Socrates, who did indeed advance what is called the physico-teleological demonstration for the existence of God, did not conduct himself in this way. He

[82] Kant, *Critque of Pure Reason*, p. 423.
[83] David Hume, *Dialogues Concerning Natural Religion and the Posthumous Essays* (Indianapolis: Hackett Publishing, 1980), p. 56.
[84] *Concluding Unscientific Postscript*, vol. 1, pp. 203f.
[85] *Fragments*, p. 42
[86] T.H. Croxall, *Kierkegaard Commentary* (New York: Harper & Bros., 1956), p. 172.
[87] *Fragments*, p. 43.

constantly presupposes that the god exists, and on this presupposition he seeks to infuse nature with the idea of fitness and purposiveness.'[88]

It may be seen then, that the traditional arguments for God's existence are not rejected out of hand but may be acceptable if their limits are allowed for. Namely, 'the belief in God which the proof is supposed to support is actually supporting the proof, rather than the other way around.'[89] At no point in any of his writings does Kierkegaard allow Climacus to deny that God can be known rationally. The target is those who would use demonstrations as the foundations of faith, making God out to be the distant impersonal object of speculation. Kierkegaard himself knew God's reality from personal faith and subjective experience, things which textbook reasons could not replace. God is to be encountered as a living being, present in ways accessible to all people, not an object relegated to the field of philosophical scrutiny. Kierkegaard draws a parallel case with the pretensions of some scientists: 'Tell him [the natural scientist] that any man has all he needs in his conscience and in Luther's *Small Catechism*, and the natural scientist will look down his nose. In an imposing way he wants to make God into a coy beauty, a devil of a fellow, whom not everyone can understand.'[90] Maybe for Kierkegaard God is to be known far more easily than many of his critics would allow. Through Climacus he defended the philosophy that 'objective speculation and subjective existence are opposite and incompatible movements. Thus, to the extent that I try to prove God's existence by speculation, I make God's reality appear doubtful by removing myself from the existential standpoint which actually offers assurance.'[91] The key is to 'let go' of such proofs, recognizing their limits, and try to relate to God in faith,

> So long as I am holding on to the demonstration (that is, continue to be the one who is demonstrating), the existence does not emerge, if for no other reason than that I am in the process of demonstrating it, but when I let go of the demonstration, the existence is there. Yet this letting go, even that is surely something; it is after all, *meine Zuthat* [my contribution]. Does it not have to be taken into account, this diminutive moment, however brief it is - it does not have to be long, because it is a leap.[92]

The notion of the leap is well-known in Kierkegaardian studies. In this context it refers to the necessity of a personal act of commitment, 'It directs our attention to the necessity of choice and the inescapability of

---

[88] Ibid., p. 44.
[89] Evans, *Passionate Reason*, p. 68.
[90] *Journals and Papers*, 2809, VII 1 A 186 *n.d.*, 1846.
[91] Evans, *Passionate Reason*, pp. 70-1.
[92] *Fragments*, p. 42-3.

the leap. It reminds us that theological affirmation is grounded in presuppositions that are chosen, not proven.'[93]

3. The Unknown God and Negative Theology

Returning to the theism found in *Philosophical Fragments* I now wish to turn to Climacus' description of 'the god' as 'the unknown'. In discussing the limits of human knowledge Climacus asserts that, 'this, then is the ultimate passion of thought: to want to discover something that thought cannot think.'[94] By this it is being implied that human thought attempts to transcend itself, an impossible and somewhat paradoxical task. He then explains that in this situation of constant striving to know more there will always be something beyond, and hence unknowable, to reason.

> But what is this unknown against which the understanding in its paradoxical passion collides and which even disturbs man and his self-knowledge? It is the unknown. But it is not a human being, insofar as he knows man, or anything else that he knows. Therefore let us call this unknown the god [*Guden*]. It is only a name that we give to it.[95]

This statement is in the midst of Climacus' description of the limits of, not necessarily knowledge in general, but of what he refers to as Socratic knowledge. This was discussed in detail earlier and refers to the theory of Socratic recollection, namely, that we posses all necessary truth within ourselves and need only to 'recollect' that which we already know. According to Stephen M. Emmanuel the use of 'the unknown' in this manner is an indictment upon the Socratic position - 'that he is unable to advance further than to the paradoxical realization that he cannot know the highest truth is itself evidence of the inherent conceptual limitations of the Platonic-Socratic view.'[96] Thus he would agree with the position which understands Climacus to be but a personification of the aesthetic-ethical lifeview, not the proponent of a valid theological position on behalf of Kierkegaard himself.

A different interpretation is put forward by David Law in *Kierkegaard as Negative Theologian* and Michael Hardin in an article on Kierkegaard's spirituality in the *Scottish Journal of Theology*.[97] Although these two scholars seem to have arrived at their positions

---

[93] Westphal, *Kierkegaard's Critique of Reason and Society*, p. 94.
[94] *Fragments*, p. 37.
[95] Ibid., p. 39.
[96] Emmanuel, *Kierkegaard and the Concept of Revelation*, p. 48.
[97] Michael Hardin, 'Reflections on the Spirituality of Soren Kierkegaard', *Scottish Journal of Theology* (1992) 45, pp. 325-340.

quite independently of each other, there are some marked similarities between them. First, both fail to distinguish between 'God' and 'the god' in the Climacus texts, taking either of Climacus' terms to denote the Christian God.[98] Second, their interpretation of Kierkegaard's writings lays little stress upon the pseudonymity and irony, hence there is minimal distinction between the views of Climacus and those of Kierkegaard.[99] Due to this the result is that Climacus' thought is treated entirely seriously, detecting within his theism strands of 'apophatic', or negative theology. Law offers the following evidence for his position:

> The unknown that is God, however, is not unknown because the individual lacks knowledge. God is unknown because human reason is simply not capable of grasping Him. To gain purchase on God, reason would have to be above God. God would then be subject to its laws and open to examination and explication. God, however, is the creator of the world and it is He who has ordained its laws and principles, including those of reason. Consequently God is above reason and as such is unknown ... In this emphasis on the breakdown of reason when confronted by the Divine we can see a very powerful apophatic motif coming to the fore. Because reason is incapable of grasping God, God becomes the Unknown, a concept that bears a striking resemblance to the hidden God of negative theology.[100]

Law is not claiming a direct influence between negative theology and Kierkegaard, merely an uncanny similarity, although Kierkegaard was aware of its proponents through his theological studies.[101] Hardin also suggests that Kierkegaard's approach to God is similar to the apophatic tradition, although he also suggests that Kierkegaard knew more about Western mysticism, which he rejected.[102]

Kierkegaard's criticisms of mysticism are few and far between. In *Either/Or* his personification of the ethical lifeview, Judge William, rejects mysticism largely on the grounds that mystics become alienated from the rest of society as all relationships other than that with God become insignificant.[103] This is quite understandable when it is realized that the ethical lifeview depends entirely upon society for verification of its value system. Kierkegaard makes some direct criticism in the *Journals*, for instance in 1840 he commented that 'mysticism does not have the patience to wait for God's revelation'.[104] Ten years later,

---

[98] Law, *Kierkegaard as Negative Theologian*, p. 163; Hardin, 'Reflections on the Spirituality of Soren Kierkegaard', p. 333.
[99] Law, *Kierkegaard as Negative Theologian*, p. 5.
[100] Ibid., p. 163.
[101] *Journals and Papers*, 1430, X 4 A 567 *n.d.*, 1852.
[102] Hardin 'Reflections on the Spirituality of Soren Kierkegaard', pp. 327, 329.
[103] *Either/Or*, vol. 2, p. 245.
[104] *Journals and Papers*, 2795, III A 8 July 11, 1840.

contrasting Hegelian Idealism and mysticism, he stated that 'The system begins with "nothing"; the mystic always ends with "nothing".'[105]

Negative theology lays great stress on the hiddenness and incomprehensibility of God and may be found in a diverse collection of theologies. Beginning in the Patristic period it is possible to cite figures such as Clement of Alexandria and the Cappadocian Fathers, moving on to include Dionysius the Areopagite and then Meister Eckhart in the Middle Ages. They cannot be said to constitute a self-conscious 'school' of negative theology as they were part of very different traditions and range across several centuries. Instead they may be seen to share a few common characteristics. It is not difficult to see similarities between some of these and Climacus. Clement states that 'God is invisible and beyond expression by words'.[106] From the Eastern tradition, Basil the Great asserts that 'knowledge of the divine essence involves perception of His incomprehensibility, and the object of our worship is not that of which we comprehend the essence, but of which we comprehend that the essence exists'.[107] His brother, Gregory of Nyssa states that, 'the simplicity of the True Faith assumes God to be that which He is, viz., incapable of being grasped by any term, or any idea, or any other device of our apprehension, remaining beyond the reach not only of the human but also of the angelic and of all supramundane intelligence, unthinkable, unutterable, above all expression in words.'[108]

However, could it be that the similarity is at best merely superficial? Let us consider the following statement made by Climacus in *Fragments*: 'the paradoxical passion of the understanding is, then, continually colliding with this unknown, which certainly does exist but is also unknown and to that extent does not exist.'[109] It would seem from this and the general tenor of his stance that his 'unknown' is more the result of agnosticism than it is a description of God's essential nature. Climacus' 'god' is but an impersonal concept, a term he has coined to designate an unknown facet of existence. Yet the above representatives of negative theology all claimed that God is knowable, albeit to the limited extent that He chooses to reveal something of himself to us - through the Incarnation, the Bible, the traditions of the Church and so

---

105 Ibid., 2797, X2 A 340 *n.d.*, 1850.

106 Clement of Alexandria, 'The Stromata, or Miscellanies', in *Ante-Nicene Fathers*, 2nd series, vol. II (Peabody: Hendrickson, 1995), p. 463.

107 Basil the Great, 'Letters and Selected Documents', in *Nicene and Post-Nicene Fathers*, 2nd series, vol. VIII (Peabody: Hendrickson, 1995), p. 275.

108 Gregory of Nyssa, 'Against Eunominus', in *Nicene and Post-Nicene Fathers*, 2nd series, vol. VIII (Peabody: Hendrickson, 1995), p. 99.

109 *Fragments*, p. 44.

on. It is therefore God's essential nature, the extent of his intrinsic 'Godness' as it were, which eludes us, and is hence unknown.

Clearly Climacus' use of the term is not the same as found in negative theology, so we must look elsewhere for a correct understanding of its use. Evidence for this claim can be found in a journal entry of 1847 where Kierkegaard states that, 'in paganism God was regarded as the unknown. More recently it has been assumed presumptuously that to know God is a trifle.'[110] There is a clear contrast being made between the claims of rationalist and Idealist philosophy with those of pagan antiquity. Through his aesthetic lifeview Climacus attempts to maintain a speculative distance from the theological topics of his discussion, he is not a believer nor does he seriously pretend to be one. Climacus may therefore be understood to represent the 'pagan' viewpoint just described, yet I have been careful to show that such a view is not shared by Kierkegaard who remains within Christian orthodoxy. With regard to 'the unknown' it is interesting to observe that the same use of terms can be found in Martensen's *Christian Dogmatics* when he states that 'the God of theism is known amongst heathens merely as "the unknown God".'[111] This is a direct reference to Paul's debate in front of the Areopagus in Athens as described in Acts 17:23. Calling attention to one of their altars bearing the inscription 'To an unknown god', Paul begins his address by saying 'what therefore you worship as unknown, this I proclaim to you'. As Martensen was not only one of the most prominent Danish theologians of Kierkegaard's time, but also, and more importantly, his erstwhile tutor during his university studies, it is more than likely that there is a direct link between them on this point.

We can also find descriptions of God as the unknown in Luther's writings. Luther takes the concept of the unknown God in a different direction from that of negative theology. In *The Bondage of the Will* he writes: 'To the extent, therefore, that God hides Himself and wills to be unknown to us, it is no business of ours,' and 'God must therefore be left to himself in his own majesty, for in this regard we have nothing to do with him, nor has he willed that we should have anything to do with him. But we have something to do with him insofar as he is clothed and set forth in his Word, through which he offers himself to us.'[112] The emphasis is on the will of God in some way remaining hidden from us, being therefore unknown mainly as a result of his choice to conceal himself, rather than due to the limitations and finitude of human reason itself. Luther makes an important distinction between God as preached

---

[110] *Journals and Papers*, 1351, VIII 1 A 30 *n.d.*, 1847.

[111] Martensen, *Christian Dogmatics*, p. 85.

[112] Luther, 'The Bondage of the Will', in *Career of the Reformer, Luther's Works*, vol. 33 (Philadelphia: Fortress Press, 1972), p. 139.

(the Word of God) and God hidden (God himself). We cannot, indeed we must not, pry into the secrets of the Divine will, and so Luther carefully advises all who follow to occupy themselves with the revelation of God Incarnate in Jesus.[113] As I have already argued, by far the greater part of Kierkegaard's theology is highly Christocentric and Kierkegaard owes a great debt to Luther's theology of the cross. It would therefore be safe to claim that Kierkegaard was strongly influenced by the Lutheran tradition on this point and that the similarities with negative theology are noteworthy, but incidental. However, they do help to show that his theology may be placed in a broader context than allowed by some of his critics. For both Luther and Kierkegaard the process of doing theology was undergirded and held together by a specific conception of faith. Both argued that, without such faith, theology becomes an impossible undertaking. It is my intention in the next and final chapter to examine this claim and explain the details of Kierkegaard's doctrine of faith.

---

[113] Ibid., pp. 140; 145-7.

Chapter Six

Kierkegaard's Doctrine of Faith and Rationality

This final chapter considers certain aspects of Kierkegaard's doctrine of faith. This important topic has been left till now as it is the culminating point of his theological reflections, although as we have already seen, Kierkegaard's understanding of faith is to a certain degree implicit within the other themes discussed in the previous chapters. It is important to offer some more specific treatment of it at this point so that it may be seen how, just like his doctrine of God and criticisms of natural theology, Kierkegaard develops his doctrine of faith from his Christology. Through a careful consideration of this subject it is hoped that the argument presented in this chapter will serve to counter the hostile charges of fideism that are made against him. For, just as his Christology has been the cause of many misunderstandings, so has Kierkegaard's doctrine of faith met with a variety of misinterpretations by opponents and supporters alike.

I will begin with an examination of the relationship between faith and reason. Starting with a comparison of some similar ideas from Luther, Hamann and Pascal, it is argued that, contrary to the frequent claims of his radical unconventionality, Kierkegaard may instead be understood to stand within a valid and credible theological tradition. Second, I show how Kierkegaard went counter to post-Kantian Idealism in his conception of the reason *per se*, as contradistinguished from the understanding, and of its relation to faith. The third and final section considers certain specific aspects of Kierkegaard's doctrine of faith in detail. This is done by focusing on three specific areas, discussing the various relationships between faith and knowledge, then faith and the will, before concluding with an examination of his famous statement from the *Postscript* that 'truth is subjectivity'.

1. Faith and Reason

The influence of classical Lutheranism becomes very much apparent in Kierkegaard's treatment of faith and reason. This claim is of course no real surprise to us when we remember that, as I attempted to prove in chapter four, Kierkegaard did actually derive many of his most important theological insights from Luther's theology of the cross. Although he claimed not to have read much by Luther before writing *Fragments*[1] it can be seen that there is certainly a level of influence within Kierkegaard's output during the early 1840s. This influence becomes more apparent in the *Journals* and the authorship from the late 1840s. Therefore I wish to begin this chapter by outlining some of Luther's thoughts on the subject faith and reason.

However, Luther was not the sole influence upon Kierkegaard's theological development. In view of this I will discuss two other figures in the Christian tradition who also deserve to be mentioned in this context. First, Johann Hamann, a contemporary of Kant whom Kierkegaard very much admired for his critique of Enlightenment Rationalism from the perspective of the Lutheran faith. Next the French thinker Blaise Pascal will be mentioned for similar reasons, although his critique was delivered against rationalist elements within Roman Catholicism. I will then show how ideas from all three figures served to influence Kierkegaard's own thoughts on faith and reason. The term 'fideist' is so often used with reference to all four, assuming a negative verdict on their achievements. However, my aim is to deliver a more positive evaluation and thereby illustrate how this so-called 'fideism' is in fact a valid and realistic approach to the problem of religious knowledge.

Luther on Faith and Reason

From the beginning Luther is careful to distinguish between those areas in which the unaided human reason is valid, as opposed to those in which it is not. He does not question the fact that in secular matters, or the 'Kingdom of Earth' (*regnum mundi*), the reason is an important if not vital instrument in regulating our lives. It is personified as 'the inventress and mistress of all the arts, of medicine and law, of whatever wisdom, power, virtue and glory men possess in this life'.[2] However, although reason is regarded as being God-given, it is by no means infallible. So despite its being taken to be the highest authority in secular matters, it is certainly not an autonomous faculty.

---

[1] *Journals and Papers*, 2453, VIII A 465 *n.d.*, 1847.

[2] Brian Gerrish, *Grace and Reason, A Study in the Theology of Luther* (Oxford: Clarendon Press, 1962), p. 17.

It is emphasized that the right use of reason is an essential component in theology, but only when operating in conjunction with the testimony of Scripture and the conscience.[3] So, clearly, Luther is not content to allow human reason to operate entirely on its own grounds. God-given it may be, but it does share the fallen nature of its human recipient and, like the conscience, it too is bound by the limitations of a sinful will. If Luther sounds vitriolic in his criticisms of reason as being blind, or even on the occasions when he calls it 'the Devil's whore', it is because reason, when dominated by the fallen will, negates all claims to neutrality or objectivity and thereby limits itself to operating within the narrow confines of a sinful view of existence.[4] Because of this it fails to comprehend the nature of its own sin and that of others. In this sense it is merely of the 'flesh'. However, this is not always to be understood as negatively as might be suggested. When Luther talks of the limitations of the 'works of natural reason' he implies 'what a man can do without grace, solely by means of his native capacities'.[5] Thus, of itself, reason or any other natural human ability cannot bring us any closer to God than we already are and we stand in need of God's gift of grace.

There is a fundamental dualism in Luther's thought here between the 'Kingdom of Earth' and the spiritual 'Kingdom of Christ' (*regnum Christi*). The former is also referred to by him as the 'Kingdom of Reason' (*regnum rationis*). In the spiritual realm the unaided reason is quite impotent, and God's gift of faith is required to transform reason in order to allow it some legitimacy in this sphere. Luther does not claim that reason becomes perfected in this process but that it becomes more aware of its limitations and fallenness. As Gustav Aulén explains,

> Luther speaks of the Christian as *simul iustus et peccator*, the meaning is not that he is at once and at the same sense sinless and sinful. It is that two different principles are present together in him, so that he can be regarded from two aspects: on the one hand, he is a child of God, alive unto God, justified; on the other, he is not worthy of this Divine vocation. And the more deeply he recognizes his Divine vocation, the more he becomes conscious of his own sin: as Luther again says, *Quo quique magis pious est, eo plus sentit illam pugnam*.[6]

In view of this it is important that we understand the different conceptions of reason implied. Gerrish detects within Luther's thoughts on reason the following threefold distinction: first, the 'natural reason',

---

[3] Bernard Lohse, *Martin Luther, An Introduction to His Life and Work* (Edinburgh: T&T Clark, 1987), p. 161.
[4] Ibid., p. 159.
[5] Gerrish, *Grace and Reason*, p. 70.
[6] Gustav Aulén, *Christus Victor* (London: SPCK, 1970), p. 155n3.

God's gift appropriate for discernment in secular matters. Second, the 'arrogant reason' which attempts to trespass onto spiritual affairs for which it is neither equipped nor properly orientated, this is what is sometimes referred to as the 'Devil's whore'. Finally, there is the 'regenerate reason' subject to the Word of God and which is described as the handmaid of faith. This latter concept refers to reason in its broadest definition, encompassing human rationality as a whole.[7] Open to the work of the Holy Spirit this becomes a 'new reason' (*nova ratio*).[8] It is not perfected by this process, but its perspective becomes altered and corrected. This reason then, is not taken as a purely human faculty but is instead defined according to its object 'the wisdom of the Cross of Christ, that is, faith'.[9] Without such orientation reason remains within an inferior state, unable to penetrate beyond the temporal sphere and so recognize God or his works as they really are. From this latter standpoint Luther contends that God remains unknown and unreachable.

Hamann and the 'Counter Enlightenment'

Where Luther had sought to correct the errors of late medieval Catholicism, Hamann sought to refute the excesses of the Enlightenment's confidence in the powers of reason. He was part of a German 'Counter-Enlightenment' against the *Aufklärung* that arose particularly in East Prussia in the eighteenth century, an anti- rationalist in the cause of a pietistic Lutheran faith.[10] It is quite ironic that in order to do this he employed methods inspired directly by the philosophical scepticism of David Hume. Yet Hamann was to do so in staunch defence of the very kind of Christian faith Hume had wished to refute. For instance, consider the following passage from his *An Enquiry Concerning Human Understanding*, where Hume puts it that:

> The Christian Religion not only was at first attended with miracles, but even at this day cannot be believed by any reasonable person without one. Mere reason is insufficient to convince us of its veracity: And whoever is moved by Faith to assent to it, is conscious of a continued miracle in his own person, which subverts all the principles of his understanding, and

[7] Gerrish, *Grace and Reason*, p. 26.

[8] Ibid., p. 72.

[9] Gerhard Ebeling, *Luther: An Introduction to His Thought* (London: Collins, 1970), p. 87.

[10] Isaiah Berlin, *Against the Current: Essays in the History of Ideas* (Oxford: OUP, 1981), pp. 6, 162.

> gives him a determination to believe what is most contrary to custom and experience.[11]

This was meant as a rather subtle ironic rejection of Christian faith on the grounds of its alleged irrationality. Referring to this quote Hamann argues that Hume's statement proves that 'one can preach the truth in jest and without knowing it or desiring to do so'.[12] On the same matter Hamann also quotes the following from Luther: 'God has set these things in a place which all your oratory will never find, nor your philosophy, nor your politics; it is called Faith, containing all things which we can neither see nor grasp. To seek to make them visible, evident, and within our reach, as you do, is to reap heartache and lamentation.'[13] What had for Hume made Christianity implausible, in Hamann's eyes served to give it greater strength and credibility. Hamann therefore turned Hume's critique on its head. Both figures rejected orthodox rationalist apologetics, arguing that the allegedly certain foundations of *a priori* reason were in fact uncertain and reason was therefore inadequate to the task. Hume then used this to argue against religious belief. Hamann argued that a better foundation lay elsewhere than the claims of speculative and theoretical philosophies. Isaiah Berlin offers the following description of Hamann's philosophical stance:

> He was by temperament not merely indifferent, but deeply opposed, to those who seek to find some intelligible order in the universe, capable of being reduced to, and communicated by means of, a theoretical system. He belonged to those thinkers ... whose hatred of tidy, rational schemes leads them to look for the exceptional and the irregular, if only because these serve to undermine reliance on general laws, and to confute those who suppose that they can catch and order the teeming variety of reality within their artificial constructions. Monist, dualist, pluralist systems were, for him, equally delusive chimeras, efforts to confine the unconfinable, contain the wildly conflicting, unpredictable, often chaotic, data of direct experience, and reduce them to regularities and symmetries by means of logical or metaphysical links - he describes them as walls of sand built to hold back the waves of an ocean.[14]

Reason might be needed to systematize facts and figures within logic, the natural sciences and the general realm of day to day banality, but the depth of reality eludes it. Neither rationalism nor empiricism had the

---

[11] David Hume, *An Enquiry Concerning Human Understanding and A letter from a Gentleman to his Friend in Edinburgh* (Indianapolis: Hackett Publishing, 1977), p. 90.
[12] J.G. Hamann, in Ronald Gregor Smith, *J.G. Hamann 1730-1788: A Study in Christian Existence, with Selections from his Writings* (London: Collins, 1960), p. 241.
[13] Luther, in E.W. Zeeden, *The Legacy of Luther* (London: Hollis & Carter, 1957), p. 191.
[14] Berlin, *Against the Current*, p. 166.

ability to furnish anything more than a one-sided description of part of the picture. A true philosopher would try to explain, but not rationalize, life in all its contradictions, after all says Hamann 'God is a poet, not a mathematician'.[15]

To Hamann the *Aufklärung*, like its counterparts in Britain and France, had questioned everything save itself. Its self-glorified 'objective' reason was the enemy to true faith, denying the uniqueness of the individual in his or her particular situation. He questioned its authority and opened up the way for a rebirth of things the *Aufklärung* despised: 'the non-rational powers of feeling and longing, of the unknown, of tradition and the mystery of organic growth.'[16] He went so far as to claim that the truths of the Christian faith do, and should, appear but folly to anybody who approaches them from a rationalist standpoint. Yet this is no reason to deny their validity, nor charge them with irrationality, rather it must be accepted that reason cannot pass judgement on what is beyond its scope. Anticipating Kierkegaard's critique by nearly one hundred years, Hamann declared:

> Reason is inclined to serve an unknown God, but is infinitely remote from knowing him. It does not wish to know him - and what is even more astonishing, when it does know him it ceases to serve him. This is why God discloses so late and so slowly, for he knows that the knowledge of him is a stumbling-block and an offense to man, that he is foolishness and a thorn in the flesh to him as soon as he wishes to reveal himself and make himself known to him. When Jesus said that he was the Son of God, thus disclosing the most comforting, important and new truth, the Jews lifted stones, rent their garments, and condemned him as a malefactor. The Athenians were devoutly ready to fall down before an unknown God; but immediately this unknown God was disclosed to them, they cared no more: they mocked and thought they were, not something new, but matters of indifference, not worth investigating and knowing in their context, or receiving fresh insight about.[17]

Instead of reason, Hamann saw faith (*Glaube*) as forming the true basis of our knowledge of God. It is possible for all people to experience God directly, for just as all knowledge came directly from the senses, so God communicates through the Bible, the process of history and nature itself if only we would listen.[18] True religion is the direct experience of God's presence as recognized by faith. Ultimately this is Christocentric,

[15] Ibid., p. 168.
[16] Zeeden, *The Legacy of Luther*, p. 194.
[17] Hamann, in Smith, *J.G. Hamann 1730-1788: A Study in Christian Existence, with Selections from his Writings*, p. 137.
[18] Berlin, *Against the Current*, pp. 166f.

contained in 'the primal message of the Word become flesh'.[19] Hamann saw little or no difference between faith, belief and revelation, deriving the core of his definition of faith from Hume: 'I studied Hume even before I wrote my *Socratic Memoirs* and this is the source to which I owe my doctrine of faith ... Our own existence and the existence of all things outside us must be believed and cannot be demonstrated in any other fashion.'[20] According to Hume, belief 'is an operation of the soul, when we are so situated, as unavoidable as to feel the passion of love, when we receive benefits; or hatred, when we meet with injuries. All these operations are a species of natural instincts, which no reasoning or process of the thought and understanding is able, either to produce, or to prevent.'[21] Faith is thereby equated with a direct experience of reality, including experience of God, the truth of which is grounded not in philosophical argument but in instinct. In the *Socratic Memorabilia* Hamann states that,

> One can believe the proof of a proposition without approving the proposition. The reasons of a Hume may be ever so well grounded, and the refutation of them just borrowed propositions and doubts; so faith wins and loses just as much with the most adept babbler and the most honorable and objective pleader. Faith is not a work of reason and therefore cannot succumb to an attack by reason; because believing happens as little by means of reasons as tasting and seeing.[22]

Similar thoughts are contained in a letter Hamann wrote in 1787: 'Just as all kinds of unreason presuppose the existence of reason and its misuse, so must all religions bear a relation to the faith in a single, independent and living truth, which, like our existence, must be older than our reason, and hence cannot be known from the genesis of reason but by a direct revelation of the truth.'[23]

Pascal and the Submission of Reason

> One must know when it is right to doubt, to affirm, to submit. Anyone who does otherwise does not understand the force of reason. Some men run counter to these three principles, either affirming that everything can be proved, because they know nothing about proof, or doubting everything, because they do not know when to submit, or always submitting, because

[19] Hamann, in Smith, *J.G. Hamann 1730-1788: A Study in Christian Existence, with Selections from his Writings*, p. 259.
[20] Berlin, *Against the Current*, p. 171.
[21] Hume, *An Enquiry Concerning Human Understanding*, p. 30.
[22] Hamann, in Smith, *J.G. Hamann 1730-1788: A Study in Christian Existence, with Selections from his Writings*, p. 182.
[23] Ibid., p. 258.

> they do not know when judgement is called for. Sceptic, mathematician, Christian; doubt, affirmation, submission.[24]

Pascal's *Pensées* might not be within the Lutheran tradition, but the critique of reason presented within them bears a striking resemblance to those made by Luther and Hamann. Writing in the period between those two thinkers, Pascal is like them in that he does not reject reason, but instead offers a qualification of its scope and abilities.[25] Just as Hamann's 'anti-rationalism' is directed against the rationalist philosophy of the *Aufklärung* on behalf of Lutheran pietism, so Pascal's 'anti-rationalism' upholds Catholicism against the rationalism inspired by Cartesian philosophy.

In the *Pensées* he claims that there are 'two excesses: to exclude reason, to admit nothing but reason'.[26] Pascal felt himself to be confronted with two erroneous viewpoints based upon these excesses: rationalism and superstition. Both extremes had their consequences: 'If we submit everything to reason our religion will be left with nothing mysterious or supernatural. If we offend the principles of reason our religion will be absurd and ridiculous.'[27] It is clear from this that he was adamant in rejecting any moves towards irrationalism. But on the other hand, a complete reliance on the powers of human reason alone in theological matters, without any openness to revelation, was little better. Ultimately such an allegedly 'natural' theology could only lead to scepticism.[28] Because of this he argued that 'reason's last step is the recognition that there are an infinite number of things which are beyond it. It is merely feeble if it does not go as far as to realize that. If natural things are beyond it, what are we to say about supernatural things?'[29] Pascal therefore concludes: 'Submission *and* use of reason; that is what makes true Christianity.'[30]

It could be argued that this amounts to nothing but a cowardly surrender of reason's powers in the face of a difficult conflict. However, this was not what Pascal had in mind - he did not lack intellectual integrity and he was by deserved reputation one of the most eminent scientists of his generation.[31] Without reason where would his scientific

---

[24] Blaise Pascal, *Pensées* (London: Penguin, 1966), p. 83.
[25] Cf. James Byrne, *Glory, Jest and Riddle: Religious Thought in the Enlightenment* (London: SCM Press, 1996), p. 82.
[26] Pascal, *Pensées*, p. 85.
[27] Ibid., p. 83.
[28] Ernst Cassirer, *The Philosophy of the Enlightenment* (Princeton: Princeton University Press, 1972), p. 146.
[29] Pascal, *Pensées*, p. 85.
[30] Ibid., p. 83, italics mine.
[31] Cf. Peter Gay, *The Enlightenment: An Interpretation. The Rise of Modern Paganism* (New York: W.W. Norton & Co., 1966), p. 314.

theories find a basis? In common with most seventeenth century intellectuals he held mathematical, geometrical reasoning to be supreme in scientific enquiry, yet he differed from them in his belief that in theological matters it fell short of the mark. When 'reason' (*la raison*) is mentioned in this context, it is not reason in its widest sense, that being the entire human capacity for rational thought and discourse. Instead *la raison* denotes the 'presumptive use of a priori and metaphysical reasoning'.[32] In theological matters he was far more eager to advocate the use of 'the heart' (*la coeur*), including within this broad category instinct, will, feeling and intuition.[33] Here his was not a search for mathematical certainty but one in which the whole person is grasped existentially, hence his famous statement: 'The heart has its reasons of which reason knows nothing'; and also, 'It is the heart which perceives God and not the reason. That is what faith is: God perceive by the heart, not by reason.'[34] This leads him to state that 'faith certainly tells us what the senses do not, but not the contrary of what they see; it is above, not against them'.[35] Finally, like Luther in particular, Pascal is unavowedly Christocentric in his dealing with the problem of religious knowledge: 'Not only do we only know God through Jesus Christ, but we only know ourselves through Jesus Christ; we only know life and death through Jesus Christ. Apart from Jesus Christ we cannot know the meaning of our life or death, of God or ourselves.'[36]

Kierkegaard's 'Anti-Rationalism'

Many commentators have been swift to discern some influence from the above-mentioned figures in Kierkegaard's writings. This applies especially to those texts that are attributed to Climacus. In the case of Luther and Hamann, evidence may be taken straight from the text of *Fragments* where each is briefly quoted in relation to 'the paradox'.[37] I will now examine some elements of the discussion of faith and reason in *Fragments* in which these quotations occur, with the purpose of

---

[32] F. Coleman, *Neither Angel Nor Beast, The Life and Work of Blaise Pascal* (London: Routledge & Kegan Paul, 1986), pp. 4-5.
[33] Ibid.
[34] Pascal, *Pensées*, p. 154.
[35] Ibid., p. 85.
[36] Ibid., p. 148.
[37] *Fragments*, pp. 52f. On the early influence of Hamann on Kierkegaard see Lowrie, *A Short Life of Kierkegaard*, pp. 108f. Cf. also Gouwens, *Kierkegaard as Religious Thinker*, pp. 46f. It is interesting to note that Gouwens seems far more hesitant than Lowrie in his discussion of Hamann's influence on Kierkegaard's philosophical development. Added to this, for some reason Gouwens classes Hamann's influence, alongside that of Lessing, as 'philosophical', as opposed to Luther and Pascal whom he discusses under the heading of 'Christian theologians and traditions'.

illustrating the extent of their influence. Material will, as usual, also be taken from Kierkegaard's *Journals* and some later writings where the influence of these figures becomes more pronounced. In doing this, I will offer an interpretation of the text in line with the views of Luther, etc., as outlined above, for which the term 'anti-rationalist' may be deemed more accurate than irrationalist. Through this I wish to claim that for Kierkegaard, the statement that the Christian revelation is truly a 'paradox', is one made by those outside of faith not by those who are transformed by it.

As explained previously, Kierkegaard holds the Incarnation to be the decisive Christian revelation. In Climacus' terminology this is referred to 'the moment in time'.

> Let us recapitulate. If we do not assume the moment, then we go back to Socrates, and it was precisely from him that we wanted to take leave in order to discover something. If the moment is posited, the paradox is there, for in its most abbreviated form the paradox can be called the moment. Through the moment, the learner becomes untruth; the person who knew himself becomes confused about himself and instead of self-knowledge he acquires the consciousness of sin etc., for just as soon as we assume the moment, everything goes by itself.[38]

This divine revelation calls into question any previously held notions of self-certainty and human autonomy, and so its recipient now stands in awe and confusion at the new situation. That humanity is fallen and sinful might not come as too great a shock to the worldly wise, but that God in Christ now wants 'to annul this absolute difference'[39] is an altogether different matter which constitutes a real stumbling block.

This point is vividly illustrated by Anti-Climacus through his tale of the day-labourer whom a mighty emperor chose to be his son-in-law. Previously this labourer had no idea that the emperor even knew he existed. The chance of catching the merest glimpse of the great emperor would have been something to relate in pride to his descendants, but to be welcomed into the imperial family surpasses even his wildest dreams. Not able to believe his good fortune, nor find seemingly logical reasons for it, the labourer finally exclaims, 'Such a thing is too high for me, I cannot grasp it; to be perfectly blunt, to me it is a piece of folly.'[40] Relating this to the Incarnation, Anti-Climacus explains the nature of the perceived paradox further. It revolves around the fact that, by virtue of God's initiative in and through the

---

[38] Ibid., p. 51.
[39] Ibid., p. 47.
[40] *The Sickness Unto Death*, p. 85.

Incarnation, each person may enjoy a personal relationship with Him on an individual basis.

> Therefore, this human being exists before God, may speak with God any time he wants to, assured of being heard by him - in short, this person is invited to live on the most intimate terms with God! Furthermore, for this person's sake, also for this very person's sake, God comes to the world, allows himself to be born, to suffer, to die, and this suffering God - he almost implores and beseeches this person to accept the help that is offered to him! Truly if there is anything to lose one's mind over, this is it! Everyone lacking the humble courage to dare to believe this is offended. But why is he offended? Because it is too high for him, because his mind cannot grasp it, because he cannot attain bold confidence in the face of it and therefore must get rid of it, pass it off as a bagatelle, nonsense, and folly, for it seems as if it would choke him.[41]

It must be remembered that Climacus, unlike Anti-Climacus, is a caricature of a non-Christian attitude. He never claims to have faith (the 'passion', or 'happy passion' in his vocabulary) and so appears to stand outside its effects. Is it therefore surprising to hear him ask,

> But is a paradox such as this conceivable? ... The understanding certainly cannot think it, cannot hit upon it as its own, and if it is proclaimed, the understanding cannot understand it and merely detects that this will be its downfall. To that extent the understanding has strong objections to it; and yet, on the other hand, in its paradoxical passion the understanding does indeed will its own downfall. But the paradox too wills the downfall of the understanding, and thus the two have a mutual understanding, but this understanding is present only in the moment of passion.[42]

So, the learner cannot understand the situation, but at the same time he yet wants to. He is thereby put in the predicament of, either, accepting what has been revealed even though it seems to conflict with all his expectations; or, rejecting it on the grounds of its conflicting with what he previously understood to be possible. Either 'the paradox', or the 'understanding', but not both. As Kierkegaard put it in his *Journals*, 'When a person first begins to reflect upon Christianity, it undoubtedly is at first a cause of offense before he enters into it; yes, he may have wished that it had never come into the world, or at least that the question had never arisen in his consciousness.'[43] This statement accords with Hamann's view that the Christian faith appears as folly to those outside, especially if they chose to judge it entirely according to

---

[41] Ibid., pp. 85-6.
[42] *Fragments*, p. 47.
[43] *Journals and Papers*, 1710, II A 596 *n.d.*, 1837.

reason alone.[44] It is also possible to discern a parallel with Luther's claim that reason is blind when asserting its own authority over and against that of the Christian revelation. Reason in this context is not an impartial judge but is biased towards its own interests.[45] Because of this it is unwilling to allow any apparent surrender of its authority even though it may feel compelled to do so. We can therefore understand Climacus' earlier statement that, 'the understanding has strong objections to it; and yet, on the other hand, in its paradoxical passion the understanding does will its own downfall.'[46] Only in faith does reason wish to be subordinate to another. Climacus likens this relationship to one of 'erotic love', in that self love is surrendered in selfless commitment to another with all the risk and vulnerability that that may bring.[47] Personal goals and desires are thereafter to be passed over as priority is given to the needs and wishes of another.[48]

Without faith, reason rejects Christianity, not only as a paradox, but as an 'offense'. Yet this is in reality an inversion of the actual situation, for judgements made in this manner are themselves the real offense; 'for offense is the erroneous accounting, is the conclusion of untruth ... offense is in its essence a misunderstanding of the moment.'[49] So it is not that Christianity is foolishness, but that in its prior state, reason is judged and found to be wrong in its assumptions.

> The expression of offense is that the moment is foolishness, the paradox is foolishness - which is the paradox's claim that the understanding is the absurd but which now resounds as an echo from the offense ... but since the paradox has made the understanding the absurd, what the understanding regards as very important is no distinguishing mark.[50]

Reason tries to transcend its own limits, but bound by these limitations and clouded by sin it cannot fulfil its self-set aim. Kierkegaard himself was in sharp disagreement with any attempts to prove otherwise. His more specific target, usually Hegelian philosophy, was sometimes loosely referred to simply as 'German philosophy' in contradistinction to Kierkegaard's 'Danish Philosophy':

> Danish philosophy ... will be different from German philosophy in that it definitely will not begin with nothing or without any presuppositions whatever or explain everything by mediating, because, on the contrary, it

[44] Zeeden, *The Legacy of Luther*, p. 198.
[45] Lohse, *Martin Luther, An Introduction to His Life and Work*, p. 159.
[46] *Fragments*, p. 47.
[47] Ibid., p. 48.
[48] Cf. Evans, *Passionate Reason*, p. 93.
[49] *Fragments*, p. 51.
[50] Ibid., p. 52.

> begins with the proposition that there are many things between heaven and earth which no philosophy has explained. By being incorporated in philosophy, this proposition will provide the necessary corrective and will also cast a humorous-edifying warmth over the whole.[51]

This is reminiscent of Pascal's statement that, 'Reason's last step is the recognition that there are an infinite number of things which are beyond it.'[52] It is also possible to hear echoes of Luther's claims that unaided reason is unable to operate within the *regnum Christi* but must remain in the *regnum mundi*, 'In this God is seeking only that man may have the humility to bring his reason into captivity and be subject to divine truth.'[53] The problem lies both with the inadequacies of reason, and with the nature of the *regnum Christi*; as the latter is qualitatively different from the *regnum mundi* and requires faith before reason. With this in mind Climacus makes the following indirect reference to Luther: 'When the understanding cannot get the paradox into its head, this did not have its origin in the understanding but in the paradox, which was paradoxical enough to have the effrontery to call the understanding a clod and a dunce.'[54] Although Luther did not use the exact words 'a clod and a dunce', it would seem from what has been said so far that his theology does at times express this view.[55]

Hamann is quoted by Climacus in the same passage: 'Once again, it is not the understanding that discovers it [i.e. the offense], but the understanding merely parrots the paradox, however strange that may seem, for the paradox itself says: Comedies and novels and lies must be probable, but how could I be probable?'[56] The last sentence is taken from Hamann: 'Is it not an old notion which you often heard from me: Incredible but true? Lies and romances must be probable, hypotheses and fables; but not the truth and fundamental doctrine of our faith.'[57] So, what might seem improbable when viewed from the standpoint of 'reason' is actually proclaimed to be true and believable. Climacus quotes him again, 'you think that it is an objection, but the truth in the mouth of a hypocrite is dearer to me than to hear it from an angel and

---

[51] *Journals and Papers*, 3299, V A 46 *n.d.*, 1844.

[52] Pascal, *Pensées*, p. 85. Cf. *Journals and Papers*, X 3 A 609 *n.d.*, 1850 where Kierkegaard approvingly refers to this passage in Pascal and supports Pascal's belief that we can only know God when we allow ourselves to be transformed by him in faith.

[53] Luther, in Gerrish, *Grace and Reason*, p. 19. It is also possible to see parallels with Hamann's thoughts here, although Kierkegaard argues that the relationship is not as obvious as is at first apparent. Cf. *Journals and Papers*, 1559, X 2 A 225 *n.d.*, 1849.

[54] *Fragments*, p. 53

[55] Cf. Westphal, *Kierkegaard's Critique of Reason and Society*, p. 107; *Fragments*, 1962, pp. 225f.

[56] *Fragments*, p. 52.

[57] *Fragments*, 1962, p. 225.

an apostle.'[58] This backs up his position that the offended person can only see a paradox, but this is no real objection and is only to be expected when they are faced with the real Gospel. Climacus himself is unable to go further than this position, but now compare what has been said with some of Kierkegaard's own words from his *Journals*,

> For every third party who is not a believer the content of faith is the absurd [i.e. the paradox], and that in order to become a believer everyone must be alone with the absurd ... What is lacking here is the tension of the dialectical. To understand that for reason it is the absurd, to talk about it in this way quite calmly to a third party, granting that it is the absurd, maintaining the stress that the other must regard it as the absurd - and then still believe it. At the same time it naturally follows that for the believer it is not the absurd ... This is the tension, the tension in the life of faith, in which one is to keep oneself. But everywhere the tendency is to present faith directly. An attempt in this direction is science or scholarship, which wants to comprehend faith.[59]

According to this and what I have explained beforehand, it would seem that Kierkegaard's views on faith and reason have much in common with Pascal and Hamann,[60] and are also in continuity with those of Luther. He has not posited Christianity as being paradoxical in itself, but rather states that that is how it appears to one viewing it with human reason and without faith. However it would be unwise to leave the discussion there, as his doctrine of faith is more complex than has been shown so far. I now wish to illustrate this by discussing Kierkegaard's thought on faith and reason with reference to the Idealist philosophy of his contemporaries.

2. Reason and Understanding

So far I have discussed Kierkegaard's critique of 'reason' although most of his material, especially that from *Fragments*, seems instead to refer to the 'understanding'. On the surface this may appear to be a trivial distinction. However, the importance of whether or not to maintain the philosophical distinction between 'reason' and 'understanding' when interpreting Kierkegaard's writings has been hotly debated. In the case of the two pioneers of Kierkegaard scholarship in the English language, David Swenson and Walter Lowrie, the debate between them on this

---

[58] *Fragments*, p. 52. Cf. also *Journals and Papers*, 1542, II A 2 *n.d.*, 1837.

[59] *Journals and Papers*, 8, X2 A 592 *n.d.*, 1850.

[60] Although, with regard to Kierkegaard's relation to Hamann, it can be seen that Hamann was prepared to allow faith a far more direct access to God, where Kierkegaard emphasized the indirect nature of religious knowledge.

matter took place over many years and it has influenced translations of his works since the 1930s. I wish to examine the nature of the debate and its implications for Kierkegaard's criticisms of natural theology. This will be done by first outlining the distinction between reason and understanding as made by Kant, then as made by Hegel. After this I will provide a brief outline of the distinction made by Samuel Taylor Coleridge, whom I wish to argue does adhere to a position similar to Kierkegaard and, like Kierkegaard, he sought to preserve a more traditional Christian theology in an intellectual climate dominated by post-Kantian Idealism. Following this I will illustrate the relationship between the reason/understanding and the 'paradox' of the Christian faith in Kierkegaard's thought.

Kant on Pure Reason

The distinction between reason and understanding is introduced by Kant in the *Critique of Pure Reason*. Kant states that:

> All our knowledge begins with sense, proceeds thence to understanding [*Verstand*], and ends with reason [*Vernunft*], beyond which nothing higher can be discovered in us for elaborating the matter of intuition and subjecting it to the highest unity of thought. At this stage of our enquiry it is my duty to give an explanation of this, the highest faculty of knowledge, and I confess I find myself here in some difficulty. Of reason, as of the understanding, there is a merely formal, that is, logical use, in which it makes abstraction of all content of knowledge; but there is also a real use, inasmuch as it contains in itself the source of certain concepts and principles, which it does not borrow either from the senses or from the understanding. The former faculty has been long defined by logicians as the faculty of mediate conclusions, in contradistinction to immediate ones.[61]

The understanding then is 'the faculty of judging' or 'the faculty of rules'[62] and is based upon experience, whereas reason, or rather 'pure reason' in this context, is 'the faculty of principles'.[63] The latter is superior, being a higher faculty which unites the former's abilities and so transcends them. Therefore,

> The understanding may be a faculty for the production of unity of appearances by virtue of rules; reason is a faculty for the production of unity of the rules of the understanding under principles. Reason, therefore, never applies directly to experience, or to any sensible object; rather it applies to

---

[61] Kant, *Critique of Pure Reason*, p. 236.
[62] Ibid., pp. 79, 236.
[63] Ibid., p. 236.

> the understanding, in order to provide the multiple knowledge of the understanding with *a priori* unity by means of concepts - a unity which may be called rational unity, and which is of a nature very different from that of the unity produced by the understanding.[64]

In view of this it is apparent that Kant's philosophy depends upon the clear distinction being made between reason (*Vernunft*) and understanding (*Verstand*). If it can be claimed that Kierkegaard does follow him in making this distinction, then there are two possible interpretations of his stance regarding the paradox: either it requires the surrender of the understanding, a lesser faculty and there is no necessary threat to reason *per se* and so the charge of irrationalism may be dismissed. Or, the paradox requires the surrender of reason itself, and Kierkegaard holds the Christian revelation to be irrational yet believable because that is the case! Once this option is put forward the way is open to the by now familiar charges of irrationalism, or even that Christian truth-claims are nonsensical. Obviously my argument centres around the fact that the latter is incorrect and is the result of a profound misunderstanding of Kierkegaard's terminology. Before refuting this misunderstanding directly, it is appropriate to hear about the views he wished to refute himself - in which case, let us talk about Hegelian philosophy.

Hegel and Speculative Reason

Hegel also makes a distinction between reason (*Vernunft*) and understanding (*Verstand*), although he sometimes refers to *Vernunft* as 'positive reason' or 'speculation'.[65] The understanding is, as in Kantian thought, which Hegel adopted and then modified, inferior to reason. Yet for Hegel this is not a static relationship as the understanding constituted an early phase in the dialectical development of thought itself, with reason as the pinnacle. The understanding is analytic and abstract and fails to perceive the full nature of reality, and in his view a total reliance upon the understanding was detrimental to 'real' philosophy. Such a failing characteristic was typified by the Enlightenment which he refers to in his *Lectures on the Philosophy of Religion* as 'that vanity of understanding' and hence 'the most vehement opponent of philosophy'.[66] With the understanding thus

[64] Ibid., p. 238.
[65] Reardon, *Religion in the Age of Romanticism*, pp. 35f.
[66] Hegel, *The Christian Religion*, p. 290.

relegated to the fields of mathematical and logical enquiry, the reason was seen to be applicable to all areas of inquiry, including the religious.[67]

The concept of reason in Hegelian philosophy came to encompass what had previously been defined as faith (*Glaube*) in Hamann's terminology, that is it came to denote a direct experience of reality, including God. As faith was thus replaced by reason, the debate between faith and reason in theology became the debate between reason and understanding. This distinction appears in Hegel, but it had also been developed through the writings of Jacobi, Herder, Schelling and Schleiermacher.[68] However, in Hegel it reaches its most fully developed form as reason is posited as being capable of grasping all things. Religious truth becomes 'rational' and hence he is led to claim: 'That to which reason has access is no mystery or secret; in the Christian Religion, one knows the mystery. Mysteries exist only for the understanding and for thought based on sense experience.'[69] In this form of philosophy even the very nature of God himself is found to be accessible to reason.[70] Where understanding can see only limitations and contradictions, reason can comprehend the totality of existence, grasping its very structure and so unites all that seemed to be contradictory.[71] Elements of this view permeated through to German Romanticism and to Danish intellectuals such as Henrik Steffens (the Norwegian born pupil of Schelling) and Hans Martensen.[72] With Kierkegaard's vehement animosity towards Hegelian thought reaching fame of near mythical proportions, it would be quite unlikely to find him adopting this distinction. Therefore, if he does distinguish between reason and understanding it cannot be according to the manner here described.

Coleridge on Reason and Understanding

A different form of this distinction may be discerned in English philosophy a generation before Kierkegaard in the thought of Samuel Taylor Coleridge. Although his philosophy was in many ways a conscious development from Kant, it would be wrong to claim that Coleridge merely echoed the Kantian project without making his own

---

[67] Hans Frei, 'David Friedrich Strauss', in (eds.) Smart et al, *Nineteenth Century Religious Thought in the West* (Cambridge: CUP, 1988), p. 217.

[68] George Price, *The Narrow Pass, A Study of Kierkegaard's Concept of Man* (London: Hutchinson & Co., 1984), p. 94.

[69] Hegel, *The Christian Religion*, p. 80.

[70] Ibid., p. 91.

[71] Peter Hodgson, 'George William Freidrich Hegel', in (eds.) Smart et al, *Nineteenth Century Religious Thought in the West*, p. 85.

[72] John Elrod, *Being and Existence in Kierkegaard's Pseudonymous Works* (Princeton: Princeton University Press, 1981), pp. 12, 30-35.

significant contribution. Instead, his theology exhibits greater influence from a variety of sources that include Plato, Luther and the Cambridge Platonists, over anything derived from German Idealism.[73] His concept of reason was far more subtle, more dynamic than that allowed for in Kant's rationalist religion. In his great work on the Christian faith *Aids to Reflection*, Coleridge rejected 'Minimi-fidianism', the term he coined for the dry 'rational' theologies in circulation which had confined themselves 'to draw religion down to the Believer's intellect, instead of raising his intellect up to religion'.[74] He also dismissed 'Ultra-fidianism' or religious beliefs 'not only above but contrary to Reason, and against the evidence of our proper senses'.[75] For Coleridge, 'Faith elevates the soul not only above Sense and sensible things, but above Reason itself. As Reason corrects the errors which Sense might occasion, so supernatural Faith corrects the errors of natural Reason judging according to Sense.'[76] At times the mood of his comments on the state of Christian thought closely resembles that of Kierkegaard, 'This was the true and first apostasy - when in Council and in Synod the divine Humanities of the Gospel gave way to speculative Systems, and Religion became a Science of Shadows under the name of Theology, or at best a bare Skeleton of Truth, without life or interest, alike inac[c]essible and unintelligible to the majority of Christians.'[77]

In fact, the existence of certain parallels in the thought of Coleridge and Kierkegaard has long been noticed by scholars of English literature and intellectual history. Some have therefore described Coleridge, being the earlier of the two, as the original pioneer of existentialism instead of Kierkegaard.[78] However, it must be understood that the two are parallel, not in conscious succession. Coleridge was one of a few thinkers, who like Kierkegaard, 'belonged to that rare class of minds which are prepared to set themselves against the master-currents of their time, and to go on fighting the zeitgeist, alone if need be, with unremitting courage and determination.'[79] It is somewhat surprising that, save for some material in one recent study,[80] there is a complete lack of theological comparisons between the two in Kierkegaard scholarship.

---

[73] Claude Welch, 'Samuel Taylor Coleridge', in (eds.) Smart et al, *Nineteenth Century Religious Thought in the West*, p. 4.
[74] Samuel Taylor Coleridge, *Aids to Reflection*, in *The Collected Works of Samuel Taylor Coleridge*, vol. 9 (London: Routledge, 1993), p. 214.
[75] Ibid., p. 208.
[76] Ibid., p. 207
[77] Ibid., p. 192
[78] Basil Willey, *Samuel Taylor Coleridge* (London: Chatto and Windus, 1972), p. 257.
[79] Ibid., p. 213.
[80] Jamie Ferreira, *Transforming Vision, Imagination and Will in Kierkegaardian Faith* (Oxford: Clarendon Press, 1991), pp. 91ff.

A full discussion of the distinction between reason and understanding is found in *Aids to Reflection*. There we read that 'understanding' is 'the Faculty judging according to Sense',[81] whilst,

> On the contrary, Reason is the Power of universal and necessary Convictions, the Source and Substance of Truths above Sense ... Contemplated distinctively in reference to formal (or abstract) truth, it is the speculative Reason; but in reference to actual (or moral) truth, as the fountain of Ideas and the Light of the Conscience, we name it the practical Reason. Whenever by self-subjection to this universal Light, the Will of the Individual, the particular Will, has become a Will of Reason, the man is regenerate: and Reason is then the Spirit of the regenerated man, whereby the Person is capable of quickening inter-communion with the Divine Spirit.[82]

Reason includes not only the intellect, but also the will and the conscience. The reason-understanding distinction illustrates 'the difference between head-knowledge and heart-knowledge - the knowledge which is made up of intellectual abstractions from sense-data, and that which springs from involvement with our whole being'.[83] This existential concept of reason is not viewed as an indication of human autonomy but as a gift from God, part of the Divine Image imparted to us.[84] A neglect of the true nature and origin of reason and the subsequent usurpation of its place by the understanding had led to the failings of the previous century. The results of this process had been disastrous: 'Materialism, determinism, atheism, utilitarianism, the "godless revolution", "moral science exploded as mystic jargon", the "mysteries of religion cut and squared for the comprehension of the understanding".'[85] The general tenor of this criticism seems to put him in line with, not only those great 'anti-rationalists' Luther, Pascal and Hamann, but also Kierkegaard. The extent of this latter similarity shall now be discussed.

Kierkegaard and Faithful Reason

Turning now to Kierkegaard's writings, it remains to be seen whether a similar terminology really is to be encountered. In the 1966 edition of *Fragments*, translated by David Swenson, the Danish term *Forstand* which Kierkegaard uses (the cognate for the Kantian or Hegelian *Verstand* or understanding) is translated as reason. There are no

---

[81] Coleridge, *Aids to Reflection*, p. 215.
[82] Ibid., p. 217.
[83] Willey, *Samuel Taylor Coleridge*, p. 163.
[84] Coleridge, *Aids to Reflection*, p. 148.
[85] Basil Willey, *Nineteenth Century Studies* (Harmondsworth: Penguin, 1964), p. 37.

instances of *Fornuft* (*Vernunft*) in the Danish text.[86] It would therefore seem that the argument against the Socratic hypothesis relates to the limits of rationality itself. Swenson gives his reasons for this choice in a letter to Walter Lowrie dated September 14, 1937. First, he argues that Kierkegaard is not employing the Kantian distinction (which in his opinion is 'foreign' and 'irrelevant' to his thought), neither is he referring to the Hegelian distinction. Also, he claims that by using 'understanding' the way would be open for interpreters to claim that 'the Absolute Paradox' is not objectively a paradox in the pro*per sen*se, and that it is thereby within the sphere of some higher principle of human reason. He therefore explains,

> A paradox which merely offends my private understanding is subject to being resolved through a better understanding within the limits of what it is possible to understand as a human being; such a paradox is relatively and transitorily a paradox, a paradox for a limited and imperfect understanding, a paradox for some imperfect individual, but not a paradox for the race. Hence it is not the Absolute Paradox in Kierkegaard's sense. [So] if I use the word Understanding ... I am aware that I will evoke the suggestion that human nature contains a higher principle, the Reason, which does not need to be set aside, and for which the Absolute Paradox is not paradoxical. I am convinced that such a thought is flatly contradictory of the entire spirit, purpose and letter of Kierkegaard's work. If there is such a principle in me, then there is no Absolute Paradox, then the Teacher is not God, then the entire virile Christian terminology of the new birth, of the believer being a new creature, etc., falls down like a house of cards, and becomes a mere rhetorical exaggeration, an immature and irrelevant adornment of what is essentially the Socratic position.[87]

Finally, he puts it that *Forstand* is a concrete rather than abstract concept. Thus it may be held to refer to:

> the entire rational self-consciousness of man as man, and includes of course a sense of values. If it did not, it could have no bearing upon the apprehension of the divine. Thus the Reason ... stands for the essential and reflective common sense of mankind, in which each individual participates, though of course, with respect to his actual as opposed to his ideally potential grasp, at any one time, only imperfectly.[88]

---

[86] Cf. Andrew Burgess, '*Forstand* in the Swenson-Lowrie Correspondence and in the "Metaphysical Caprice"', in (ed.) Robert Perkins, *International Kierkegaard Commentary: Philosophical Fragments and Johannes Climacus* (Macon: Mercer University Press, 1994), p. 117.

[87] Swenson, *Something About Kierkegaard*, pp. 219-20.

[88] Ibid., p. 220.

Is this in accord with what Kierkegaard puts forward? In a journal entry in 1850 he rejects abstract concepts of reason, specifically Kant's 'pure reason': 'people have a rattle-brained, conceited notion about human reason, especially in our age, when one never thinks of a thinker, a reasoning man, but thinks of pure reason and the like, which simply does not exist, since no one, be he a professor or what he will, is pure reason. Pure reason is something fantastical.'[89]

There is however an objection to certain aspects of this interpretation. Whilst not denying that *Forstand* refers to more than the abstractions of Kant's pure reason, it does seem a little perturbing to allege, as Swenson appears to do, that the Christian revelation is paradoxical to the extent that it defies any hope of rational explanation; even if we do allow for the ironic, partly rhetorical style of the aesthetic works (which Swenson does not). It could therefore be more appropriate to use the term 'understanding' instead, as is done in the 1985 Princeton translation of *Fragments*. Yet even though there is this change of term, the basic concept beneath still remains largely the same. This is illustrated in Evans' *Passionate Reason* where he chooses to use both terms interchangeably in order to discourage interpretations defending reason's ability to comprehend the paradox of the Incarnation.[90] The majority of scholars appear to agree with the contents of this view, and at the same time reject the thesis that Kierkegaard conceives that this revelation is nonsensical. For instance Stephen Emmanuel claims 'revelation is not absurd or paradoxical in that it violates fundamental principles of logic, but in the sense that it disturbs our common sense view of ourselves and our values'.[91] This point returns us to Kierkegaard's rejection of complete human autonomy and his affirmation of our intrinsic need for God's help and revelation. When this is borne in mind it can be argued that he 'is not against reason as such but rather against the absolute claims of reason, a reason that poses itself as the supreme power, capable of explaining everything and solving all contradictions with its own dialectics. Thus the first task of faith is that of unmasking the totalising claims of reason'.[92]

Kierkegaard's polemic is directed against more than Kant's concept of the understanding, but it should not be alleged that he is advocating a leap into irrationalism. However, I must admit that I am reluctant to

[89] *Journals and Papers*, 7, X 2 A 354 *n.d.*, 1850.

[90] Evans, *Passionate Reason*, p. 188, n7.

[91] Emmanuel, *Kierkegaard and the Concept of Revelation*, p. 49.

[92] M. Nicoletti, 'Politics and Religion in Kierkegaard's Thought: Secularization and the Martyr', in George B. Connell and C. Stephen Evans (eds.), *Foundations of Kierkegaard's Vision of Community: Religion, Ethics and Politics in Kierkegaard* (Atlantic Highlands, N.J. and London: Humanities Press, 1992), p. 186.

embrace entirely the interpretations offered by Swenson and his followers. Clearly his use of *Forstand* differs from Kant's *Vorstand* as employed in *The Critique of Pure Reason.* He is not referring to abstract reasoning. But the view that revelation is paradoxical to reason because it 'disturbs our common-sense view of ourselves and our values',[93] fails to deliver the full weight of Climacus' or Kierkegaard's own arguments. Also the persistent use of the term 'reason' in translations, even in some of the most recent publications, leads to the assertion that for Kierkegaard 'faith is always non-rational'.[94] In order to prevent this frequent charge of irrationalism, even by those well disposed to Kierkegaard's thought, something further needs to be said with regard to the concepts employed.

To argue that revelation, specifically the Incarnation, is against the understanding as defined by for instance Coleridge, is not to say that it 'merely offends my private understanding'.[95] Instead, 'the Understanding then (considered exclusively as an organ of human intelligence,) is the Faculty by which we reflect and generalize.'[96] It is not a private, subjective matter but rather, this-worldly reasoning, 'the mind of the flesh',[97] or more precisely:

> the 'scientific' reasoning of the eighteenth century, of Bentham and Paley, the kind of reasoning that separates, analyses, measures, classifies, knows in terms of cause and effect, is concerned with means rather than ends. It gives accuracy, it eliminates error. Within its proper limits this is an indispensable kind of thinking - for science, for much of the routine of life, for knowledge of the finite.[98]

In his *Journals* Kierkegaard criticizes the understanding for its constant enquiring and deliberating in religion without ever reaching a valid conclusion, turning theology into 'a chaos of reflections and deliberations'.[99] The understanding's thirst for knowledge fails to take its human limitations into account and therefore takes on a task that remains forever incomplete.

Hegel, although joining these two in their criticisms of the Enlightenment and the understanding, posits reason as being able to comprehend the essence of existence itself, and on this point he differs dramatically from them. Consider these two statements, the first from

---

[93] Cf. Emmanuel, *Kierkegaard and the Concept of Revelation*, p. 49.
[94] Vardy, *Kierkegaard*, p. 56.
[95] Swenson, *Something About Kierkegaard*, p. 219.
[96] Coleridge, *Aids to Reflection*, p. 224.
[97] Willey, *Samuel Taylor Coleridge*, p. 227.
[98] Welch, 'Samuel Taylor Coleridge', in (eds.) Smart et al, *Nineteenth Century Religious Thought in the West*, p. 8.
[99] *Journals and Papers*, 3710, X2 A 624 *n.d.*, 1850.

Coleridge's *Aids to Reflection*, the second from Kierkegaard's *Journals* of 1843:

> Many things may be paradoxical, (that is contrary to the common notion) and nevertheless true: nay, paradoxical, because they are true. How should it be otherwise, as long as the imagination of the Worldling is wholly occupied by surfaces, while the Christian's thoughts are fixed on the substance, that which is and abides, and which, because it is the substance, the outward senses cannot recognize. Tertullian had good reason for his assertion, that the simplest Christian (if indeed a Christian) knows more than the most accomplished irreligious philosopher.[100]

> Faith has hopes for this life also, but, note well, by virtue of the absurd, not by virtue of human understanding; otherwise it is only common sense, not faith.[101]

There is a clear distinction being made between worldly understanding and a different God-centred reasoning. The difference is absolute and, in both cases may be equated with Luther's distinction between the regenerate reason (*nova ratio*) and unregenerate reason ('the flesh').[102] In this case it can be argued that Kierkegaard is not claiming that the paradox, or absurd, is to be conquered by any higher human reason. Instead, 'he sets out to show that both the man in the street's hovel of common sense and the speculative philosopher's palace of thought are both built in the sand.'[103] Each and every human project designed to meet God on our own terms can only fail, for God meets us on his terms through the paradox of the Incarnation. Yet he does not impart to us some higher reason that can resolve the paradox. In another journal entry Kierkegaard writes:

> Hugo de St Victore states a correct thesis (Helfferich, *Mystik*, Vol. I, p. 368): 'Faith is really not supported by the things which go beyond reason, by any reason, because reason does not comprehend what faith believes; but nevertheless there is something here by which reason becomes determined or is conditioned to honor faith which it still does not perfectly succeed in grasping.' This is what I have developed (for example, in *Concluding Unscientific Postscript*) - that not every absurdity is the absurd or the paradox. The activity of reason is to distinguish the paradox negatively - but no more.[104]

Kierkegaard puts similar words into the mouth of Climacus:

---

[100] Coleridge, *Aids to Reflection*, p. 17.
[101] *Journals and Papers*, 5, IV A 108 *n.d.*, 1843.
[102] Cf. Gerrish, *Grace and Reason*, pp. 70ff.
[103] Thompson, *Kierkegaard*, p. 171.
[104] *Journals and Papers*, 7, X A 354 *n.d.*, 1850.

> How then does the learner come to an understanding with this paradox, for we do not say that he is supposed to understand the paradox but is only to understand that this is the paradox. We have already shown how this occurs. It occurs when the understanding and the paradox happily encounter each other in the moment, when the understanding steps aside and the paradox gives itself, and the third something, the something in which this occurs (for it does not occur through the understanding, which is discharged, or through the paradox, which gives itself - consequently in something), is that happy passion to which we shall now give a name. We shall call it faith.[105]

Reason remains limited, unable to transcend the paradox and must now submit to faith. 'Christianity ... always turns the concepts of the natural man upside down and gets the opposite meaning out of them.'[106] Paradoxically, the autonomous, worldly reason has to 'die' in order to function correctly in the new life of the believer. As Stephen Dunning argues, it is at this point Kierkegaard's theology of the cross really comes to the fore:

> The obvious meaning of the cross is, of course, death. Theologically, Christ died to redeem the world from sin and thereby makes it possible for believers to 'die' to the sin of their own lives. The epistemological death is the need to know, the compulsion to understand God's revelation ... This is the crucifixion of knowledge. It is not a sacrifice of the intellect, for it presupposes the passion of thought that leads to the collision with the paradox. But it does force the intellect to choose between its own claim to sovereignty and that of God. And the result of such a dilemma is offense - or a yielding that is tantamount to death. Of course, even this death is not the final word. A final parallel emerges between the theological resurrection to a new identity and eternal life, on the one hand, and a new epistemic state of faith, a faith that is 'by virtue of the absurd'. Just as death has lost its sting (1 Cor. 15:55), so also the paradox is no longer an offense to one who believes.[107]

The issue is one of autonomy. Kierkegaard criticizes, under the broad title of *Forstand*, both faculties describable as reason and understanding. Although he does not always make it directly obvious which of the two he implies, it is possible to discern the object of his polemic according to the nature of the specific argument at the time. At times he dismisses the view that *Forstand* as an analytic or abstract faculty is capable of operating successfully in theological enquiry. This criticism refers to

---

105 *Fragments*, p. 59.

106 *Journals and Papers*, 7, X A 354 *n.d.*, 1850.

107 Stephen Dunning, 'Paradoxes in Interpretation: Kierkegaard and Gadamer', in Matustík and Westphal (eds.), *Kierkegaard in Post/Modernity* (Bloomington and Indianapolis: Indiana University Press, 1995), p. 129.

Verstand and the hollow rationalism of the previous century. He also rejects the Hegelian concept of reason, or *Vernunft*, which was claimed to be able to rationalize all contradictions. In their place Kierkegaard defends a reason that is defined by its object, the paradox. Like Luther, and Coleridge, this reason is fundamentally linked to God-given faith and all its successes are attributable to this vital link. However, although it can accept things that appear paradoxical to the secular mind, it does not follow that these now become rationalized. Instead it recognizes that some things are destined to remain beyond its reach, being above, but not against it. The standpoint of faith allows for this willing, yet careful subordination to divine authority where the rationalist or Hegelian would wish to assert his own powers of reason. However, if Kierkegaard is suggesting that, what may be called this 'faithful reason' is defined by its object, and therefore relates to the God of traditional Christianity, is it not rational that this very God who by nature defies our comprehension will operate in ways that are at times above reason? In which case, although it seems absurd to the atheist and agnostic, Kierkegaard's surrender of *Forstand* becomes 'reasonable'. To conclude, in Kierkegaard's own words from the *Gospel of Sufferings*:

> For indeed it is not required of anybody that he should be able to comprehend the working of God's love, but this is required, that one shall be able to believe, and believing to comprehend, that He is love! It is no terrible thing that thou canst not comprehend the purposes of God, of still He is indeed eternal love, but it is a terrible thing if thou canst not comprehend them because He is unfathomable subterfuge.[108]

3. Kierkegaard's Doctrine of Faith

> I believe that one of the things Christianity says is that sound doctrines are all useless. That you have to change your *life*. (Or the direction of your life.) It says that wisdom is all cold; that you can no more use it for setting your life to rights than you can forge iron when it is cold. The point is that a sound doctrine need not take hold of you; you can follow it as you would a doctor's prescription. - But here you need something to move you and turn you in a new direction. - (I.e. this is how I understand it.) Once you have turned around, you must stay turned around. Wisdom is passionless. But faith by contrast is what Kierkegaard calls a passion.[109]

Wittgenstein presents us here with a typical interpretation of Kierkegaard's doctrine of faith. We find in this interpretation a clear

[108] Søren Kierkegaard, *The Gospel of Sufferings* trans. A.S. Aldworth and W.S. Ferrie (Cambridge: James Clark, 1982), p. 70.

[109] Ludwig Wittgenstein, *Culture and Value* (Oxford: Basil Blackwell, 1980), p. 53.

stress upon the effects of faith over what it is that faith believes.[110] This, added to Kierkegaard's frequent statements that Christianity is not a doctrine,[111] lead some to claim that he places no importance on what is believed, preferring instead to focus on the strength of the faith itself and its effects on the believer.[112] I wish to challenge this and similar interpretations, and to propose an alternative. Whilst by no means undermining the importance of the strength of the believer's faith, and the transforming effects of that faith upon him, it will be shown that there is a vital propositional content to Kierkegaard's understanding of faith: if Christian faith is not based firmly on belief in the actual fact of the Incarnation, it is not Christian faith at all. On this point, like many others, we can easily form a comparison between him and Luther as both of them are concerned primarily with soteriology rather than epistemology. I have chosen to examine his doctrine of faith under three headings. First, 'Faith and Knowledge', in which the relationship between faith, belief and doctrine is discussed. Second, in 'Faith and Volition' I explain the role of the will in coming to faith and the resultant importance Kierkegaard gives to human freedom in this context. Finally, 'Faith and Subjectivity' tackles the meaning of that well-known quotation from Kierkegaard that 'truth is subjectivity'[113] and shows how this is to be related to his doctrine of faith.

Faith and Knowledge

In 1849 Kierkegaard put down in his journal that 'A dogmatic system ought not to be erected on the basis: to comprehend faith, but on the basis: to comprehend that faith cannot be comprehended'.[114] This claim is closely linked with the assertions discussed in the previous section, in Kierkegaard's own words, that 'reason's activity is to recognize the paradox negatively - precisely no more than that',[115] or

[110] This and other of Wittgenstein's comments on the nature of faith, in particular with reference to his concept of 'language games', have led some philosophers to attribute to him a position entitled 'Wittgensteinian Fideism'. D.Z. Phillips lists the general traits of this position as 'to claim that only religious believers understand religious belief, that religious belief or believers cannot be criticized, that anything called religion determines what is meaningful, and that religious belief cannot be overthrown by any personal or cultural event' (D.Z. Phillips, *Wittgenstein and Religion* (London: Macmillan, 1993), p. xii). However, not only is this a misinterpretation of Wittgenstein's thought (Phillips refers to it as 'anti-intellectualism and conservatism'. Ibid., p. 81), but it is incorrect to form too close a link with Kierkegaard and Wittgenstein's interpretation of him. (Cf. Ferreira, *Transforming Vision*, p. 130, n54.)

[111] E.g. *Concluding Unscientific Postscript*, vol. 1, p. 326.

[112] Cf. Cupitt, *The Sea of Faith*, p. 153.

[113] *Concluding Unscientific Postscript*, vol. 1, p. 189.

[114] *Journals and Papers*, 3564, X 1 A 561 *n.d.*, 1849.

[115] Ibid., 7, X 2 A 354 *n.d..*, 1850.

alternatively through Climacus, 'we do not say that he [the learner] is supposed to understand the paradox but is only to understand that this is the paradox.'[116] He stands in blatant opposition to the Hegelian claim that reason can penetrate all the mysteries of Christianity and thereby replace faith with direct, immediate knowledge. In *Practice in Christianity* we read,

> The whole of modern philosophy has done everything to delude us into thinking that faith is an immediate qualification, that it is the immediate - which in turn is linked up with having abolished the possibility of offense, having made Christianity into a teaching, having abolished the God-man and the situation of contemporaneity. What modern philosophy understands by faith is really what is called having an opinion or what in everyday language some people call 'to believe'. Christianity is made into a teaching; this teaching is then proclaimed to a person, and he believes that it is as the teaching says. Then the next stage is to 'comprehend' this teaching, and this philosophy does. All of this would be entirely proper if Christianity were a teaching, but since it is not, all this is totally wrong.[117]

In the above passage Kierkegaard uses his pseudonym Anti-Climacus to make the basic distinction between belief-that and belief-in, or to put it differently, belief and faith. As seems to be usual with Kierkegaard's terminology, it is possible to run into some difficulty with interpretation. The Danish word used is *Tro*, which can be translated as either belief or faith.[118] However, for once Kierkegaard uses a pseudonym to clarify his position and Climacus explains the two senses: 'faith ... in its direct and ordinary meaning'[119] or faith '*sensu laxiori*',[120] that is merely belief-that and not the matter of concern here; 'but secondly, faith must be taken in the wholly eminent sense,'[121] or '*sensu strictissimo*'.[122] This two-fold distinction is not by any means confined to Kierkegaard, and Alistair Hannay attributes it to scholasticism.[123] The contemporary British philosopher Basil Mitchell distinguishes between 'faith in the sense of "believing that"', and '"faith" in which it means "trusting reliance upon God"';[124] and C.S. Lewis compares 'faith' as 'simply belief - accepting or regarding as true the doctrines of Christianity', with 'Faith in the second or higher

116 *Fragments*, p. 59; cf. also *Concluding Unscientific Postscript*, vol. 1, p. 214.
117 *Practice in Christianity*, p. 141.
118 Hannay, *Kierkegaard*, p. 101; Law, *Kierkegaard as Negative Theologian*, p. 86.
119 *Fragments*, p. 87.
120 *Concluding Unscientific Postscript*, vol. 1, p. 322.
121 *Fragments*, p. 87.
122 *Concluding Unscientific Postscript*, vol. 1, p. 322.
123 Hannay, *Kierkegaard*, p. 101.
124 Basil Mitchell, *Faith and Criticism* (Oxford: Clarendon Press, 1994), p. 65.

sense'.[125] I can believe for certain that God has chosen to reveal Himself to the world through Christ, but I can choose to ignore this fact or reject it. But if I believe in him, then I move on to include a level of trust and commitment in addition to intellectual acceptance, in which case I have faith. Hence we hear Climacus saying 'one does not have faith that the god exists ... That is improper use of language'.[126] Faith at this level does not just refer to intellectual assent, but must include as well a person's response to it, therefore 'Christianity is not a doctrine but an existence-communication'.[127]

So, why is it that Kierkegaard seems to go to such great lengths to stress the response nature of faith over that of its content? I have already indicated something of the answer in the above paragraph, namely that he was aware of those who equated having faith in Christ with the intellectual act of comprehending a proposition about him.[128] Kierkegaard usually had Hegel in mind, with such statements as 'faith is essentially the consciousness of absolute truth', and 'faith comprehends',[129] lending themselves quite freely to this interpretation. This fails to understand what Christianity really requires, therefore 'Christianity itself must indeed regard as false Christians those who merely know what Christianity is'.[130] As Julia Watkin explains 'Belief in propositions, however, is distinct from the existential faith-commitment to an ethical-religious lifestyle [i.e. Christianity], and the propositional form of belief can distract from the existential commitment in a number of ways that can seriously blinker the individual in the endeavour to enter into and deepen the God-relationship'.[131] We must not assume from this that Kierkegaard held the propositional content of faith to be unimportant, instead he rejects the view that Christianity is concerned with propositions about God rather than God Himself.[132] The interpretation quoted from Wittgenstein at the beginning of this section, 'that sound doctrines are all useless'[133] is therefore an incorrect interpretation of Kierkegaard's position.

---

[125] C.S. Lewis, *Mere Christianity* (Glasgow: Collins, 1988), p. 122.
[126] *Fragments*, p. 87.
[127] *Concluding Unscientific Postscript*, vol. 1, p. 570.
[128] Consider the following passage from the *Journals*: 'The difficulty of my task is that I do indeed say: On the whole the doctrine as it is taught is entirely sound. Consequently that is not what I am contending for. My contention is that something should be done with it.' (*Journals and Papers*, 6702, X3 A 635 *n.d.*, 1850.)
[129] Hegel, *The Christian Religion*, p. 216.
[130] *Concluding Unscientific Postscript* vol. 1, p. 371.
[131] Watkin, *Kierkegaard*, p. 82.
[132] Cf. *Fragments*, p. 62.
[133] Wittgenstein, *Culture and Value*, p. 53.

It is quite false to attribute to Kierkegaard the view that, 'it does not ultimately matter what is the content of belief so long as it is adhered to with sufficient intensity', but instead recognize it as stemming from a misunderstanding amongst his would be disciples.[134] Richard Swinburne refers to this erroneous definition of faith as 'trust without the belief-that', or the 'Pragmatist View of Faith', attributing it to the influence of both Kierkegaard and William James.[135] Yet Kierkegaard's theology is quite orthodox in that it holds that not only is there an intellectual content to faith, a belief-that, or beliefs-that expressible in propositions, but this content is openly discernible to Christian and non-Christian alike (compare with Luther's 'simple Gospel' which all can understand, yet none expected).[136] Consider the following extract from the *Postscript*:

> That one can know what Christianity is without being a Christian must, then, be answered in the affirmative. Whether one can know what it is to be a Christian without being one is something else, and it must be answered in the negative. On the other hand, the Christian must indeed also know what Christianity is and be able to tell us - provided he himself has become one ... In other words, a person who actually has become a Christian must certainly have had a period when he was not a Christian; he must in turn have had a period when he found out what Christianity is; then, in turn, if he has not totally forgotten how he himself existed before he became a Christian, he must be able for his part to say what Christianity is by comparing his earlier life with his Christian life.[137]

All the warnings that 'Christianity is not a doctrine',[138] or that 'faith is not a knowledge'[139] are put into the mouths of his pseudonyms in order to prevent the readership from assuming that 'belief-that' is synonymous with 'belief-in', as derivable from Hegel ('for faith is also knowledge'[140]). As already explained, the latter includes the former, but the former alone is inadequate. When such assertions are made they are done so in the context of spelling out that 'faith does not result from straightforward scholarly deliberation',[141] but is instead the result of a gift from God.[142] So then, when Hegel claims,

---

[134] Mitchell, *Faith and Criticism*, p. 35.
[135] Richard Swinburne, *Faith and Reason* (Oxford: Clarendon Press, 1981), p. 116n.
[136] Cf. Gerrish, *Grace and Reason*, p. 115.
[137] *Concluding Unscientific Postscript*, vol. 1, p. 372.
[138] Ibid., p. 380.
[139] *Fragments*, p. 62.
[140] Hegel, *The Christian Religion*, p. 329
[141] *Concluding Unscientific Postscript*, vol. 1, p. 29.
[142] *Eighteen Upbuilding Discourses*, p. 44; cf. *Fragments*, pp. 46f.

> In faith the true content is certainly already found, but it still lacks the form of thinking. As we observed earlier, all forms - those of feeling, representation, etc. - can indeed have the content of truth, but they themselves are not the true form, which makes the true content necessary. Thinking is the absolute judge, before which the content must verify and attest its claims. Philosophy has been criticized for placing itself above religion. But as a matter of fact this is false because philosophy has only this and no other content, although it gives it in the form of thinking; it places itself only above the form of faith, while the content is the same in both cases.[143]

To this Kierkegaard retorts: 'Is knowledge higher than faith? By no means.'[144] We cannot attain perfect knowledge of God, and even if we could that would not necessarily lead directly to faith. Nor is thinking about faith to be substituted for faith itself:

> Precisely because Christianity is not a doctrine, it holds true, as developed previously, that there is an enormous difference between knowing what Christianity is and being a Christian. With regard to a doctrine, this distinction is unthinkable, because the doctrine is not related to existing. I cannot help it that our age has reversed the relation and changed Christianity into a philosophical theory that is to be comprehended and being a Christian into something negligible. Furthermore, to say that Christianity is empty of content because it is not a doctrine is only chicanery. When a believer exists in faith, his existence has enormous content, but not in the sense of a yield of paragraphs.[145]

Kierkegaard's thoughts on the relationship between faith and knowledge can be illustrated further by his comments on that between intellect and action.

> Certainly Christianity has never been a mystery, has in fact abhorred mystery, in the sense of being only for a few superlative people who have been initiated. No, God has chosen the poor and the despised - but the initiation was not lacking. It is not an intellectual initiation but an ethical initiation, personality's enormous respect for being admitted into the Christian community, a respect expressed not in assurances and frills but existentially in action.[146]

There is an indispensable practical element to faith that differentiates it from mere knowledge or belief. Kierkegaard's words bring to mind James' warning that faith and action must go together if

---

[143] Hegel, *The Christian Religion*, p. 292.
[144] *Journals and Papers*, 2283, IV C 99 *n.d.*, 1842-43.
[145] *Concluding Unscientific Postscript*, vol. 1, p. 380.
[146] *Journals and Papers*, 2793, X2 A 341 *n.d.*, 1850.

faith is to have any meaning at all.[147] '"But is it not of absolute importance, then, first of all to understand?" No, ethically, the important thing is that you do it, that which is so infinitely easy to understand that you understand it immediately.'[148] Whatever we can understand we must act upon, however little that may seem at first, because it is the action arising from trust which helps make the transition from knowledge to faith. This point is made by Kierkegaard's comparison between the 'witness', who demonstrates what he believes by the conduct of his own life, and the 'teacher' or 'professor', who understands all the details yet keeps his distance.[149] There is a qualitative difference between the person who speculates about the nature of from the outside, and the person who experiences the content of faith as a reality in their own life.

A similar illustration may be found in his essay 'Of the Difference between a Genius and an Apostle' published in 1848. Read for instance what he says regarding the minister who approaches Christianity from the wrong angle:

> The pernicious thing is when the whole train of his thought is affected, when the price of his orthodoxy is an emphasis in an entirely wrong place, when he calls for faith in Christ, when he preaches faith in Him on grounds which simply cannot be the object of faith. If a son were to say, 'I obey my father, not because he is my father but because he is a genius, or because his orders are profoundly intelligent,' then that filial obedience is affected. The son accentuates something entirely wrong, he emphasizes the intellectual aspect, the profundity in a command, whereas a command is, of course, indifferent to that qualification. The son wishes to obey by virtue of the father's intellectual profundity; and to obey by virtue thereof is just not possible, for his critical attitude as to whether the command is profound undermines the obedience. And so, too, it is affectation to speak of adopting Christianity and believing Christ because of the great profundity of the doctrine. By putting the accent in entirely the wrong place one only makes a show of orthodoxy. The whole of modern philosophy is therefore affected, because it has done away with obedience on the one hand, and authority on the other, and then, in spite of everything claims to be orthodox.[150]

For Kierkegaard Christianity is to be embraced first and foremost on the grounds of its divine authority, not necessarily for its intellectual content, as this will come over time - the very opposite to Hegel ('the

---

[147] James 2: 14-26 (NRSV).

[148] *Journals and Papers*, 2874, X3 A 169 *n.d.*, 1850.

[149] Ibid., 4967, X3 A 5 *n.d.*, 1850.

[150] *The Present Age and of the Difference Between a Genius and an Apostle*, trans. Alexander Dru (New York: Harper Torchbooks, 1962), pp. 103-4.

faith of the community rests solely on reason itself', i.e. on its philosophical coherence).[151]

Like Luther before him, he stresses the importance of not confusing philosophy with theology, or reason with faith.[152] Faith is the obedient response to a divine call and once the believer has faith it shapes that believer's life in all respects. Here again we may draw parallels with Luther's concept of a *nova ratio*, in that 'reason must first be illuminated by faith, before it issues in works'.[153] In a certain sense, Kierkegaard follows the theological approach of '*fides quaerens intellectum*' so often associated with Anselm: 'I do not try, Lord, to attain your lofty heights, because my understanding is in no way equal to it. But I do desire to understand Your truth a little, that truth that my heart believes and loves. For I do not seek to understand so that I may believe; but I believe so that I may understand.'[154] As Trevor Hart succintly puts it, this may be described as 'faith thinking'.[155]

This is not to say that faith becomes 'a sort of provisional form of higher knowledge' as Price claims,[156] but is an example of '*fides caritate formata*, faith quickened and warmed by love of God above all'.[157] Although the believer must have accepted certain propositions about God as valid in order to come to believe in the first place, such knowledge is only the starting point and by far the greater amount of learning is done within the framework of faith. In this respect his position on theological enquiry parallels that of enquiry within other fields.[158] For instance, in order to carry out a scientific experiment successfully, the persons involved must accept certain scientific theories as being valid before they can begin. Without doing so they have no credible basis to work from, nor could they have any way of calculating the validity of the experiment if they chose to proceed. So it is with faith and knowledge, there has to be something known about God as a starting point upon which that faith is grounded. This then becomes the basis of all further knowledge about God that is gained as faith develops. Kierkegaard's main concern is with justifying faith, rather than a purely epistemological faculty. Therefore, what he says on faith must be interpreted within the context of soteriology rather than being an open question on the validity of faith's content. He sought not so much to

---

[151] Hegel, *The Christian Religion*, p. 258.
[152] Cf. Gerrish, *Grace and Reason*, p. 42.
[153] Luther, in Gerrish, *Grace and Reason*, p. 82.
[154] Anselm, *Proslogion*, in Arthur Hyman and James Walsh (eds.), *Philosophy in the Middle Ages, The Christian, Islamic and Jewish Traditions* (Indianapolis: Hackett Publishing Co., 1973), p. 150.
[155] Trevor Hart, *Faith Thinking* (London: SPCK, 1995), p. 1.
[156] Price, *The Narrow Pass*, p. 129.
[157] Collins, *The Mind of Kierkegaard*, p. 267.
[158] Cf. Hart, *Faith Thinking*, p. 21.

question the doctrinal content of Lutheran Christianity as to call others to humble themselves before God. In which case this leads us on to consider what Kierkegaard has to say regarding the importance of the will. Yet, before departing from the question of faith and knowledge, it would seem that some of Kierkegaard's thoughts are well expressed by the following quotation from Thomas à Kempis:

> All perfection in this life is accompanied by a measure of imperfection, and all our knowledge contains an element of obscurity. A humble knowledge of oneself is a surer road to God than a deep searching of the sciences. Yet learning itself is not to be blamed, nor is the simple knowledge of anything whatsoever to be despised, for true learning is good in itself and ordained by God; but a good conscience and a holy life are always to be preferred.[159]

Faith and Volition

With his alleged downplay of the intellectual element of faith and assertion of the value of personal commitment, some have asked whether Kierkegaard is proposing a volitionist doctrine of faith. Certain passages in his writings do lend themselves to such an interpretation. Defining the Christian concept of faith Kierkegaard writes: 'What is it to believe? It is to will ... God-fearingly and unconditionally obediently, to defend oneself against the vain thought of wanting to comprehend and against the vain imagination of being able to comprehend.'[160] It might seem to follow that if faith cannot be reached by the mere intellectual assent to propositions, the transition must be attributed to some other human ability, possibly the will for instance. However, despite his often overtly critical attitude towards it, Kierkegaard still remains a conscious product of the Lutheran tradition. To claim that faith could be gained by force of willpower is to go so far as to claim that faith could be gained by human effort rather than Divine initiative.

If Kierkegaard held to such a voluntarist position he would, in effect, be affirming justification by works, in which case he would be going against both the spirit and the letter of the Lutheran creed. This he does not do: 'One becomes a Christian only by the grace of God in Christ. Luther's confession lives on in Kierkegaard: salvation is by divine grace in Jesus Christ.'[161] However, it is possible to go to the

[159] Thomas à Kempis, *The Imitation of Christ* (Harmondsworth: Penguin, 1983), p. 31.
[160] *Journals and Papers*, 1130, X A 368 *n.d.*, 1849.
[161] Holmes Hartshorne, *Kierkegaard Godly Deceiver*, p. 27. We find several references to this topic within Kierkegaard's direct work *Judge For Yourself!*, for instance 'there appeared a man from God and with faith, Martin Luther; with faith (for truly this required faith) or by faith he established faith in its rights. His life expressed works - let us never forget that - but he said: a person is saved by faith alone.' (*Judge For Yourself!*, p. 16.)

opposite pole and derive from the Lutheran doctrine of *sola fide* a position which places so much emphasis upon God's grace that humanity becomes purely passive in its own salvation. Luther's assertion that God takes us 'just as we are'[162] was made in order to accentuate his love and grace, not to encourage inaction on the side of the believer. Likewise, Luther's doctrine of predestination, despite its harshness to many contemporary ears, stressed the sovereignty of God over and against the theologies of his time which attributed salvation to human initiative and works; it did not seek to promote complacency.

The theologically trained Kierkegaard was well aware of his Lutheran heritage. He was also unhappily aware of the 'prodigious illusion' of 'Christendom' which surrounded him at the time of writing: 'All these people, even those who assert that no God exists, are all of them Christians, call themselves Christians, are recognized as Christians by the State, are buried as Christians by the Church, are certified as Christians for eternity!'[163] As far as a fair proportion of his society was concerned, being a loyal Dane involved being a baptized and confirmed Lutheran, regardless of personal belief (or lack of it).[164] Thus Christianity in 'Christendom' was in reality little more than conforming to civic virtue, a hangover from Enlightenment moral religion; as he ironically observes: 'The thing of becoming and of being a Christian is now a triviality.'[165] Yet Christianity is not the passive acceptance of the social status quo, nor can it be reduced to secular ethics. Therefore 'faith is a choice', either we choose, individually, personally, to become a Christian, or we reject Christianity as something we do not wish to associate ourselves with.[166] But we cannot become part of it by association, nor by accident of birth.

The importance of the will is emphasized for another reason. Some believers could well claim that, as God has already predestined all events, we have no responsibility for our own actions - whatever happens happens by virtue of his will and causation, whatever I appear to choose has already been chosen for me.

> It is deceitful to talk like this ... 'Whatever happens to me that I cannot prevent it, wherever way I am led I cannot go another other way - this is God's will.' Well, thanks for that! It certainly leaves out the difficulty, the difficulty that a man shall himself choose. It appears to be so *geschwindt* [quick] and easy, this statement which sounds so Lutheran, and yet when it is supposed to be true in the highest sense it is rarely seen: I cannot do

[162] Cf. Gerrish, *Grace and Reason*, p. 115.
[163] *The Point of View*, pp. 22-3.
[164] Watkin, *Kierkegaard*, p. 13. Cf. *Judge For Yourself!*, p. 194.
[165] *The Point of View*, p. 74.
[166] *Practice in Christianity*, p. 141.

> otherwise; God help me, Amen. In this we hear immediately that the person who is speaking is someone who knows what it is to choose.[167]

If choice and responsibility are taken away entirely then all that is left is fatalism. However harsh our situation, however much life seems to be beyond our control, we cannot renounce the freedom and responsibility of our own actions. Some of Kierkegaard's harshest criticism in this area is reserved, not for Hegel, but for Augustine and Luther for not giving enough attention to the need to 'strive' for salvation before God.[168] The stress upon grace, designed to combat justification by works doctrines, seemed to reduce the imitation of Christ to something of no consequence. Kierkegaard's criticism of Lutheranism is extreme, similar to that made by the Council of Trent.[169] However, Luther really believed that faith must produce good works as a necessary consequence, thereby distancing his theology from the apparent misunderstandings above.[170] Yet, we must allow for Kierkegaard's strongly polemical and satirical style and interpret his words accordingly. His real objects of attack were those who misunderstood Luther's teachings, using arguments against monasticism, penances and indulgences in favour of embracing worldly living and secularized values.[171] What he attacks is 'Christendom's' perversion of *sola fide* as a gross misunderstanding of the original Augustinian-Lutheran position.

Kierkegaard insisted that faith is not produced by means of an intellectual conclusion regarding the truth of doctrine.[172] In the context of faith 'the conclusion of belief is no conclusion but a resolution'.[173] If it were blatantly obvious to all that all the details of Christianity were true, how could we be free to accept or reject it? Just as he held the traditional proofs of God's existence to be useful in a limited capacity, not as proofs but as bringing someone a little closer to faith; so Kierkegaard felt that there would always be a gap between intellectual conclusion and faith's resolution. The former cannot go so far as to make the 'paradox' of the Christian revelation seem so probable that accepting it would follow as a matter of course. From the learner outside of faith its contents appear improbable.[174] Therefore human freedom is maintained and 'belief is not a knowledge but an act of freedom, an expression of will'.[175] This is why the understanding

---

[167] *Journals and Papers*, 1256, IX A 109 *n.d.*, 1848.
[168] Ibid., 2551, XI 1 A 297 *n.d.*, 1854.
[169] Cf. Swinburne, *Faith and Reason*, p. 111.
[170] Gerrish, *Grace and Reason*, p. 123; Swinburne, *Faith and Reaon*, p. 115.
[171] *Journals and Papers*, 2521, X3 A 217 *n.d.*, 1850; ibid., 2528, X3 A 510 *n.d.*, 1850.
[172] *Fragments*, p. 93; *Concluding Unscientific Postscript*, vol. 1, p. 29.
[173] *Fragments*, p. 84.
[174] *Journals and Papers*, 7, X2 A 354 *n.d.*, 1850; cf. *Fragments*, p. 94.
[175] *Fragments*, p. 83.

cannot make the final move from knowledge to faith, from seen to unseen, if it could we would be faced with some form of an intellectual categorical imperative. There always remains an element of risk and uncertainty.[176] But, our will cannot make the final move unaided, we are not autonomous and in the final analysis faith is God-given.[177] In this sense therefore 'faith is not an act of will, for it is always the case that all human willing is efficacious only within the condition [of faith] ... But if I do not possess the condition ... then all my willing is of no avail.'[178] This is very similar to the view of 'faith seeking understanding' with regard to faith and knowledge. As Kierkegaard explained in his *Journals*:

> Two wills in thc world cannot be tolerated. God is the only one. To be sure, God has given man and the human world the power of having a will. But as punishment for willing its own will the world must take the consequence of its not really existing for God of his handing it over. However, as soon as a will wills to become involved with God, this will must go. That is the meaning of dying to the world. That a will wills to involve itself with him is precisely what God wants, but the next comes as a matter of course if God and this will are to be bound together.[179]

The human will is not annihilated but transformed as the believer is brought into a right relationship with God. It is not a matter of voluntarism, but of obedience: 'If the fear of God be the beginning of wisdom, then the learning of obedience is the perfecting of wisdom.'[180] In contradistinction to Kant, Kierkegaard holds that it is only when the believer recognizes his need for God and realizes that he cannot grasp autonomy, that, paradoxically, he can become himself.

> Just as knowing oneself in one's own nothingness is the condition for knowing God, so knowing God is the condition for the sanctification of a human being by God's assistance and according to His intention. Wherever God is in truth, there He is always creating. He does not want a person to be spiritually soft and to bathe in the contemplation of His glory, but in becoming known by a person He wants to create in him a new human being.[181]

---

[176] *Concluding Unscientific Postscript*, vol. 1, p. 209.
[177] *Fragments*, p. 103.
[178] Ibid., p. 623.
[179] *Journals and Papers*, 5038, XI A 239 *n.d.*, 1854.
[180] *The Gospel of Sufferings*, p. 58.
[181] *Eighteen Upbuilding Discourses*, p. 325.

Faith and Subjectivity

Kierkegaard made the frequent assertion that 'subjectivity is truth'.[182] He did so as a means to draw his readers' attention away from objective speculation on doctrines and towards an active life of personal devotion. This was done in the context of distinguishing between (justifying) faith and mere belief-that. However it is debated what is implied by subjectivity in this context, and it is possible to hear many objections voiced against Kierkegaard's position.

> Truth, they would want to say, has nothing to do with subjectivity; it has an objectivity found in the Scriptures, in history, and in the teachings of the Church. To say that subjectivity is truth is to tread the most dangerous of paths: to found eternal truth on individual emotion and conjecture. Such emotionalism and individualism must be avoided at all costs. Man's salvation is to be found, not in his own conjectures, but in the objective truth presented by the Church.[183]

If the interpretation of Kierkegaard's theology which I have presented so far is true, then these accusations are incorrect, and what Kierkegaard meant by subjectivity stands in need of careful interpretation. I have not argued that he denies the possibility for those outside of faith to make philosophical observations about it (such a position would result in the 'Wittgensteinian Fideism' that I mentioned earlier). Nor have I denied that they, like the believer, may know its contents in the form of propositional knowledge (although unlike the believer, they have not experienced the non-propositional self-revelation of God in Christ to which it refers).

What has been argued throughout is that knowledge does not equal faith, and that talking about faith is very different from having it. The full force of Kierkegaard's criticism is levied against 'this woeful preaching of Christianity - objectively quite correct - by men who really have no intimation of Christianity. Nothing, nothing has to such a degree confused, yes, abolished Christianity as the unchristian way in which it is preached'.[184] The living truth of Christianity is not so much determined by attention to doctrinal detail, but proclaimed by the reality of personal witness.

> Whether speculative thought is in the right is a different question. What is asked here is only how its explanation of Christianity is related to the Christianity that it explains. And how should they be related? Speculative

---

[182] E.g. *Concluding Unscientific Postscript*, vol. 1, p. 343.

[183] D.Z. Phillips, *Faith and Philosophical Enquiry* (London: Routledge and Kegan Paul, 1970, p. 205.

[184] *Journals and Papers*, 2793, X A 341 *n.d.*, 1850.

> thought is objective, and objectively there is no truth for an existing individual but only an approximation, since by existing he is prevented from becoming entirely objective. Christianity, on the other hand, is subjective; the inwardness of faith in the believer is the truth's eternal decision. Objectively there is no truth; an objective knowledge about truth or the truths of Christianity is precisely untruth.[185]

This point is related to the difference Kierkegaard makes between the teacher and the witness, to which I referred earlier. The teacher, or rather a caricature of a speculative thinker, approaches faith from a distance as a matter of objective enquiry, something distinct from the truth of his own personal existence. This is the view of an observer, yet the believer is not an observer but a participant. The objective truth of Christianity is not denied by Kierkegaard, but he realizes that anybody can examine the truth of a set of doctrines. In the *Postcript* we hear that '*Objectively the emphasis is on* what *is said; subjectively the emphasis is on* how *it is said.*' Regarding the 'how' in this context, 'this is not to be understood as manner, modulation of voice, oral delivery, etc., but it is to be understood as the relation of the existence of the existing person, in his very existence, to what is said'.[186] There is therefore an intrinsic link between the commitment and the content of faith. Aware of the misinterpretations of this topic in circulation even then, Kierkegaard explains in his *Journals* that,

> In all the usual talk that Johannes Climacus is mere subjectivity etc., it has been completely overlooked that in addition to all his other concretions he points out in one of the last sections that the remarkable thing is that there is a How with the characteristic that when the How is scrupulously rendered the What is also given, that this is the How of 'faith'.[187]

So Christianity is subjective because in the life of the believer its doctrines spring from the page and into existence: 'What is truth but to live for an idea?'[188] If Christianity remains just objective, then it might be because we are offended by it and reject it. Or, we are not really interested and wish to maintain a speculative distance from it.[189] If we are not offended by it then we accept it as the truth and in this way it becomes for us 'subjective'.

---

185 *Concluding Unscientific Postscript*, vol. 1, p. 224.
186 Ibid., pp. 202-3.
187 *Journals and Papers*, 4550, X 2 A 299 *n.d.*, 1849. Cf. *Concluding Unscientific Postscript*, vol. 1, pp. 610-11.
188 Ibid., 5100, I A 75 August 1, 1835.
189 Cf. Ibid., 4567, X 4 A 667 *n.d.*, 1852.

Faith is described as being 'a sphere by itself'.[190] The real proof of Christianity to one who believes is provided by the existence of this faith within him: 'the inner proof, *argumentum spiritus sancti,*' and 'It is not reasons which justify the faith in God's son, but just the opposite - faith in God's son is the testimony'.[191] Because it is upon faith that every other detail of the believer's life depends, 'Faith, is quite correctly, "the point outside the world" which therefore also moves the whole world.'[192] It is also 'the point outside the world' because there can be no objectively verifiable evidence to prove the truths of its content conclusively. There always remains the freedom to choose. Otherwise faith becomes synonymous with the conclusion of knowledge. For the believer, '*an objective uncertainty, held fast through appropriation with the most passionate inwardness*, is the truth, the highest truth there is for an *existing* person. At the point where the road swings off (and where that is cannot be stated objectively, since it is precisely subjectivity), objective knowledge is suspended.'[193] As Climacus explains,

> But the definition of truth stated above is a paraphrasing of faith. Without risk, no faith. Faith is the contradiction between the infinite passion of inwardness and the objective uncertainty. If I am able to apprehend God objectively, I do not have faith; but because I cannot do this, I must have faith. If I want to keep myself in faith, I must continually see to it that I hold fast the objective uncertainty, see to it that in the objective uncertainty I am 'out on 70,000 fathoms of water' and still have faith.[194]

Faith cannot avoid the element of risk, and it is through an exercise of will that the gift of faith must be embraced despite the objective uncertainty. 'Objectively the emphasis is on what is said; subjectively the emphasis is on how it is said.'[195] Willing to undertake the risk and whatever may result from it constitutes the 'passion' of faith, it is 'the relation of the existing person, in his very existence, to what is said'.[196] To explain this further let us turn to Anti-Climacus' definition of faith as: 'that the self in being itself and in willing to be itself rests transparently in God.'[197] Faith is understood as being wholly open to the will of God, not through passive resignation but by actively choosing

---

[190] Ibid., 10, X B 79 *n.d.*, 1850; cf. *Concluding Unscientific Postscript*, vol. 1, p. 327.
[191] Ibid., 3608, X A 481 *n.d.*, 1849.
[192] Ibid., 2803, X A 529 *n.d.*, 1850.
[193] *Concluding Unscientific Postscript*, vol. 1, p. 203.
[194] Ibid., p. 204.
[195] Ibid., p. 202.
[196] Ibid., p. 203.
[197] *The Sickness Unto Death*, p. 82.

to accept what is given. For Kierkegaard the believer is one who truly becomes himself in this Divine-human relationship.

And it is as a two-way relationship that his doctrine of faith is best described. I now wish to end this chapter with a brief summary of this doctrine. Kierkegaard, either directly, or through his pseudonyms, declares that faith is not a knowledge; because although the believer knows what is believed in the form of doctrinal statements, the real importance is that he relates to the object of belief Christ, the God-man. Hence he places the very experience of God's self-revelation over the ability to elucidate it in the form of propositions, though the latter should result from the latter. Otherwise there is the danger 'that he becomes learned instead of becoming a Christian'.[198] We are told that faith is an act of will, but it is not brought about by mere will-power. Through grace faith is given, and out of grace we are permitted to respond freely whether to believe, or be offended.[199] In this sense faith may be understood both as a gift and a task.[200] Finally, in the life of faith, truth is subjectivity because the believer is not an impartial observer but a concerned witness. If Christianity is true it follows that he stakes his life on it, but to the observer might be intellectually intriguing, but it is kept at an objective distance. As John Mullen puts it, in Kierkegaard's eyes, 'chessboards and logic problems are for sharpening one's wit, but one's relationship to God is not.'[201] In the last year of his life Kierkegaard wrote the following comments on faith in his journal:

> In the New Testament faith is presented as having not an intellectual but an ethical character, it signifies the relationship of personality between God and man. Therefore faith is demanded (as an expression of devotedness), believing against [worldly] reason, believing although one cannot see (wholly a qualification of personality, and ethical). The apostle speaks of the obedience of faith. Faith is set to a test, is tested, etc.[202]

Kierkegaard's doctrine of faith, if examined closely, can be seen to be well within the orthodox Lutheran tradition and hence within the mainstream of Protestant Christianity. Beneath the rhetoric we can find him accepting the traditional three elements of faith: knowledge (*notitia*), assent (*assensus*), and trust (*fiducia*). Yet in true Lutheran

---

198 *Concluding Unscientific Postscript*, vol. 1, p. 611.
199 Cf. *Practice in Christianity*, pp. 141ff.
200 Lee Barrett, 'The Paradox of Faith in Kierkegaard's *Philosophical Fragments*: Gift or Task?, in Robert Perkins (ed.), *International Kierkegaard Commentary: Philosophical Fragments and Johannes Climacus* (Macon: Mercer University Press, 1994), p. 284.
201 Mullen, *Kierkegaard's Philosophy*, p. 148.
202 *Journals and Papers*, 1154, XI A 380 *n.d.*, 1854-55.

style he subordinates the first two to trust in a Living God.[203] To the atheist, or agnostic, this act of total commitment to an objective uncertainty may well seem to be a paradox. Where is the proof? The only real proof, replies Kierkegaard, is faith, if you have it. It must be revealed and believed. It is something that you must work out as you live it and nobody else can do it for you. Yet ultimately this is the point to which all apologetics arrives, the reasoning comes to an end and a choice must be made whether to reject or accept the God who comes to us in Christ.

---

[203] Cf. Swinburne, *Faith and Reason*, p. 111; cf. also Owen, *Christian Theism*, p. 3. I must emphasize that, although both Swinburne and Owen clarify this three-fold distinction within Christian faith, and, that they provide useful descriptions of faith as defined within Lutheran theology, neither sets Kierkegaard within the context of their respective discussions.

Bibliography

1. Works by Kierkegaard

Attack Upon 'Christendom', trans. Walter Lowrie (Princeton: Princeton University Press, 1968).

Christian Discourses, ed. and trans. Howard V. Hong and Edna H. Hong (Princeton: Princeton University Press, 1997).

The Concept of Anxiety, ed. and trans. Reidar Thomte (Princeton: Princeton University Press, 1980).

The Concept of Irony, with Continual Reference to Socrates, ed. and trans. Howard V. Hong and Edna H. Hong (Princeton: Princeton University Press, 1989).

Concluding Unscientific Postscript, ed. and trans. Howard V. Hong and Edna H. Hong, 2 vols. (Princeton: Princeton University Press, 1992).

Eighteen Upbuilding Discourses, ed. and trans. Howard V. Hong and Edna H. Hong (Princeton: Princeton University Press, 1990).

Either/Or, ed. and trans. Howard V. Hong and Edna H. Hong, 2 vols. (Princeton: Princeton University Press, 1987).

Fear and Trembling and *Repetition*, ed. and trans. Howard V. Hong and Edna H. Hong (Princeton: Princeton University Press, 1983).

For Self-Examination and *Judge for Yourself!*, ed. and trans. Howard V. Hong and Edna H. Hong (Princeton: Princeton University Press, 1990).

Gospel of Sufferings, trans. A.S. Aldworth and W.S. Ferrie (Cambridge: James Clarke, 1982).

Philosophical Fragments and *Johannes Climacus*, ed. and trans. Howard V. Hong and Edna H. Hong (Princeton: Princeton University Press, 1985).

Philosophical Fragments, trans. David Swenson with intro. and commentary Niels Thulstrup, revised Howard Hong (Princeton: Princeton University Press, 1962).

The Point of View, trans. Lowrie, W. (London: OUP, 1950).

Practice in Christianity, ed. and trans. Howard V. Hong and Edna H. Hong (Princeton: Princeton University Press, 1991).

The Present Age and *Of The Difference Between a Genius and an Apostle*, trans. Alexander Dru, intro. Walter Kaufman (New York: Harper Torchbooks, 1962).

The Sickness Unto Death, ed. and trans. Howard V. Hong and Edna H. Hong (Princeton: Princeton University Press, 1980).

Soren Kierkegaard's Journals and Papers, 7 vols. ed. and trans. Howard V. Hong and Edna H. Hong (Bloomington and London: Indiana University Press, 1967-78).

Stages on Life's Way, ed. and trans. Howard V. Hong and Edna H. Hong (Princeton: Princeton University Press, 1988).

2. Literature about Kierkegaard

Barrett, L., 'Kierkegaard's "Anxiety" and the Augustinian Doctrine of Original Sin', in Robert L. Perkins (ed.), *International Kierkegaard Commentary: The Concept of Anxiety* (Macon, Georgia: Mercer University Press, 1985), pp. 35-62.

Barrett, L., 'The Paradox of Faith in Kierkegaard's *Philosophical Fragments*: Gift or Task?', in Robert L. Perkins (ed.), *International Kierkegaard Commentary: Philosophical Fragments and Johannes Climacus* (Macon, Georgia: Mercer University Press, 1994), pp. 261-284.

Bigelow, P., *Kierkegaard and the Problem of Writing* (Tallahassee: Florida State University Press, 1987).

Brandt, F., *Søren Kierkegaard* (Copenhagen: Det Danske Selskab, 1963).

Burgess, A., 'Forstand in the Swenson-Lowrie Correspondence and in the "Metaphysical Caprice"', in Robert L. Perkins (ed.), *International Kierkegaard Commentary: Philosophical Fragments and Johannes Climacus* (Macon, Georgia: Mercer University Press, 1994), pp. 109-128.

Collins, J., *The Mind of Kierkegaard* (Princeton: Princeton University Press, 1983).

Croxall, T.H., *Kierkegaard Commentary* (New York: Harper & Bros., 1956).

Davis, William C., 'Kierkegaard on the Transformation of the Individual in Conversion,' *Religious Studies* 28 (1992), pp. 145-163.

Diamond, M., 'Kierkegaard and Apologetics', *The Journal of Religion* 44 (1964), pp. 122-32.

Dunning, S., *Kierkegaard's Dialectic of Inwardness, A Structural Analysis of the Theory of Stages* (Princeton: Princeton University Press, 1985).

Dunning, S., 'Paradoxes in Interpretation: Kierkegaard and Gadamer', in Matustík and Westphal (eds.), *Kierkegaard in Post/Modernity* (Bloomington and Indianapolis: Indiana University Press, 1995), pp. 125-41.

Elrod, John W., *Being and Existence in Kierkegaard's Pseudonymous Works* (Princeton: Princeton University Press, 1975).

Elrod, John W., *Kierkegaard and Christendom* (Princeton: Princeton University Press, 1981).

Emmanuel, Stephen M., *Kierkegaard and the Concept of Revelation* (Albany: State University of New York, 1996).

Emmanuel, Stephen M., 'Kierkegaard on Knowledge and Faith,' *Kierkegaardiana* 15 (1991), pp. 136-146.

Evans, Stephen C., *Kierkegaard's 'Fragments' and 'Postscript': The Religious Philosophy of Johannes Climacus* (New Jersey: Humanities Press, 1983).

Evans, Stephen C., 'Is Kierkegaard an Irrationalist? Reason, Paradox and Faith', *Religious Studies* 25 (1989), pp. 347-62.

Evans, Stephen C., *Passionate Reason, Making Sense of Kierkegaard's 'Philosophical Fragments'* (Bloomington and Indianapolis: Indiana University Press, 1992).

Evans, Stephen C., 'Empiricism, Rationalism, and the Possibility of Historical Religious Knowledge', in C.S. Evans and M. Westphal (eds.), *Christian Perspectives on Religious Knowledge* (Grand Rapids: William B. Eerdmans Publishing, 1993), pp. 134 - 160.

Evans, Stephen C., *Faith Beyond Reason* (Edinburgh: Edinburgh University Press, 1998).

Ferguson, H., *Melancholy and the Critique of Modernity, Søren Kierkegaard's Religious Psychology* (London: Routledge, 1995).

Ferreira, M. Jamie, *Transforming Vision, Imagination and Will in Kierkegaardian Faith* (Oxford: Clarendon Press, 1991).

Ferreira, M. Jamie, 'The Point Outside the World: Kierkegaard and Wittgenstein on Nonsense, Paradox and Religion', *Religious Studies* 30 (1994), pp. 29-44.

Ferreira, M. Jamie, 'Leaps and Circles: Kierkegaard and Newman on Faith and Reason,' *Religious Studies* 30 (1994), pp. 379-97.

Gardiner, P., *Kierkegaard* (Oxford: OUP, 1988).

Garelick, Herbert M., *The Anti-Christianity of Kierkegaard, A Study of Concluding Unscientific Postscript* (The Hague: Martinus Nijhoff, 1965).

Garff, J., 'The Eyes of Argus. The Point of View and Points of View with Respect to Kierkegaard's "Activity as an Author"', *Kierkegaardiana* 15 (1991), pp. 29-54.

Garff, J., '"My Dear Reader!" Kierkegaard Read with Restrained Affection,' *Studia Theologia* 45 (1991), pp. 127-147.

Glebe-Møller, J. 'Wittgenstein and Kierkegaard', *Kierkegaardiana* 15 (1991), pp. 55-68.

Gouwens, D., *Kierkegaard as Religious Thinker* (Cambridge: CUP, 1996).

Hamilton, C., 'Kierkegaard on Truth as Subjectivity: Christianity, Ethics and Ascetism', *Religious Studies* 34 (1998), pp. 61-79.

Hannay, A., *Kierkegaard* (London: Routledge, 1991).

Hardin, M., 'Reflections on the Spirituality of Søren Kierkegaard', *Scottish Journal of Theology* 45 (1992), pp. 325-340.

Holmes Hartshorne, M., *Kierkegaard Godly Deceiver, The Nature and Meaning of His Pseudonymous Works* (New York: Columbia University Press, 1990).

Kirmmse, B., ' "Out with It!": The Modern Breakthrough, Kierkegaard and Denmark', in Alastair Hannay and Gordon Marino (eds.), *The Cambridge Companion to Kierkegaard* (Cambridge: CUP, 1998), pp. 15-47.

Law, D., *Kierkegaard as Negative Theologian* (Oxford: Clarendon, 1993).

Law, D., 'How Christian is Kierkegaard's God?', *Scottish Journal of Theology* 48: (1995), pp. 301-348.

Lowrie, W., *A Short Life of Kierkegaard* (Princeton: Princeton University Press, 1970).

Mackay, L., *Kierkegaard: A Kind of Poet* (Philadelphia: University of Pennsylvania Press, 1971).

McKinnon, A., 'Søren Kierkegaard', in Smart et al. (eds.), *Nineteenth Century Religious Thought in the West*, Vol. 1 (Cambridge: CUP, 1988), pp. 181-214.

McKinnon, A., 'Kierkegaard's Accounts of Faith: Their Relative Centrality', *Studia Theologica* 46 (1992), pp. 147-59.

Miller, E.L., 'At the Centre of Kierkegaard: An Objective Absurdity', *Religious Studies* 33 (1997), pp. 433-441.

Mullen, J.D., *Kierkegaard's Philosophy, Self-Deception and Cowardice in the Present Age* (London: University Press of America, 1995).

Nicoletti, M., 'Politics and Religion in Kierkegaard's Thought: Secularization and the Martyr', in George B. Connell and C. Stephen Evans (eds.), *Foundations of Kierkegaard's Vision of Community: Religion, Ethics and Politics in Kierkegaard* (Atlantic Highlands, NJ, and London: Humanities Press, 1992), pp. 183-95.

Norris, C., 'De Man Unfair to Kierkegaard? an allegory of (non)-reading', in Birgit Bertung (ed.), *Kierkegaard Conferences 1: Kierkegaard - Poet of Existence* (Copenhagen: C.A. Reitzel, 1989), pp. 89-108.

Pattison, G., *Kierkegaard and the Crisis of Faith* (London: SPCK, 1997).

Piety, M.G., 'Kierkegaard on Religious Knowledge', *History of European Ideas.* 20 (1995), pp. 105-11.

Pojman, Louis P., *The Logic of Subjectivity: Kierkegaard's Philosophy of Religion* (Alabama: The University of Alabama Press, 1984).

Pojman, Louis P., 'Kierkegaard's Epistemology,' *Kierkegaardiana.* 15 (1991), pp. 147-152.

Polke, T.H., *The Biblical Kierkegaard* (Macon, Georgia: Mercer University Press, 1997).

Poole, R. *Kierkegaard: The Indirect Communication* (Charlottesville and London: University Press of Virginia, 1993).

Poole, R. 'The Unknown Kierkegaard: Twentieth-century receptions', in Alastair Hannay and Gordon Marino (eds.), *The Cambridge Companion to Kierkegaard* (Cambridge: CUP, 1998), pp. 48-75.

Price, G. *The Narrow Pass, A Study of Kierkegaard's Concept of Man* (London: Hutchinson & Co., 1963).

Rae, M., *Kierkegaard's Vision of the Incarnation, by Faith Transformed* (Oxford: OUP, 1997).

Roberts, R.C., *The Socratic Knowledge of God,* in Robert L. Perkins (ed.), *International Kierkegaard Commentary: The Concept of Anxiety* (Macon, Georgia: Mercer University Press, 1985), pp. 133-52.

Rohde, P., *Søren Kierkegaard* (London: George Allen & Unwin, 1963).

Rudd, A., *Kierkegaard and the Limits of the Ethical* (Oxford: Clarendon Press, 1993).

Stern, K., 'Kierkegaard on Theistic Proof', *Religious Studies,* 26 (1994), pp. 219-226.

Swenson, D.F., *Something About Kierkegaard* (Macon, GA: Mercer University Press, 1983).

Taylor, Mark C., *Kierkegaard's Pseudonymous Authorship, A Study of Time and the Self* (Princeton: Princeton University Press, 1975).

Thomas, J. Heywood., *Subjectivity and Paradox* (Oxford: Basil Blackwell, 1957).

Thompson, J., *Kierkegaard* (London: Victor Gollancz, 1974).

Thulstrup, N., *Commentary on Kierkegaard's 'Concluding Unscientific Postscript' with a new introduction* (Princeton: Princeton University Press, 1984).

Vardy, P., *Kierkegaard* (London: Fount, 1996).

Walsh, S., 'Living Poetically: Kierkegaard and German Romanticism', *History of European Ideas*. 20 (1995), pp. 189-94.

Watkin, J., *Kierkegaard* (London: Geoffrey Chapman, 1996).

Weston, M., 'Philosophy and Religion in the Thought of Kierkegaard', in M. McGhee (ed.), *Philosophy, Religion and the Spiritual Life. Royal Institute of Philosophy Supplement* 32 (1991), pp. 9-29.

Weston, M., *Kierkegaard and Modern Continental Philosophy* (London and New York: Routledge, 1994).

Westphal, M., *Kierkegaard's Critique of Reason and Society* (University Park, Pennsylvania: The Pennsylvania State University Press, 1987).

Westphal, M., 'Christian Philosophers and the Copernican Revolution', in C.S. Evans and M. Westphal (eds.), *Christian Perspectives on Religious Knowledge* (Grand Rapids: William B. Eerdmans Publishing, 1993), pp. 161-179.

Westphal, M., *Becoming A Self: A Reading of Kierkegaard's Concluding Unscientific Postscript* (Indiana: Perdue University Press, 1996).

Williams, C., 'Kierkegaardian Suspician and Properly Basic Beliefs', *Religious Studies*. 30 (1994), pp. 261-7.

Wind, H.C., 'The Metaphysics of Love. Theology, Myth and Metaphysics with Special Reference to Søren Kierkegaard', *Studia Theologica*, 43 (1989), pp. 211-25.

3. Other Literature

À Kempis, Thomas, *The Imitation of Christ*, trans. Sherley-Price, L. (Harmondsworth: Penguin, 1952).

Alford, S., *Irony and the Logic of Romantic Imagination* (New York: Peter Lang, 1984).

Anselm of Canterbury, *Proslogion*, in Hyman A. and Walsh J. (eds.), *Philosophy in the Middle Ages, The Christian, Jewish and Islamic Traditions* (Indianapolis: Hackett Publishing, 1973), pp. 149-151.

Aristotle, *The Art of Rhetoric*, trans. J.H. Freese (London: Heinenmann, 1926).

Aristotle, *Metaphysics*, ed. and trans. John Warrington (London and New York: J.M. Dent & Sons and E.P. Dalton & Co.,1956).

Aulén, G., *Christus Victor* (London: SPCK, 1970a).

Aulén, G., *The Drama and the Symbols, A Book on Images of God and the Problems They Raise* (London: SPCK, 1970b).

Ayer, A.J., *Language, Truth and Logic* (Harmondsworth: Penguin, 1980).

Baillie, D.M., *God Was in Christ, An Essay on Incarnation and Atonement* (London: Faber and Faber, 1963).

Baillie, J., *The Sense of the Presence of God. Gifford Lectures 1961-2* (London: OUP, 1962).

Barnes, T.D., *Tertullian: A Historical and Literary Study* (Oxford: Clarendon, 1971).

Barclay, W., *New Testament Words* (London: SCM, 1964).

Barclay, W., *The Daily Study Bible: The Letters to the Corinthians* (Edinburgh: The Saint Andrew Press, 1965).

Barth, K., *Church Dogmatics* I.2., G.W. Bromiley and T.F. Torrance (eds.) (Edinburgh: T&T Clark, 1988).

Basil of Caeserea, *Letters and Selected Documents. Select Library of the Christian Church, Nicene and Post-Nicene Fathers. 2nd series, Vol. 8*, Philip Schaff and Henry Wace (eds.) (Peabody, Mass.: Hendrickson, 1995).

Behler, E., *German Romantic Literary Theory* (Cambridge: CUP, 1993).

Berkhof, L., *Systematic Theology* (Edinburgh and Pennsylvania: Banner of Truth, 1994).

Berlin, I., *Against the Current, Essays in the History of Ideas* (Oxford: OUP, 1981).

Berlin, I., *The Magus of the North, J.G. Hamann and the Origins of Modern Irrationalism*. Henry Hardy (ed.) (London: John Murray, 1993).

Bettenson, H., *The Early Christian Fathers* (Oxford: OUP, 1969).

Blandshard, B., *Reason and Belief* (London: Allen & Unwin, 1974).

Bonhoeffer, D., *Christology* (London: Collins, 1978).

Brunner, E., *The Mediator* (London: Lutterworth, 1963).

Byrne, J., *Glory, Jest and Riddle, Religious Thought in the Enlightenment* (London: SCM Press, 1996).

Cassirer, E., *The Philosophy of the Enlightenment* (Princeton: Princeton University Press, 1979).

Chadwick, H., *Early Christian Thought and the Classical Tradition: Studies in Justin, Clement and Origen* (Oxford: Clarendon Press, 1966).

Cicero, *De Oratore*, trans. H. Rackham (London: Heinenmann, 1960).

Clement of Alexandria, *Fathers of the Second Century: Hermas, Tatian, Athenagoras, Theophilus and Clement of Alexandria* in *Ante-Nicene Fathers 2nd series, Vol. 2*, Alexander Roberts and James Donaldson (eds.) (Peabody, Mass.: Hendrickson, 1995).

Coleman, F., *Neither Angel nor Beast, The Life and Work of Blaise Pascal* (London: Routledge & Kegan Paul, 1986).

Coleridge, S.T., *Aids to Reflection* in *The Collected Works of Samuel Taylor Coleridge*, Vol. 9, K. Cobern and B. Winer (eds.) (London: Routledge, 1993).

Copleston, F., *History of Philosophy, Vol. VI, Wolffe to Kant* (London: Search Press, 1977).

Copleston, F., *History of Philosophy, Vol. VII, Fichte to Nietzsche* (London: Search Press, 1963).

Cranston, M., *The Romantic Movement* (Oxford: Blackwell, 1994).

Cupitt, D., *The Sea of Faith* (London: BBC, 1984).

Eagleton, T., *The Ideology of the Aesthetic* (Oxford: Blackwell, 1991).

Ebeling, G., *Luther, An Introduction to his Thought*, trans. R.A. Wilson (London: Collins, 1970).

Erasmus, D., *Praise of Folly*, trans. B. Radice (London: Penguin, 1985).

Evans, C.S., *The Historical Christ and The Jesus of Faith, The Incarnational Narrative as History* (Oxford: Clarendon, 1996).

Ferré, F., *Language, Logic and God* (New York: Harper & Row, 1961).

Feuerbach, L., *The Essence of Christianity*, trans. George Eliot (London: Harper & Row, 1957).

Frei, H., 'David Friedrich Strauss', in Smart et al. (eds.), *Nineteenth Century Religious Thought in the West*, Vol. 1 (Cambridge: CUP, 1988), pp. 215-91.

Gay, P., *The Enlightenment, An Interpretation. The Rise of Modern Paganism* (New York: W.W. Norton & Co., 1966).

Gerrish, B., *Grace and Reason, A Study in the Theology of Luther* (Oxford: Clarendon, 1962).

Gerrish, B., 'Friedrich Schleiermacher', in Smart et al (eds.), *Nineteenth Century Religious Thought in the West*, Vol. 1 (Cambridge: CUP, 1988), pp. 123-56.

Gregory of Nyssa, *Dogmatic Treatises, etc.* in *Select Library of the Christian Church, Nicene and Post-Nicene Fathers, 2nd series, Vol 5*, Philip Schaff and Henry Wace (eds.) (Peabody, Mass.: Henrickson, 1995).

Grillmeier, A., *Christ in Christian Tradition. Volume 1: From the Apostolic Age to Chalcedon (451)*, trans. J. Bowden (London: Mowbrays, 1965).

Gunton, C., *A Brief Theology of Revelation* (Edinburgh: T&T Clark, 1995).

Gunton, C., *Christ and Creation* (Carlisle and Grand Rapids, Mich.: Paternoster and Eerdmans, 1992).

Gunton, C., *Yesterday and Today; A Study in the Contimuities in Christology* (London: DLT, 1983).

Hall, S., *Doctrine and Practice in the Early Church* (London: SPCK, 1991).

Hardy, D.W., 'Christ and Creation', in T.F. Torrance (ed.), *The Incarnation.* (Edinburgh: Handsel Press, 1981), pp. 88-110.

Hart, T., *Faith Thinking* (London: SPCK, 1995).

Hebblethwaite, B., *The Incarnation, Collected Essays in Christology* (Cambridge: CUP, 1987).

Hegel, G.W.F., *The Christian Religion, Lectures on the Philosophy of Religion, Part III. The Revelatory, Consumate, Absolute Religion*, ed. and trans. Peter Hodgson (Missoula: Scholars Press, 1979).

Helm, P., *Faith and Understanding* (Edinburgh: Edinburgh University Press, 1997).

Hengel, M., *The Cross of the Son of God* (London: SCM, 1986).

Hepburn, R.W., *Christianity and Paradox: Critical studies in Twentieth Century Theology* (London: Watts, 1958).

Heron, A., 'Homoousios with the Father', in T.F. Torrance (ed.), *The Incarnation* (Edinburgh: Handsel Press, 1981), pp. 58-87.

Hilary of Poitiers, *Hilary of Poitiers and John of Damascus*, in *A Select Library of the Christian Church, Nicene and Post-Nicene Fathers, Vol. 9, 2nd series*, Philip Schaff and Henry Wace (eds.) (Peabody, Mass.: Henrickson, 1995).

Hodgson, P.C., 'George William Friedrich Hegel', in: Smart et al (eds.), *Nineteenth Century Religious Thought in the West*, Vol. 1 (Cambridge: CUP, 1988), pp. 81-122.

Hume, D., *Dialogues Concerning Natural Religion, and the Posthumous Essays* (Indianapolis: Hackett Publishing, 1980).

Hume, D., *An Enquiry Concerning Human Understanding and A Letter from a Gentleman to his Friend in Edinburgh* (Indianapolis: Hackett Publishing, 1977).

Kant, I., *Critique of Pure Reason* (London: Everyman, 1996).

Kant, I., *Religion Within the Limits of Reason Alone* (New York: Harper and Row, 1960).

Lewis, C.S., *Mere Christianity* (Glasgow: Collins, 1988).

Lohse, B., *Martin Luther, An Introduction to His Life and Work* (Edinburgh: T&T Clark, 1987).
Luther, M., *Career of the Reformer:1. Luther's Works, Vol. 31* (ed.), Harold J. Grimm (gen. ed.) Helmut T. Lehman (Philadelphia: Muhlenberg Press, 1957).
Luther, M., *Career of the Reformer:3. Luther's Works, Vol. 33* (ed.), Philip S. Watson (gen. ed.) Helmut T. Lehmen (Philadelpia: Fortress Press, 1984).
Macquarrie, J., *Jesus Christ in Modern Thought* (London: SCM Press, 1990).
Martensen, H., *Christian Dogmatics: A Compendium of the Doctrines of Christianity,* trans. William Urwick (Edinburgh: T&T Clark, 1878).
Mascall, E., *Existence and Analogy.* (London: Longmans, 1949).
Mascall, E., *Whatever Happened to the Human Mind?* (London: SPCK, 1980).
Mason, J., *Philosophical Rhetoric, The Function of Indirection in Philosophical Writing* (London and New York: Routledge, 1989).
McGrath, Alister E., *Luther's Theology of the Cross: Martin Luther's Theological Breakthrough* (Oxford: Basil Blackwell, 1985).
McGrath, Alister E., *The Making of Modern German Christology: From the Enlightenment to Pannenberg* (Oxford: Basil Blackwell, 1986).
Mitchell, B. (ed.), *The Philosophy of Religion* (Oxford: OUP, 1989).
Mitchell, B., *Faith and Criticism* (Oxford: Clarendon Press, 1994).
Morris, T.V., *The Logic of God Incarnate* (Ithaca and London: Cornell U.P., 1986).
Osbourne, E., *The Emergence of Christian Theology* (Oxford: Clarendon Press, 1993).
Owen, H.P., *Christian Theism, A Study in its Basic Principles* (Edinburgh: T&T Clark,1984).
Pascal, B., *Pensées*, trans. Krailsheimer, A. (London: Penguin, 1966).
Phillips, D.Z., *Faith and Philosophical Enquiry* (London: Routledge & Kegan Paul, 1970).
Phillips, D.Z., *Wittgenstein and Religion* (London: Macmillan, 1993).
Plato, *The Last Days of Socrates*, trans. Tredennick, H. and Tarrant, H. (London: Penguin, 1993).
Plato, *Protagoras and Meno*, trans. Guthrie, W.K.C. (London: Penguin, 1968).
Plato, *Timaeus*, trans. Lee, H.D.P. (London: Penguin, 1965).
Prestige, G.L., *God in Patristic Thought* (London: SPCK, 1952).
Quintillian, *Institutio Oratoria.*, trans. H.E. Butler (London: Heinenmann, 1920).
Reardon, B., *Hegel's Philosophy of Religion* (London and Basingstoke: Macmillan, 1977).
Reardon, B., *Religion in the Age of Romanticism* (Cambridge: CUP, 1985).
Roberts, J., *German Philosophy, An Introduction* (Oxford: Polity Press, 1990).
Russell, B., 'Mathematical Knowledge as Based on the Theory of Types', in *Logic and Knowledge, Essays 1901-50* (London and New York: Routledge, 1992), pp. 57-102.
Ryle, G., *Plato's Progress* (Cambridge: CUP, 1966).
Schleiermacher, F., *On Religion, Speeches to its Cultured Despisers* (Cambridge: CUP, 1995).
Schleiermacher, F., *The Christian Faith* (Edinburgh: T&T Clark, 1989).
Schwöbel, C., *God: Action and Revelation* (Kampen: Kok Pharos, 1992).
Sellers, R.V., *Two Ancient Christologies* (London: SPCK, 1940).

Simpson, D. (ed.), *The Origins of Modern German Critical Thought - German Aesthetic and Literary Criticism from Lessing to Hegel* (Cambridge: CUP, 1988).

Smith, R.G., *J.G. Hamann 1730-1788: A Study in Christian Existence, with Selections from his Writings* (London: Collins, 1960).

Spinoza, B., *Ethics and On the Correction of the Understanding*, trans. Andrew Boyle, intro. T.S. Gregory (London and Melbourne, Everyman's Library, 1986).

Strauss, D.F., *The Life of Jesus Critically Examined* (London: SCM, 1973).

Sturch, R., *The Word and the Christ, An Essay in Analytic Christology* (Oxford: Clarendon, 1991).

Swinburne, R., *The Christian God* (Oxford: Clarendon Press, 1994).

Swinburne, R., *The Existence of God* (Oxford: Clarendon Press, 1991).

Swinburne, R., *Faith and Reason* (Oxford: Clarendon Press, 1981).

Tertullian, *The Writings of Tertullian, Vol. II,* in *Ante-Nicene Christian Library: Translations of the Writings of the Fathers Down to A.D. 325, Vol. 15*, Alexander Roberts and James Donaldson (eds.) (Edinburgh: T&T Clark, 1870).

Thomas, J. Heywood, 'J.G. Fichte and F.W.J. Schelling', in Smart et al (eds.), *Nineteenth Century Religious Thought in the West*, Vol. 1 (Cambridge: CUP, 1988), pp. 41-80.

Thomas, J. Heywood, *Subjectivity and Paradox* (New York: Macmillan, 1957)

Torrance, A., 'The Christ of History and the Question of Criteria', unpublished paper presented as second of Hensley Henson Lectures at the University of Oxford (1998).

Torrance, T.F., *God and Rationality* (Edinburgh: T&T Clark, 1997).

Torrance, T.F., *Space, Time and Incarnation* (Edinburgh: T&T Clark, 1997).

Torrance, T.F., *Theological Science* (Edinburgh: T&T Clark, 1996).

Von Löwenich, W., *Luther's Theology of the Cross*, trans. Herbert J.G. Bouman (Belfast: Christian Journals, 1976).

Welch, C., 'Samuel Taylor Coleridge', in Smart et al (eds.), *Nineteenth Century Religious Thought in the West*, Vol. 1 (Cambridge: CUP, 1988), pp. 1-29.

Wheeler, K., *Romanticism, Pragmatism and Deconstruction* (Oxford: Blackwell, 1993).

Willey, B., *Nineteenth-Century Studies* (Harmondsworth: Penguin, 1964).

Willey, B., *Samuel Taylor Coleridge* (London: Chatto and Windus, 1972).

Wittgenstein, L., *Culture and Value*, trans. P. Winch (Oxford: Basil Blackwell, 1980).

Zeedcn, E.W., *The Legacy of Luther* (London: Hollis & Carter, 1954).